Discla

This book covers my research, over
of the Lygon Arms, in Broadway, Wo. _____.___. __.

The Lygon Arms is an old and venerable hostelry, highly regarded by
residents and visitors alike. Today it seamlessly belies its complex
evolution.

The original buildings are of some antiquity, and on an even older
site. The ambitions of some of its owners are reflected in its new
builds, extensions, and renovations. In addition, several buildings, of
differing centuries, neighbouring properties of some antiquity, were
woven together by one owner to make the whole.

The struggles of owners and innholders tell different tales. Their
journey makes fascinating reading.

Broadway itself is an ancient settlement, with its own story to tell; its
history reflects, in part, the history of England. The very location of
the village impacted its development, just as the Hotel's location
impacted and contributed to its journey, and its attraction to
'excursionists.'

I have, where possible, triangulated evidence and used source
documents. I appreciate that this book is a starting point, and that
further evidence may well shed more light on specific events or facts.

The past is always a puzzle; it would be pleasing to think that a
second edition might incorporate additional information from new
sources, further deeds, and documents.

I hope until then you find this book on the Lygon Arms 'words in their best order,' and a fascinating read.[1]

---

1. Samuel Coleridge 1827.

Acknowledgements

The Directors and Management of London and Regional who have supported my work in any way they practically could.

Jayne Bridges a good friend and professional editor who helped me considerably to polish the final document.

My husband, Douglas, who accepted that the long hours of research and writing would preoccupy me and supported me throughout.

Julian Hunt, a Worcestershire man, librarian, and professional historian who has on occasion very helpfully challenged my research and provided some extremely helpful sources, vital to the final text.

Jerold Northrop Moore, an American-born, long-term Broadway resident, best known for his biography and other writings on the life and music of Sir Edward Elgar, a family friend who has shared his experience as a professional writer and given me gentle encouragement over the years.

Gordon Russell Design Museum – Guardians of some of the Lygon Arms archives.

Ray Leigh MBE, Gordon Russell Design Director 1967, Managing Director 1971.

Graeme Nesbitt, General Manager of the Lygon Arms, and his staff.

Adam Lynk, photographer, for the use of some of his photographs of the Lygon Arms

Colwyn Thomas, a stalwart and key member of staff, still working at the Lygon Arms since he joined in 1969.

My late father-in-law, John van den Driessche, recruited from Shoreditch Technical Institute, a trained cabinet maker, an early employee of Gordon Russell's. He was just one of my many first-hand sources.

James Algar and his colleagues at Vale Press who helped and guided me in producing and printing this book.

Published by Elizabeth Eyre

Printed by Vale Press,6 Willersey Business Park, Willersey WR12 7RR   www.valegroup.co.uk

A catalogue record for this book is available from the British Library.
ISBN 978-1-7398400-1-3

Contents

Chapter 1: Location, location, location: A haven of hospitality at one with its setting 11

Chapter 2: The internationally recognised sign of the Lygon Arms Hotel, linking the Hotel to two of England's most powerful families, post 1066 15

Chapter 3: 13th century, humble beginnings – a previous building on the site of the White Hart Inn (Lygon Arms) 23

Chapter 4: 14th century, the village becomes a town, a More substantial dwelling is built on a burgage plot, the site of the Lygon Arms, main street Broadway 33

Chapter 5: 1532–2024, an Introductory overview. The Inns long journey to become the Lygon Arms of today 41

Chapter 6: 1532, Thomas White and the White Hart Inn 49

Chapter 7: 1532–1620, The White and the Sambache family, early proprietors of The White Hart Inn 55

Chapter 8: 1620 to 1642, the Treavis family flourish in the reign of James I, and Charles I 69

Chapter 9: Autumn 1642 – Autumn 1651, Roundheads and Royalists, a challenge for the Treavis Family at the White Hart 83

Chapter 10: 1654 – 1683, stage coaching comes to Broadway
and absentee ownership   107

Chapter 11: 1683-1809, changes, additional rooms, a scandal,
finally, the illusive stability   119

Chapter 12: 19th century, the White Hart Inn becomes
the Lygon Arms   139

Chapter 13: 1885–1912, Patronage of the Lygon Arms by
members of Broadway's Artistic Colony   169

Chapter 14: 1903 – 1909, Sydney Bolton Russell the first
few years, first steps in reviving a declining
beer house   179

Chapter 15: 1904-1907, The entrepreneurial owner
Sydney Bolton Russell   189

Chapter 16: 1905 to 1909, New challenges, running the
Hotel, refining the antiques arm of the
business, planning and expanding   197

Chapter 17: 1909-1914, Sydney Russell tackles the difficult
matter of the Assembly Rooms   205

Chapter 18: 1910-1914, The days of excursionists leading
to further expansion   219

Chapter 19: 1914-1918, the Lygon Hotel during the
Great War and its impact on its evolution   225

Chapter 20: 1919 – 1938, between the Wars   231

Chapter 21: 1939 -1945, The Second World War   249

Chapter 22: 1946 to 1985, The Russell Families' Legacy   255

Chapter 23: 1986 – 2016, The Lygon Hotel, out of private
    ownership, after more than 454 plus years   269

Chapter 24: 2016: London and Regional: The Lygon joins
    the Iconic Luxury Hotels   281

Postscripts

I-A potted history of Broadway before 1532   295

II-A snapshot–the Lygon Arms' visitor book, 1909-1912   311

III-Actors, Artists, Writers, Prime Ministers who have
    stayed......   315

IV-The Lygon Arms – a star of the silver screen   317

V-Special Features guests might like to look for in the
    Hotel   323

VI-The Remarkable Story of HMS Broadway, World War II   341

VII-The mystery of the ownership of Back Lane –
    the story so far...   347

VIII-The population of Broadway over the centuries   351

Bibliography   353

Dedication

The great traveller and lexicographer Samuel Johnson wrote, *'There is nothing which has yet been contrived by man, by which so much happiness is produced as by a good tavern or inn.'* [2]

The Lygon Estate has a significant role in the heritage and economy of Broadway; its loss at any time in the last five centuries, would have impacted the village's development.

This book pays homage to all the Inn's custodians: its owners, landlords and general managers who, each in his, her or their way, have contributed to the property we see today whether trading under the name of the White Hart Inn, the George, the Swan, the Lygon Arms Inn, the Lygon Hotel, or as today, the Lygon Arms.

I do not forget all the souls that have worked at the Inn over the centuries, sometimes in very difficult circumstances, or those that have made it successful over the years by their very patronage: those who have rested under its eaves or partaken of its fare, as it has evolved incrementally.

The book traces the evolution of the Inn, and which medieval properties came together, one building at a time, to become the whole. It covers those who have steered the ship, through both good times and rough waters; inevitably there are stories of the influencers and some of the more well-known guests, from all levels of society, over the centuries.

---

2. James Boswell, *'Life of Samuel Johnson.'* 1791, London.

Four references, spanning 256 years, sum up the journey of the Lygon Arms and its essential qualities which have contributed to its success.

1766 'The White Hart is known to be a well accustomed Inn, on the Road between Worcester and London.'[3]

1891 *'An ideal old Hotel, a romance in stone, more like what one would expect to find in a painting, or described in a novel...'* [4]

1921 *'Good food, comfort, and beautiful old-world surroundings make the Lygon Arms the premier Country Inn in the United Kingdom.'* [5]

2022 *'A genuine historic Cotswolds coaching Inn that has sympathetically retained the original features while creating true five star plus luxurious comforts and facilities.'* [6]

Elizabeth Eyre March 2024

3. Oxford Journal 9 August.
4. James. John Hissey, p 98, 'Across England in a Dog-Cart,'1891, London, R. Bentley & Son.
5. Cecil Charles Aldin, 'Old Inns,' 1921 London, Heinemann.
6. Tripadvisor, JB May 2022.

Chapter 1

Location, location, location: A haven of hospitality at one with its setting

Descending from the top of Broadway Hill (Bradewaye Hylle, previously Monte Wiccesse),[7] snaking their way down the escarpment known as Fish Hill, on a fair-weather day, travellers, coming from Oxford and beyond, are immediately rewarded by the stunning views of Broadway below and the extensive panorama of the rich, fertile Vale of Evesham beyond.

The village, a historic settlement with strong ecclesiastical, and medieval roots, still apparent today, nestles in its surroundings, nicely framed by the rising wooded North Cotswold escarpment.

---

7. Thomas Habington, p. 334. '*A Survey of Worcestershire Part I*' 1895, Oxford, The Worcestershire Historical Society. Habington Worcestershire's first historian (1560-1647) was condemned to death in the aftermath of the gunpowder plot, for giving asylum to Jesuit fathers. When his sentence was commuted, he returned home, to Hindlip Hall, in Worcestershire, where he retired from public life, to work on a parish-by-parish history of Worcestershire.

Daniel Paterson (1739–1825), a British army officer and cartographer known for his eighteen books of road maps, placed Broadway ninety-four miles from Hyde Park corner. The distance of ninety miles, hewn on an old milestone, still standing on the north side of the upper part of the high street, roughly confirms Paterson's recording of ninety-four miles from London to the White Hart, in his 1811 Road's book.[8]

The original milestone

The post war milestone is located on the north side of the upper High Street. The old milestone, defaced during the Second World

---

8. Daniel Paterson, *'a new and accurate description of all the direct and principal cross roads in England and Wales, and part of the roads of Scotland : with a variety of new measurements ... : the whole greatly augmented and improved by the assistance of Francis Freeling, Esq., Secretary to the Post-Office, and of several surveyors of the provincial districts, under the authority of the Post-Master-General'* 1811, London: Longman, Hurst, Rees, Orme, Brown, and Green

War due to the threat of invasion, the naming of the Cromwell and Charles I suites at The Lygon Arms and Broadway's war memorial near the green, are all subtle reminders that despite their outward tranquillity both the village, and the old Inn, have been bit players in some of England's darkest, most demanding times.

Approaching from Cheltenham or Evesham the traveller, whilst they see no great vista, experiences the rural setting of the wider Evesham Vale catchment.

Whichever entrance the traveller choses, Broadway is strikingly comfortable in its setting, one which had much to offer even when the first settlement was established before the Roman invasion: stone for housing, woods for fuel, streams for water, grazing, and arable land, all within easy reach.

The self-same quarried stone used for housing, a heavy but warm material, particularly the roofing stone, influences much of the look of the central village. The angle of the stone roofs at 55 degrees,[9] and the variable shanks laid from bottom to top, from long to short lengths, not only prevent rain blowing in under the tiles but, due to their physical weight,[10] impact the possible dimensions of the building below, thus imparting a degree of uniformity of footprint to the early stone buildings of Broadway. Older, larger buildings are often a composite number of smaller buildings. The stone's colour, particularly when lit by the sun, imbues its magic on these buildings.

---

9. Comment from acquaintance who had been told this by Thomas Bateman, a local architect.
10. It was also pointed out that the weight factor not only related to the Cotswold tiles, the weight of the snow on the tiles in the winter was a significant consideration.

Today, dominating yet complementing the skyline, on the north side of Broadway's high street, near to its village green, central to the village, is one of England's oldest and most famous Hotels, The Lygon Arms, a fine stone building complemented by several acres of picturesque grounds to its rear.

The Lygon Arms in all its glory October 2023

Chapter 2

The internationally recognised sign of the Lygon Arms Hotel, linking the Hotel to two of England's most powerful families, post 1066

From the early 16th century to the early 19th century the Inn, traded under the sign of the White Hart; only one reference has been found which mentions another name: the Swan, and there has been an, as yet, unsubstantiated reference to it being named the George.

Around 1828, the Inn began trading under the name of the Lygon Arms; since then, its sign, has been a prominent feature on Broadway's broad High Street.

Three influential and powerful families come together in one sign, three coats of arms, two ancient, one younger, interwoven into one: the chained bear of Urse, the Bohun Swan incorporated into the Beauchamp and Lygon Coat of Arms, including lions passant

Though instantly, and internationally recognised, the detailed heraldic references incorporated into the sign, may well have been overlooked by villagers and visitors alike. They are clues to a significant period, some say a catastrophic event, which changed England's and Worcestershire's history forever.

The sign, is based on an old coat of arms, reflecting the earliest ancestors, of William, 1st Earl Beauchamp; a specific coat of arms that he used until his death in 1816.

Coat of Arms William, 1st Earl Beauchamp (1747 - 1816)
Arms: Two lions passant double queued
Motto: Ex fide fortis – from faith (comes) strength
Supporters: A bear, muzzled collared and chained and a swan ducally gorged and chained both
with escutcheons on their shoulders charged with a fess[11] between six martlets[12]
Dimensions (height x width): 45mm x 58mm,
Heraldic Charges: lions passant (2)

---

11. Band running horizontally across the centre of the shield.
12. Six marlets on the small shields – mythical birds with no feet who cannot land – an allegory for continuous effort.

Within two years of the battle, in 1066, all English land, excluding the lands of two English lords,[13] had been distributed by King William to Norman lords. In addition to establishing Norman lords with all advantages, the occupying regime appointed all the clergy.

The Coat of Arms on the side of the sign facing west links directly to two great feudal Norman lords who fought alongside William the Conqueror, at the battle of Hastings, in 1066, thus receiving titles, land and lions passant to incorporate in their own Coats of Arms. On the left of the western face of the sign, is a muzzled bear, collared and chained. This is direct reference to Urse d'Abetot,[14] one of the sons of Lord Aumary.[15]

An ancient frieze in Worcester Cathedral depicts Urse with a rampant bear on his shield

His father was part of the invading force but died shortly after the battle, back in Normandy. In recognition of their father's loyalty and

13. Thorkill of Arden, who held seventy-one manors in Warwickshire, and Coleswain, of Lincoln who held forty-four manors.
14. Urso is Italian for bear.
15. "Aumary le Seigneur d'Abbetot"(c 1015-1066) hailed from Saint-Jean-d'Abbetot in the forest of Roumare, Normandy.

support to William, Urse and his brother, Robert d'Abetot, le Despenser,[16] who arrived in England after the battle, were richly rewarded with vast Royal land grants. Robert is thought to have built Elmley Castle, south of Bredon Hill. Urse became Commander of the Worcestershire martial army.

It was Urse who ensured the 1086 Domesday Book taxation survey[17] in Worcestershire, progressed smoothly; as a result, he was privy to most of the information about land and property ownership in the vicinity. From 1069 to his death, in 1108, he notoriously used his position as Sheriff of Worcestershire to acquire land and property by any means, especially Church land, thus becoming known, unofficially, and appropriately, as 'the avaricious bear.'

On the right of the western face of the sign, is a swan, ducally gorged (a crown around the neck) and chained (symbolising a family under the command of the King) also with lions rampant.

The counter seal of Humphrey de Bohun, 4th Earl of Hereford (1276–1322), attached to the Barons' Letter, 1301, showing the Bohun swan above the escutcheon with supporting strap, used to support a shield when not in use.

---

16. An appointment, by the legal ruling monarch, to represent the monarch in a country, a person who may have a mandate to govern the county it in their name.

17. Contrary to popular thought, the Domesday Book was the outcome of a national survey, not a geographical or statistical survey, but rather initiated to determine what taxes had been owed during King Edward the Confessor's reign. It allowed William to reassert the Crown's rights and assess where power lay after the wholesale redistribution of land following the Norman conquest.

This is a direct reference to the Bohun family. The Bohuns were part of the battle in 1066 and went on to play a prominent role in both English political and military history during the late Middle Ages. The swan, used by the family and their descendants as a heraldic badge, came to be known as the Bohun Swan.

Bohun swans collared and chained with necks entwined at the feet of the effigy of Margaret de Bohun (1311–1391), daughter of Humphrey de Bohun, 4th Earl of Hereford (1276–1322) and wife of Hugh de Courtenay, 2nd Earl of Devon (1303–1377). Located on her tomb in south transept, Exeter Cathedral, restored in the 19th century.

Aligned by marriages, over centuries, the Lygon family was able to incorporate both these ancient and noble ancestors into the 1st Earl Beauchamp coat of arms. The Beauchamps had not been at the battle in 1066; they seem to have come over from Normandy afterwards, at which point William gave forty-two lordships to Hugo de Beauchamp. [18]

---

18. p. 207-210, *'A Topographical Dictionary of England,'* ed. Samuel Lewis (London, 1848), British History Online *http://www.british-history.ac.uk/topographical-dict.* The manor of Bengeworth used to belong to the Beauchamp family. In the twelfth century, its baronial castle, situated near the old Evesham bridge, was destroyed by William d'Anville, Abbot of Evesham, in retaliation *'for depredations committed by the owner on his monastery.'*

The Beauchamps association with Urse's coat of Arms came about when his daughter Emmeline, married Walter[19] de Beauchamp, thought to be a tenant of Urse, around 1104.

In 1097, much of Emmeline's uncle's estate had passed to her father. In 1108, on his death it passed to her mother, and on her mother's death, (date unknown), as her brother had been banished from England around 1110,[20] Emmeline inherited the largest share of both their estates, thus becoming one of the wealthiest women in the new regime.

The Beauchamps association with the Bohun family began when Walter de Beauchamp's grandson, William de Beauchamp 1st Baron Abergavenny, son of Thomas Beauchamp, 11th Earl of Warwick, July 1392, married Lady Joan FitzAlan one of seven children of Richard FitzAlan, 11th Earl of Arundel, Earl of Surrey, and Elizabeth de Bohun. Elizabeth died in 1385, when Joan was ten.

The final link between these families and the Lygon's traces back to the marriage between Thomas Lygon and Joan Bracy circa 1419. Their son William was granted use of Madresfield Court[21] near Malvern, by Isabel Bracy, Joan's grandmother, in 1451.

Then around 1500, William's nephew and heir Richard Lygon married Anne Beauchamp, second daughter of the second Baron Beauchamp of Powick, who was related to Lord Beauchamp of Warwick. This marriage bestowed great wealth on the Lygon family including

---

19. One of Walter de Beauchamp's grandsons became William de Beauchamp, Earl of Warwick.
20. He was banished for murdering a member of the court.
21. In 1086, Madresfield Court was a possession of Urse d'Abetot. The house is first mentioned specifically in a charter of Henry I dated around 1120. William de Bracy lived in part of the house until 1260.

Beauchamp Court in Powick Worcestershire, land in Gloucestershire, and property in Warwickshire and Staffordshire.

Thus, the Lygon family, though substantial landowners, but minor gentry, rose up the social ladder.

More valuable to the Lygon family than the lands and property, were the connections to the Beauchamp family, their links to the Urse and Bohun ancestry, and their valuable connections to the Court.

The Lygon's wealth increased in the early 19th century when, after an extremely complex legal case,[22] a member of the Lygon family, inherited a third of the estate of William Jennens, roughly forty million. Jennens who was a bachelor cousin, godson to William III, was at the time said to be the richest commoner in England.

William Lygon was created baronet in 1806, and subsequently, in 1815, ennobled as Earl Beauchamp. The titles necessitated the creation of a Coat of Arms. It was this new Coat of Arms which wove together the Beauchamps' association with the Urse and Bohun families.

On William's death, the Coat of Arms passed to his son, the 2nd Earl, also named William, who purchased the White Hart Inn, in Broadway, in 1820.

Throughout Williams's ownership from 1820 to his early death, at the age of forty, in 1823, the Inn's sign remained that of the White Hart. The first newspaper reference mentioning the Inn under the name of the Lygon Arms was in 1828.

---

22. Said to be a basis for Jarndyce v Jarndyce, the fictional probate case in Dicken's Bleak House. It is noted others too make this claim.

On the reverse side of the Lygon sign is a Saracen's head, couped, and decorated with brilliant foliage in red, white, and gold with its shield depicting the lions passant. It is said to pay tribute to members of the Lygon family who were engaged in the 12th century crusades, though evidence of their involvement is still sketchy so must be subject to further research.

Chapter 3

13th Century
Humble beginnings – a previous building on the site of the White Hart Inn (Lygon Arms)

Inevitably, it was going to be a challenge to piece together the driver behind the erection of the first building, on the Lygon site, and how subsequent demolitions, erections and extensions gave rise to a freeman's property, which later became an Inn. Then there is the story of the Inn's considerable expansion, over almost 500 years!

This chapter covers the sketchy outline of how that very first rudimentary rural building, in the early 13th century, probably came to be erected in the northern part of Broadway, on the north side of the central section of Broadway's old Roman Saltstret, roughly where the entrance to the Hotel is today.

Several articles, in Worcestershire newspapers from 1871-1935, propose the first settled plots, on the north side of this northerly route, were developed in the reign of King John (r 1199 to 1216), by Randulf, Prior of Worcester, (1203 to 1213).[23]

'North Broadway was then little frequented by visitors. It consisted, principally of a few granges (farms*) built by Randulf, Prior of Worcester. In the reign of Henry III withy trees grew on each side of the street. A few wooden cottages were erected by those who inhabited the granges for their vassals to dwell in.*[24]

---

23. Roger Norreys, Abbot of Evesham (1191 – 1213) a cruel, dishonest, proud, self-indulgent, and immoral man, was replaced as Abbot of Evesham (1214- 1229) by Randulf.
24. *'Worcester Journal,'* 15 July 1871.

Randulf also built two other granges in this manor, the remains of one (Abbot's Grange) *can be seen at north end of the Chapel Street* (now Church Street). *The other called Pie corner, on the site of which a gentleman's house was built ......*

The chapel, erected by Randulf, contained two rows of seats one on each side of the aisle leading to the alter, a gallery and pulpit of very ancient carving now used in the Old Church (St Eadburgha's), *a clock over the door and a bell hanging under a dome supported by four pedestals now erected in the vicarage garden and a small cemetery, which for many years has been used as a garden.* (Probably late 20th century - refers to the back of Broadway Deli, there is no visible evidence today)

Much of the rest of the lengthy article, in the newspaper, from which the extract above is taken, can be corroborated.

The article is introduced in an unusual way - *'by the courtesy an influential friend resident in the neighbourhood of Broadway we are able to publish the following interesting particulars.'*

Unfortunately, the name of the author is not given.

To add to the challenge, phrases from this article are repeated in other later publications.

'Standing back at the end of a garden off the village green may be seen The Priory, or Abbots Grange. According to tradition, the building was founded by Randulf, Prior of Worcester, in the reign of King John.'[25]

25. L S Leake, p 39, *'With Pen and Pencil in Old World Worcestershire'* Cycling, 24 April 1907.

Unfortunately, as often happens, this text confuses the founding of the granges – farms and wooden cottages, in the 13th century with the later early simple stone building for the monks managing the grange in the 14th century, which was later expanded to become a substantial building used by the Abbot later.

However, there is no doubt that the land in and around Broadway, in the 13th century, was developed by the Church. The Church was extraordinarily strong in Worcestershire.[26]

Its wealth to a large degree flowed from its land holdings and their use.

AD 967, the Manor[27] of Bradanuuege or Bradanwege,[28] (Broadway), was named in documents concerning King Edgar's monastic reforms in England, as a dependency of the monastic Church of St. Mary at Pershore. It is therefore puzzling that in 1871 an *influential person* writes, the northern part of Broadway, rarely visited, was developed by the Prior of Worcester.

Several factors need to be considered:

---

26. The Church in Worcestershire included orders such as Benedictine, Franciscan, Dominican, Cluniac, and Austin Friar. The Benedictines were a central plank in Edgar's monastic reforms. Later in 1086, the Domesday Book, recorded 700 hides out of 1,200, in Worcestershire, belonged to the Church whereas in the neighbouring Warwickshire, only 175 out of about 1,135 hides belonged to the Church.
27. Manor, comes from the old French word manoir, meaning dwelling place. It does not necessarily mean a building, it could be a simple farm, a more prestigious building or just an estate of land. A feudal lord controlled the Manor and had rights to exercise certain privileges, and exact fees.
28. In the Anglo-Saxon text of the AD 972 Charter Broadway is called Bradanwege and its boundaries are outlined.

- It is correct that Broadway was in the main a land holding of Pershore, but not always. In AD 972, a Charter of King Edgar[29] restored[30] previously owned lands to the monastery and monks at Pershore, as part of Edgar's monastic reforms, reforms which put the monastery under stricter rules, those of the Benedictines. The restored lands did include those of Bradanuuege, or Bradanwege, a village of 20 manses or hides,[31] of land, with streets, streams, and ditches. So, lands were sometimes plundered and restored.

- Pershore Abbey was not always able to manage its land holdings. Several times the whole or parts of the Abbey were destroyed by fire. In 1002, according to Leland,[32] it became deserted after a fire and many of the lands reverted to the re-founded Benedictine monastery at Westminster. On this occasion records show Broadway was not one of the villages affected. There were however several fires in the 13th century destroying various parts of the Abbey.

- It is now a commonplace of early medieval social history to recognise that the thirteenth century was a time when England's population increased, the steepness of this rise is

---

29. Peter A. Stokes, 'King Edgar's Charter for Pershore (AD 972).' This single document confirmed the substantial number of estates, including Broadway, held by Pershore Abbey.
30. The monastery originally founded circa 689, by Oswald, a nephew of Ethelred, King of the Mercians, passed through many changes of fortune before and around the time of King Edgar, (r.959-975).
31. A hide, from the Anglo-Saxon word meaning 'family,' was an Anglo-Saxon unit of land, large enough to support a household. It could be 60 to 120 acres depending on the quality of the land. Tax was levied according to the hidage, (landholding), assessment.
32. John Leland or Leyland (c. 1503–1552) was an English antiquary, 'the father of English local history.'

often underestimated.[33] The 12th and 13th centuries were characterised by rising population, the colonisation of new land (through the drainage of fens, clearance of woods and expansion of farming on to upland moors) and the direct commercial management by estates of their land, whether this was dispersed among other holdings or ring-fenced within its own boundaries. The Church was a particularly active landlord, and monastic orders ran their estates from both home (demesne) farms and outlying granges, which could be large in scale (commonly 3 to 1000 acres).[34] The clearing of the church's lands for cereal crops[35] was not only profitable but urgently needed.

'Randulf, Prior of Worcester, when Abbot of Evesham (1214-1229) was chiefly occupied in opening up the Vale of Evesham: improving abbey lands - the building of mills and granges (farms),[36] the making of dovecotes and fishponds, the making of clearings in the forests. He granted licences to his free tenants to create clearings where the land seemed possible of cultivation.' [37]

If Randulf, was known for initiating the clearing of land when Abbot of Evesham, might he, as Prior of Worcester, working for the mother church, the Diocese of Worcester, to which

---

33. J Z Titow, p. 218–24. *'Some Evidence of the Thirteenth Century Population Increase.'* The Economic History Review, vol. 14, no. 2, 1961.
34. *https://historicengland.org.uk/images-books/publications/historic-farmsteads-*preliminary-character-statement-Section 4
35. Ever afterwards Broadway was said to be in a good corn area.
36. The Cistercians, a religious order arising around Dijon, came to England in the 12th century. They were well known for experimenting with new agricultural methods. They developed the grange system of farming whereby fields in the manors were cultivated by the monastic officials, rather than being divided up between demesne and rented fields.
37. p.112-127, *'A History of the County of Worcester: Volume 2,'* Victoria County History, London, 1971. *'Houses of Benedictine monks: Abbey of Evesham.'*

Pershore Abbey was linked, have supported Broadway, a few years earlier, to address the issue of available grain.

- In 1912, an article referring to Abbot's Grange, the building, in Broadway and potentially adverse development again linked the building to Randulf, in the reign of King John, says the site later became the property of the Abbots of Pershore. The reference may have confused the farm and the building, in respect of Randulf, but does seem to support the idea that this farm passed from the Diocese at Worcester to the Abbey and Convent at Pershore.

'According to Mr. Willis Bund, Broadway, which has such rich historical associations, is in danger of having one of its most interesting relics marred to meet the exigencies of modern times.

At a meeting of the Worcestershire Archaeological Society, Mr. Bund mentioned that the old Abbots' Grange is about to be turned into a lodging house. According to one writer on Broadway. the foundation of this building is attributed by tradition to Randulf, Prior of Worcester in the reign of King John. Becoming the property of the Abbots of Pershore, the Grange appears to have been used by them as a kind of country house.'[38]

- Another writer's research[39], highlight that in 1213, at the point when Randulf became Abbot of Evesham sixty acres of land was transferred from Roger of Broadway to Matilda of Cirencester without any the Abbot's involvement.

---

38. Crowquill's Jottings, p. 5, *Berrows Worcester Journal*, Saturday 7 December 1912
39. Derek Parsons, p18, *'Broadway a village history,'* Cornmill Press, 1996.

- Finally, the writings of historian John Willis Bund,[40] (1843-1928,) forcefully suggest arrangements set out in charters between the diocese, the abbey, the papal legate, and the views of the pope himself did not always align.

  'It is well known that the monastic writers of the eleventh and twelfth centuries were not above producing charters to strengthen the title of a religious house to its property; but in the wholesale fabrication of charters probably Evesham stands, "if not first, in the very first line.' [41]

In conclusion, the clearing of lands in north Broadway for grain production, as the local population rapidly increased is very plausible, though it remains unclear as to which person linked to either the arm of the local church, the Diocese at Worcester, the mother church, or Pershore Abbey, was responsible.

It seems reasonable to support the suggestion in older texts that in the early 13th century, plots of land, with rudimentary cottages for those who worked on the land, were erected, their owners being free tenants of the church. In the early 13th century, there were tenanted cottages in the more southerly original settlement area of Broadway, near St Eadburgha its church.

---

40. Bund was a Worcestershire MP, British lawyer, legal writer and professor of constitutional law and history at King's College London. He was a considerable authority on Worcestershire's history and other subjects, produced papers and wrote a great deal for the Worcester Diocesan Architectural and Archaeological Society, including many articles on the history of Evesham Abbey.

41. John Willis Bund read his paper, *'The early history of Evesham Abbey'* before the Worcester Diocesan Architectural and Archaeological Society, at the Guildhall, Worcester, on January 25, 1895.

It is also possible that in the reign of Henry III (1216 -1272), withy trees[42] grew on each side on the main street, as there were streams either side of the main street. These streams were not culverted and channelled until 1866.[43]

A plot, or a couple of plots of land with their simple cottages probably stood roughly where the core of the Lygon Arms, originally the White Hart Inn, is located today.

Mid-13th century, with the support of the Abbot, Broadway evolved from a village settlement into a medieval town or borough,[44] of around 4-600 people. As the settlement expanded, particularly near the green, where trading took place, to a degree it left behind its original historic settlement area near the church. The simple cottage dwellings fronting what was now the main street, were substantially rebuilt or newly built on larger burgage plots,[45] leased or licenced from the church.

----

42. A withy or withe is a strong flexible willow stem, typically used in thatching, basketmaking, or for constructing woven wattle hurdles. The term is also used to refer to any type of flexible rod of natural wood such as hazel or ash created through coppicing or pollarding. Hazel was often used in tying wattle and daub to a latticed wooden frame.

43. Church lands were sold in 1866 by the parish overseers to fund the works to cover over the two streams, which ran through the village, either side of its broad highway from the upper part to the lower section of its main street.

44. The word borough derives from the burghal system of Alfred the Great. Alfred set up a system of defensive strong points (Burhs); to maintain these settlements, he granted them a degree of autonomy. Only 25% of rural settlements became boroughs.

45. A burgage plot is a medieval land term for a long and narrow plot of land, rented off the Lord, which could be purchased. It had a dwelling at the street frontage, and stables, piggeries, cow bowers, mangers, and vegetable patches at the rear. Often plots were laid out similarly to the next, in width and length.

By the end of the century, a good number of Broadway residents, were enriched[46] from both agriculture and the commercial rearing of sheep.[47] [48] Increased trading, enabled by a market and fair charter, allowed freemen to pay for their tenancies in money instead of labour and sell or bequeath their properties. A new class of free tenants, or husbandmen, those free tenants with a small amount of land, had emerged.

It is from two such burgages, fronting the main street, owned by unknown freemen or husbandmen, that two became one and the Inn evolved.

---

46. This is evidenced by the number of people mentioned in 'the Lay Subsidy Roll for the County of Worcester, c1280,' edited for the Worcestershire Historical Society by J W Willis Bund and John Amphlett. It is an early surviving record of lay taxable chattels.

47. By 1273 English merchants were exporting 11,415 sacks of wool: 34.9% went to the Italians, 24.4% to the northern French towns, and 11.2% to the Brabanters (Belgium and part of the low countries.)

48. Susan Rose, 'Calais: An English Town in France, 1347-1558' Boydell & Brewer, Boydell Press, 2008.

Chapter 4

14th century
The village becomes a town, a more substantial dwelling is built on a burgage plot, the site of the Lygon Arms, main street Broadway

By the 14th Century Broadway was in two parts, Upend, shown below and Nether End.

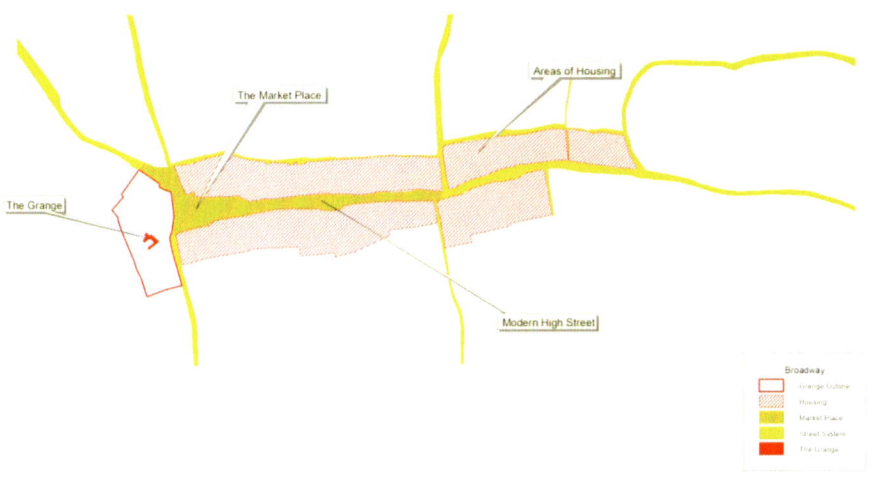

Upend, the newer medieval settlement of the village; the small track. at the rear of the plots and dwellings on the north side of main street, gave access to Broadway's common fields, wastes, and the northerly lands extending up Broadway Hill.

The older area, the original settlement to the southwest, Nether End, comprised of Bury End (also described as Very End possibly because there was only a rough track to Snowshill) and West End.

The newer northerly settlement area, parallel to Broadway's main street, which had expanded from its humble beginnings was now known as Uppey or Upend. It lay, primarily, between the green or marketplace and a track to Willersey, now the Leamington Road.

Most of the lands in Nether End: fields, closes, mores, ponds, waterways, and quarries were attached to the Lordship, in Broadway's case the Abbey and the Abbot. Trespass on these lands had consequences. This was land originally cultivated and managed either directly by the Lord: the monks, or by tenants. These could be villagers working off their burgage rents to the Lord, or freemen who had purchased their lease. Arrangements were managed through an extensive, sophisticated, complicated system of head leases, subleases, and sub-tenancies.

A simple cruck framed building[49] to house the monks managing demesne land was built on the Abbot's grange near the Green.[50] The buildings along the lane to the church could be described as cottages.

Upend was also managed through leases of lands or burgages. The medieval pattern of burgage plots, is still visible in the pattern of the buildings, footpaths, and streets particularly on the north side of the High Street, today.

---

49. Worcestershire County Archives and Archaeology (WSM17728), (WSM01292).
50. It was a centre for lay brothers who worked on the monastic estate: the original grange building had a kitchen, a refectory, residential chambers and a small chapel or oratory. There would have been a kitchen garden, barns, stables, and ancillary structures used for storing and processing crop and stock. The full extent of the grange building's immediate land or back yard is not known but appears from later maps to have extended into the gardens of what is now Farnham House, the House on the Green, to the west of the Green and the land now occupied by houses in Church Street.

20th century archaeological investigations support this arrangement and have revealed 14th century features near the green, and along the main street: foundation trenches were found in the back plots at 58 & 60, and a possible block of medieval tenements was found west of the Willersey track.

Arrangements between tenants and the Abbot were overseen by the Abbot's Steward, or Prior according to a well-developed governing church system which recorded and managed Abbey's lands, its stock, its shepherds, and herdsmen. The Steward or Prior's dwelling, known as Priors Manse, and its large adjacent barn, used to store the Lord's tithes, pre the dissolution of the Abbey and convent in 1539, were built at this time.[51]

The buildings which formed the original Inn, the White Hart, lay almost midway between these two prominent 14th century church buildings, the Grange farmhouse and Prior's Manse.

Some architects have held the opinion that when the village became a town, the early simple dwellings, the core building of the Lygon Arms, had been enhanced to become a two-storey manor house, an H shaped hall house.[52] However, a deed,[53] dated 1683, transferring ownership of the Inn, refers to the Inn as two burgages and one half burgage, 70-foot in width,[54] used as one dwelling house or Inn. This suggests that rather than a two-storey manor house being built, two neighbouring properties were brought together.

---

51. Demolished mid – 20th century.
52. Alan Brooks & Nikolaus Pevsner, 'The Buildings of England, Worcestershire,' Penguin Books Ltd. 1970
53. 29 November, 1620, Worcestershire Archives and Archaeology Service BA3464/1
54. A measurement that aligns with the Lygon frontage at that time.

To better understand how the two burgages came together a plan, known as the Enclosure Award Plan, (the outcome of the commissioner's determinations, the final dividing and enclosing of Broadway's open and common fields and commonable lands, drawn up in 1771, by government commissioners to attach to the Broadway Inclosure Act of 1772), helpfully outlines the likely footprint of two medieval burgage plots, that seem to have come together.

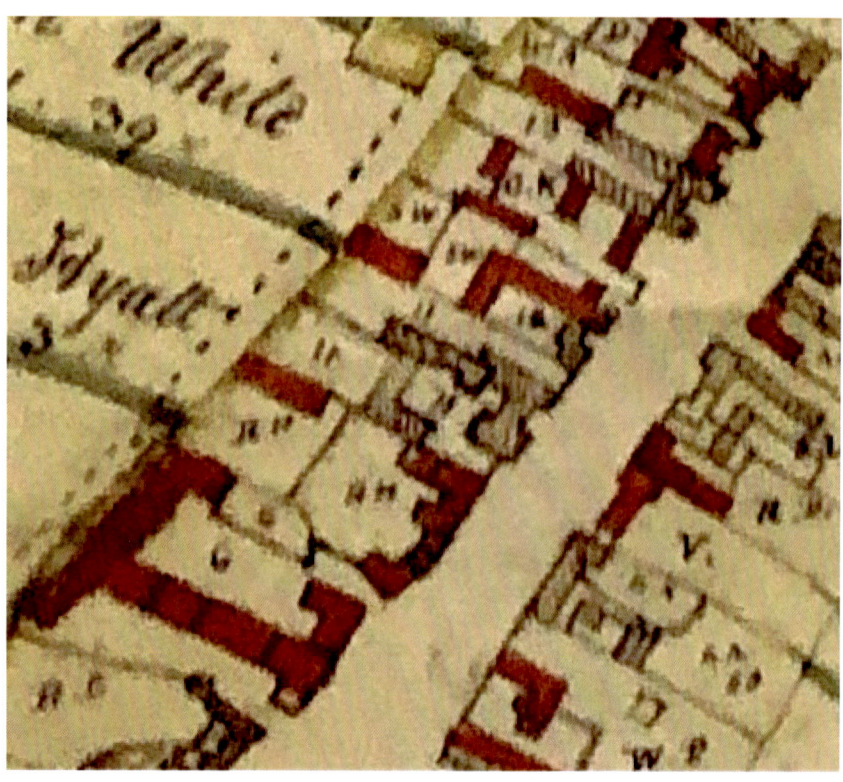

The 1771 Enclosure Award Plan identifies medieval burgage plots along Broadway's main street, and the common lands to the rear of the dotted track. Homesteads and farmsteads are coloured red, commercial or agricultural buildings are hatched grey.

Land north of the medieval track, Back Way or Back Lane, originally common land, is owned by Stephen White (SW) and Richard Hyatt (RH) in 1771. In front of the area marked Hyatt, on the Award Plan, is a grey hatched building, which in 1771 was called the White Hart Inn, (now the Lygon Arms), with outbuildings. The rear of the western burgage plot is marked number 11. The legend on the Award Plan associates 11 with John Purser; he was managing a Trust for those with an interest in the White Hart Inn in 1771.

A 1904 Survey Plan of the Lygon Arms, right, helpfully shows the thicknesses of the walls, and fireplaces which suggests how the two burgage dwellings came together.

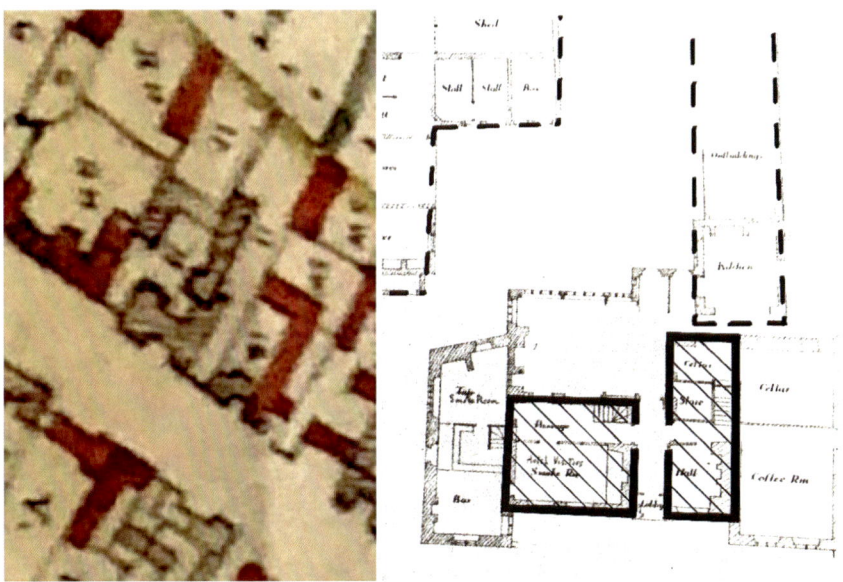

Footprint of the Inn on the 1771 Award Plan   1904 Plan- Proposed footprint of the two burgages

The dividing line of the plots is clear where the two plots meet Back Lane. The 1771 Award Plan shows the two wings added by Treavis, they are excluded on the proposed footprint of the two burgages.

The dotted lines identify outbuildings. Behind the conjoined buildings on the main street appear to be stables, outbuildings, or barns. Though there were many fewer stables in the 16th century such an assumption fits to the inventory of the White Hart dated 1556[55] which details there were attached to the property 6 horses with harnesses, one cart, one plough, four cows and one calf, and six bacon pigs and five little pigs plus poultry.

We simply do not know when the two burgage and half burgage plots came together, pre-1673. Information about the Innkeepers and their families suggest it may have been shortly after one of the buildings became an Inn, between 1545 and 1556.

An inventory dated 1556, mentions ten bedsteads which implies a suitable number of upper chambers, suggesting the Inn was probably two dwellings at that time.

Both burgages could have been at some point leased from the church, so could well have been brought together as early as 1539 when the assets of the monastery were redistributed after the January dissolution of Pershore Abbey.

It cannot be ruled out that they came together earlier before the dwelling was an Inn. In June 1349, the black death arrived in Worcestershire. As in the rest of Europe, it ravaged communities.

---

55. Worcestershire archive & archaeology Mq5844

It is said that a third of the population of Europe died. It was then Broadway reverted to a village run by a village council. Burgage plots and their buildings could have been totally abandoned, devoid of those to inherit, thus facilitating the acquisition of one burgage plot by an adjacent owner.

Irrespective of when the two burgages were brought together in the 14th century, the medieval building would not have dominated Broadway's skyline, as it does today.

An 18th century painting of smaller dwellings on Broadway's High Street, helps imagine the Inn as a two-storey building in its earlier life.

Other than references to cottages on cleared land, circa 1203-1213, in the 13th century, and thick walls, substantial fireplaces, medieval doors, and beams some of which have been shown to be of the 14th century, there are no definitive references or documents that provide information about the use of the dwelling, before 1532.

Chapter 5

1532 – 2024
An introductory overview
The Inns long journey to become the Lygon Arms of today

Chapters 3 and 4, covering the 13th and 14th century, discuss the buildings located on the site of the Lygon Arms before it became the Inn.

From the 16th century onwards, over the next almost four hundred and ninety-two years, the White Hart expanded upwards, around 1620, then outwards between 1620 and 1909. It then expanded east and west to incorporate other dwellings within its own footprint, which had originally fronted other burgages on the main street.

Land associated with the other acquired burgage dwellings was absorbed into the Lygon's Estate, as was some of the lands behind the track, known as Back Way or Back Lane, originally part of Broadway's common lands, thus adding a garden area to the Estate.

The added dwellings, to the east and west, brought with them their own history, elements within them or on their lands were themselves medieval, adding to the romance and heritage of the whole.

In addition to the expansion east and west, the adding of a wing or a bay, and the bringing together of other properties and land across the Back Way, rooms were repurposed, then renamed, outbuildings became main buildings, added facilities were built and torn down and rebuilt. 'Eggs' were broken but always in a compelling cause, as we see today. And it can be anticipated 'eggs,' will continue to be broken in years to come.

The following diagram outlines in overview the different ages of the various areas of the Lygon, some areas are acquired properties, others are extensions or new builds.

Areas mid 16th century or earlier – Known to be Inn 1532

Late 16th century

Additions By John and Ursula Treavis 1620-1630

Building over part of posting yard Giles Attwood 1772, Drawing Room above added circa 1790 Christopher Holmes

1907 – additional parlour, now bar, above bay window added to Drawing Room

1926 Garages, bedrooms, garages become conference room, now suites

Additional stables 17 and 18th century, then kitchen and bedrooms 1911, now Russell Room 1957

1960-61 The Garden Wing

1968 The Orchard Wing – demolition of the Lygon Cottage

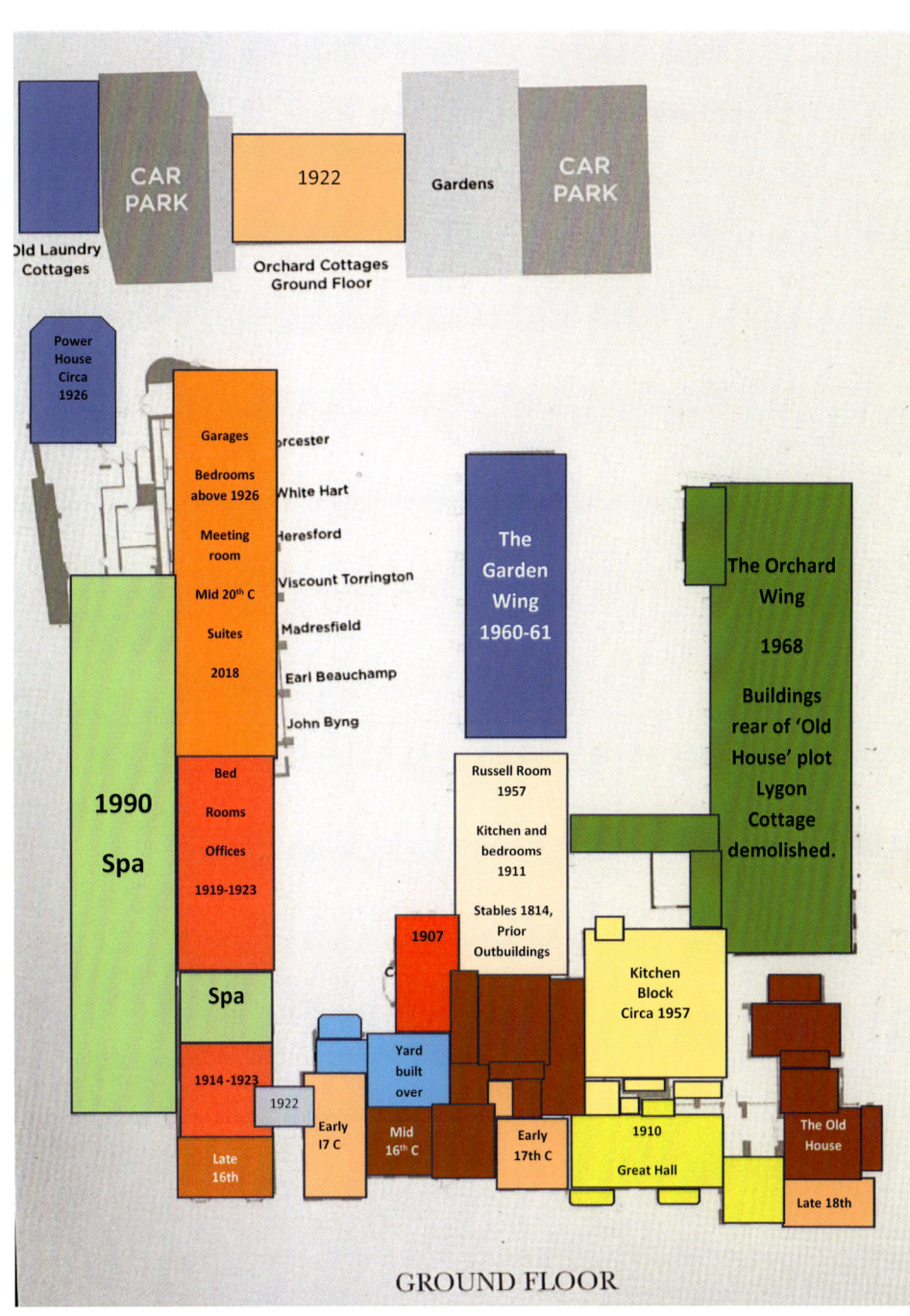

Old Laundry
Cottages

CAR PARK

1922

Orchard Cottages
Ground Floor

Gardens

CAR PARK

Power House Circa 1926

Garages

Bedrooms above 1926

Meeting room

Mid 20th C

Suites

2018

Bed Rooms

Offices

1919-1923

Worcester

White Hart

Heresford

Viscount Torrington

Madresfield

Earl Beauchamp

John Byng

1990

Spa

Spa

1914 -1923

Late 16th

1922

Early 17 C

Mid 16th C

Yard built over

1907

Russell Room 1957

Kitchen and bedrooms 1911

Stables 1814, Prior Outbuildings

Early 17th C

1910

Great Hall

Kitchen Block Circa 1957

The Garden Wing 1960-61

The Orchard Wing

1968

Buildings rear of 'Old House' plot Lygon Cottage demolished.

The Old House

Late 18th

GROUND FLOOR

The Innkeepers and owners from 1532 to 2024

16th century – White Hart

1532-1554 Owner -Thomas White and his wife Margaret

1554-1555 Owner Thomas White

1555-1556 Owner Thomas White and his second wife Joan Oakley

1556-1557 Owner William Sambache and his wife Elizabeth nee White and stepmother Joan Oakley

1557-1559 Owner Elizabeth Sambache nee White and stepmother Joan Oakley

1559-1568 Guardian Elizabeth Oakley and husband half brother Thomas

1568-1578 Owner William Sambache II, son of William and Elizabeth Sambache nee White.

17th century – White Hart – for a short time the Swan

1578- 1613 Owner William and Jane Sambache nee Severne

1613-1620 Owner William Sambache II and family

1620-1641 Owner John and Ursula Treavis and their son Thomas, possibly daughter Ann

1641-1649 Owner Ursula Treavis and son Thomas, possibly daughter Ann and husband

1649- 1654 Owner Ursula Treavis

1654-est 1656 Owner Mathew Treavis

1656-1670 Owner John Treavis son of Mathew Treavis

1670-1680 Owner Mathew Treavis
       Leaseholder William Adderley, Joseph, and Elisha Biscoe
       Innkeeper Philip Hodges

1680-1683 Trust – Katherine and Mary Treavis, Mathew's daughters
       His son Gilbert Treavis also had some interest in the Inn
       Leaseholder William Adderley, Joseph, and Elisha Biscoe
       Innkeeper Susanna Hodges wife of late Philip Hodges.

1683-1683 Owner Tomas Parry – dyer Broadway
       Innkeeper Susanna Hodges

1683 -1700 Owner Walter Parry – dyer Northampton
       Innkeeper Susanna Hodges

18th century – White Hart

1700-1713 Owner Francis Phipps, owner of the Angel Inn
       Innkeeper John and Ann Cormell

1713-1733 Owner Francis Mitchell, nephew of Francis Phipps
       Innkeeper Ann Cormell on death of her husband

1733-1740 Owner Ann Cormell
       Innkeeper Ann Cormell supported by two of her
       daughters Mary and Sarah

1740-1790 Trust in favour of Mary, Sarah, and Elizabeth Ann Cormell's

daughters, grandsons and granddaughters, and others.
Innkeepers' unknown until
1757 Anthony Stratton
1766 Giles Attwood
1770 Leaseholder and Innkeeper Giles Attwood
1776 Leaseholder and Innkeeper Christopher Holmes, and wife Martha

1790-1801 Owner Christopher Holmes, Theophilus and John Knowles

19th century – White Hart

1802-1807 Owner Martha Holmes and her brother John Knowles

1807-1820 Owner William Phelps Evesham Solicitor
Innkeepers various including one John Starling around 1814

1814-1821 Leaseholder and Innkeeper Giles Lawrence

1820-1823 Owner William Lygon, 2nd Earl Beauchamp
Innkeeper Giles Lawrence
Innkeeper Charles Drury possibly 1822 or 1823

1823-1867 Owner Honourable Henry Lygon
MP (1816-1853) Worcestershire the West Worcestershire.
and British Army Officer, served in the Peninsular War
Innkeeper Charles Drury and his wife Jane

1828 becomes Lygon Arms

1867-1874 Owner and Innkeeper Charles Drury and his wife Jane

1874-1893 Owner and Innkeeper Charles Richardson Drury and his
wife Laura

1894-Circa 1899 Owner Frances Lane
Innkeepers Robert and John Cordell

1899-1903 Owner Samuel Allsopps & Sons, Brewers, Burton on Trent
Innkeeper Robert and John Cordell

20th century

1903-1904 Owner Sydney Bolton Russell and wife Elizabeth
Innkeeper Robert Cordell

1904 -Circa 1920 Owner and Innkeeper Sydney Bolton Russell and wife
Elizabeth
Russell and Sons

1920 – 1938 Owner Innkeeper Sydney Bolton Russell and wife Elizabeth
Russell and Sons

1938- 1970 Owner Don Russell with support of Douglas Barrington

1970–1986 Owner Douglas Barrington with support of Kirk Ritchie

Corporate Ownership

1986-1998 Owners of the Savoy Hotel Group, part owned by
Wontner family

1998-2003 Blackstone Group investment company owners of the Savoy Group

2003-2005 The Furlong Hotels – a West Midlands family business

2005-2007 Acquisition by Paramount Hotels, working with Dawnay Shore
Hotels and Investment vehicle set up by Dawnay Day Structured Finance Ltd and Shore Capital Group Plc.

2007-2012 Leased by Barcelo Hotels and Resorts – a Spanish Company
January 2008 - Rebranded Barcelo Premium Properties
July 2008 - renamed Puma Hotels
2012 Barcelo Hotels withdraw from lease agreement and UK Mkt

2012–2016 Paramount Hotels – traded as Hotel Collection, which fell under the banner of Amaris Hospitality, owned by Lone Star

2016 Lygon Arms acquired by Iconic Luxury Hotels.

Chapter 6
1532, Thomas White and the White Hart Inn

In the early 16th century, Sr. Robert Byshop, the vicar of Broadway, and forty of his parishioners, appear to have come to an arrangement to ensure the great gate of St Eadburgha's church, (a gate which seems not to exist today), and several six-yard sections of the churchyard wall, proceeding eastward was repaired and *'perfected'*.

Forty parishioners were either obliged, due to their position, or had agreed, to do their part, and assist with repairs. A numbered list was drawn up.[56] In the record against the number 25 is the name Thomas White and the date 1532; in 1633 the name next to the number 25 is John Trevies, in 1710 it is Francis Phipps. John Treavis took over the White Hart in 1620, and Francis Phipps in 1700.[57] It is reasonable to conclude that in 1532 Thomas White was running the White Hart Inn, in the 19th century renamed the Lygon Arms.

A suggestion, in an earlier publication, that from 1490 onwards, if not before, that a Thomas Whyte, possibly a relative, at the request of the Abbot, provided hospitality and stabling, on a regular basis, for twelve men, is not yet sufficiently evidenced to support.

To learn more of the White family in Broadway, the clergy's records at the Abbey and Convent of Pershore might have helped, but their limited records detail leases and sub-leases connected to wool

---

56. A record of the Parish Register, 1532-1710, copied by Mr Rees Price in the early 20th century.
57. The Inn on the main street was originally known as the White Hart, the first time the Inn was called the Lygon Arms was around 1828.

trading, the size of their flocks, repair and maintenance obligations, and the work associated with monastic life. There is little information concerning those living and working in Broadway in the 15th or 16th century: the sheep farmers, shearers, softeners, dyers, weavers, or traders. In addition, on several separate occasions, the records of the Abbey in Pershore were destroyed in fires.

Parish records did not begin until after the dissolution of the monasteries, in Pershore's case around 1539, so they are of limited value.

Helpfully, records of early Chancery proceedings, 1476–1485, refer to 'Whyte of Bradway'. He is described as a husbandman,[58] a freeman with land, and recorded as having brought an action for a debt of £72[59] against one Thomas Wynnam. Whyte is most likely a farmer involved with the business of wool, leasing a burgage plot with a dwelling on it.

This man, Whyte of Broadway, also appears in the Stonor letters and papers[60] 31 July 1478. A letter from Thomas Betson, a younger member of the Stonor household, (an apprentice and factor, related to, and working for the Stonors) mentions Whyte to his master's wife, Dame Elizabeth Stonor. Betson says he needs funds to pay a number of people including Whyte of Bradway, *'to Whyte of Bradway I must pay iiij li'* (four pounds.) [61]

---

58. From the 14th century Anglo-Saxon husbonda, meaning freeholder, peasant with a dwelling, and possibly land.
59. £35,000 today
60. Stonor letters and papers, (1290-1483) are one of the most significant collections of 15th century correspondence, to shed light on the wool trade in England at that time.
61. p. 64, 'The Stonor Letters and Papers Vol. 2' by Royal Historical Society (Great Britain), Camden third series, 2019.

In the famous Cely letters and papers,[62] 1475-1488, the reference to Whyte provides a possible insight into a Whyte's position in the wool trade. Agent, William Cely, writing to his master Richard Cely, a Merchant of the Staple [63] at Calais, reported that he *'had dined with one Thomas Whyte 14 April 1484, at his master's request, to obtain information about a specific matter.'*[64]

The section goes on the illuminate that it was a delicate personal matter related to a lady, which implies Whyte had Richard Cely's confidence. In addition, Whyte sends his goodwill to Richard Cely. Few men were Master's of the Staple, a position granted by the King. Such a connection implies Whyte of Broadway had standing in the wool trade.

There are hints in a Conventual Lease dated 1490,[65] between the Abbot and Convent of Pershore and Robert Handy and Robert Hankes (Haukes or Faulkes) of Broadway, that the Whyte family in Broadway had prospered, and owned land and property in Broadway.

Reference is made in the 1490 lease to a Great Chamber, Whyte Hall, which is next to the Wool Hall, possibly where fleece was stored. A second lease dated 1535 between Anthony Daston tenanting land in

62. These papers also document the lives and lifestyle of one of England's most significant wool merchants.
63. The term 'staple' refers to the entire medieval system of trade and export taxation.
64. McLean, Elliot, p 152-153, 'The Cely Papers,' Ed Henry, London: Longmans Green, 1900
65. Library of Birmingham BLS Barnard Rees Price collection no 28, d/1, Sheldon Micellanea. (The lease is considerably damaged, the beginning and the end are practically illegible, only a few of the opening words being decipherable).

Broadway and the Abbot of Pershore[66] refer to Whyte More,[67] and Whyte Furlong.

It seems reasonable to conclude that Thomas Whyte, of Broadway, in his business dealings, had progressed from managing sheep and fleece, to become a respected wool trader at a challenging time. In the Middle Ages exports to the continent were either strictly controlled at the ports such as Calais by the Merchant Staplers, who ran and controlled a tax focussed monopoly, or linked to the merchants connected to Lombardy bankers, who cheekily bypassed the Staple at Calais, sailing their own ships, directly to the Cotswolds, via Gloucester then Tewkesbury, thus avoiding some of the taxes and improving their profit margin.

Whyte was trading when there was strife on the continent, impacting fleece exports. For much of his working life he would have traded during the Wars of the Roses (1455 -1485), the sporadic struggle between two rival branches of the Royal House of Plantagenet, Lancaster and York, both of whom had genuine claims to the English throne.

In theory, the Wars of the Roses could be, in part, ignored by major merchants, and their associates, if they had the financial clout to do so, but it must have made trading more difficult. In addition, Broadway lay uneasily between The Earl of Worcester, the Yorkist Chief Constable of England, and the Earl of Warwick who, though he had been a key player in the Yorkist cause, had switched his allegiance to the Lancastrian side.

---

66. Worcester Records at the Hive WRO BA 8965/8.
67. Open grazing land.

There is a strong possibility that Thomas Whyte, the wool trader, and Thomas White, the innkeeper in 1532 had a family connection.

Possibly Thomas White the innkeeper chose, to remain in Broadway to avoid the complications of a life which required constant travel, or maybe he had intended to be involved with the business of wool but changed direction on the birth of his daughter Elizabeth in 1520.

Calling the Inn the White Hart[68] not only incorporated the family surname but associated the Inn with a popular figure of some standing; inns relied on such associations. The personal emblem and livery of King Richard II, (r 1377 -1399), was a mature stag: a white hart. Richard's martyred great grandfather Edward II was buried in Gloucester Cathedral. The young King had held a parliament in Gloucester[69] and his memory was popular locally. Whyte was a well-known name in the country; Whyte Hall in London was the primary residence of English Monarchs from 1530.

---

68. An archaic word for a mature stag.
69. The parliament room still exists in the Church House, at Gloucester.

Chapter 7

1532–1620
The White and the Sambache family,
early proprietors of The White Hart Inn

Thomas White, the innkeeper, in 1532, possibly a relative of Thomas Whyte, involved in the business of wool, married Margaret, and had one daughter, Elizabeth, baptised circa 1520.

Little more is known of the Inn, or the family at this time, save they would have known of, perhaps even witnessed the chaos that followed the seizing of church lands, and property, belonging to Pershore Abbey and convent, 24 January 1539, by those acting on behalf the Crown.

The dissolution of the monasteries, part of the wave of national church asset grabbing and cultural destruction, became a familiar element at this point in Henry VIII's reign.

The church had much to answer for in its behaviour both collectively and individually, but it was well known that those given the task of dismantling the institutions often kept the items they seized, precious metals and robes, money, and lands, for themselves, rather than the crown.

Apart from a brief interlude, this behaviour signalled a new order of things, the move away from Catholicism in England. The White family were Catholics (as were all their neighbours) they would have had to outwardly change their allegiances very quickly, and for a brief interlude, when Mary was on the throne, back again.

In 1545, Thomas's daughter Elizabeth White, aged 25, married William Sambache I; the Sambache's were a local family. Parish records refer to members of the Sambache family as 'gents' though they were not local landowners.

Their coat of arms, 'Azure, a fesse Gules between three garbs or,' a blue shield with a red band through the centre third, between three gold sheaves of wheat,' though somewhat damaged, is said in the top left-hand corner of the large west window of St Eadburgha's church.

Coat of Arms of the Sambache Family

Thomas, and his Margaret, were still young, so most likely ran the Inn with their daughter Elizabeth, and son in law William. In 1547 Elizabeth gave birth to a son, an innkeeper in waiting, he too was christened William. Elizabeth gave birth to two other sons: Anthony, and John and a daughter Mary.

Five years later, in 1552, the parish records not only confirm the White Hart was an Inn but verify the Inn recorded the registration of guests.

When Margaret died the following year in 1554,[70] as was often the case in earlier centuries, Thomas remarried quite quickly, 18 July 1555, Joan Okeley,[71] (Oakley) the daughter of the Lord of the Manor of Wolford, whose first husband John, had died around 1545. One year later Thomas White died, aged 67.

His inventory, taken for probate purposes in early 1556, recorded by William Hodges, William Dyckyns and William Broks was proven by the ecclesiastical court with jurisdiction over the area.

In addition to listing twenty-four persons to which he owed money, on the date of his death, including a butcher, his servant, seven shillings for oats, thirty-eight shillings and eight pence for wood, six shillings and eight pence for malt, it records all the items he owned.

In the first place - two table boards, one bench, three other boards, two chairs, one round table, one painted cloth – this might have been a wall hanging with a religious purpose.
Item - three copper/zinc basins, one wash basin, two pewter basins, one pewter wash basin, eight pewter platters, seven small shallow bowls with handles, four saucers, one pewter quart pot, three pewter pint pots, and two salts.
Item- Twenty pairs of sheets, nine feather beds (mattresses), nine bolsters, eight pillows, nine bed throws, three pairs of blankets.
Item - ten bedsteads, six chests, one cupboard, two table boards, five benches, one chair, two canopies for fourposter beds,

---

70. Broadway Parish Register.
71. Broadway Parish Register.

Item – four brass pots, one warming pot, one frying pan, one dripping pan, three cauldrons, four pans,
Item – six silver spoons,
Item - three candlesticks,
Item – two spits, a pair of pothooks, two iron bars with shafts,
Item – one bess axe, one cleaver, one wood axe, two hatchets, one bill hook, a pair of fetters, two horse hooks, three augers, one adds, one hand saw – all items for the stables or the farm.
Item- metal studs, water pails, copper hardware, two barrels,
Item- wooden dishes, two trenchers,
Item- six horses with harnesses,
Item- one cart, one plough, two harrows,
Item - four cows and one calf,
Item - firewood and timber boards,
Item - plates, shovels, and spades,
Item – wheat, barley, and pulses,
Item – four geese, eight ducks and three sows,
Item – six bacon pigs and five little pigs,
Item – Thomas White's clothing, a sword, dagger, battle halberd, battle axe, forest wood knife, bows, and arrows.

The total of the value of his possessions was forty-six pounds, eleven shillings and six pence, of which seventeen pounds six shillings was owed to creditors, leaving roughly thirty pounds, which had a very healthy purchasing power in 1556.[72]

The description of the inventory items, the numbers of pots, sheets, beds, etc support the family home being an Inn, which provided accommodation and food for more than his family, for example, the

---

72. The value of his net estate, after paying his creditors, is today according, to the National Archives converter and the Bank of England Inflation calculator around £10k but at the time its value had much greater. Its purchasing power and would have bought the family: 6 horses, 24 cows, 93 stones of wool, 32 quarters of wheat, 1000 days of skilled labour.

inventory identifies ten bedsteads; discounting Thomas, and Joan's own bed, that of Elizabeth and her husband William, the beds for their three other children the inherited three beds left to the children, the remaining five beds are likely to have been for guests. This was not a period when private space was common, except in grand houses, so a room for guests may have accommodated more than one bed.

The 1556 inventory also points to the inn already being a property arising from two burgages brought together; ten bedsteads imply the property had a good number of upper chambers.

Thomas White's will does not refer to his running the Inn, or his daughter inheriting the Inn possibly because, she had previously received her inheritance or was entitled by law.[73]

The will is witnessed by, Johannes Tether, and the vicar William Dyckyns. He left to each of his daughter Elizabeth's four children one feather bed, 'which feather beds are in the parlour that hath a chimney,' probably the parlour to the east of the entrance, described on the 1904 Survey Plan as the Hall, or the room to the west, known earlier as the inglenook, which was also the kitchen.

---

73. Ancestry research bodies suggest that before 1858 probate records were created for only 10% of the population, and those who received their inheritance according to law or deceased family members were often omitted from the records, this is pertinent as the will does not mention Thomas's daughter Elizabeth's inheritance of the Inn.

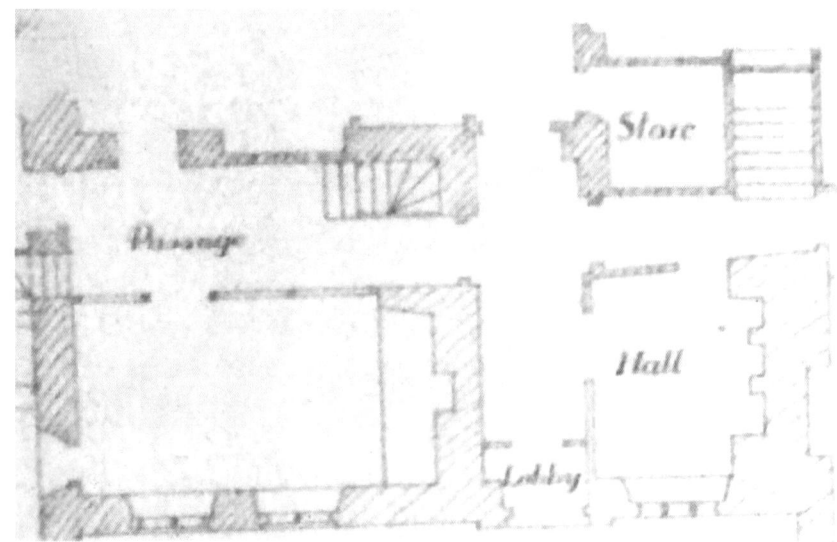

1904 Survey Plan, a section of ground floor - interpretation of the Inn's footprint in 1556.

Thomas's son in law, William, was left five butts and three tops of oak,[74] his eldest grandson William, six silver spoons.

The rest of his goods are left to his new wife, Joan, his executrix, who likely supported the business of the Inn.

Thomas White's will and inventory show no evidence of his having any commercial involvement with wool, despite in 1555, some 8,000 people in Worcestershire, being employed in some aspect of the wool trade, including local weaving, on cottage looms.

Extended family members, who lived and worked in Broadway and Wickhamford, appear to have owned land; their wills show family members being left sheep.

---

74. Tabletops.

Elizabeth's father-in-law, Richard Sambache, on his death, 1556, left property and lands to his wife which on her death were to pass to his son William but this legacy never came to pass. In 1557, a year after her father died, tragically, Elizabeth's husband, William, died.

With three sons, and a daughter not yet in their teens, Elizabeth continued to run the Inn with the help of her mother-in-law until 6 February 1559, when she married Thomas Oakley II, a son of her stepmother. This may have been a marriage of convenience, driven by the desire to keep business arrangements within the family.

From 1559, until Elizabeth's son William Sambache II (from her first marriage) came of age, in 1569, it is probable Elizabeth and her second husband, Thomas, and for a period her mother-in-law Joan, until she returned to Chastleton, supported William in running the Inn, then moved to Chastleton, around fifteen miles from Broadway, not far from Moreton in Marsh, to live with one of her daughters.

When she died circa 1566, her will shows that when she left Broadway, she had reverted to using the surname Oakley, rather than her married name White. This was understandable as the name Oakley was more well known in the Chastleton area.

Elizabeth and Thomas had one son: Edward born February circa 1560/1.

In 1558, the White/Sambache/Oakley family would have been aware of yet another notable change in ownership of Broadway's lands. *'The whole Bradwey (Broadway) Manor, its land and flocks and the advowson of the rectory and the parish church of Brodway, alias Bradwey,'* previously the holdings of the Abbot of Pershore, surrendered to Henry VIII in 1539, that passed on his death, through

Edward VI, who died aged 15, to Queen Mary Tudor, in 1553, was now owned by a court favourite William Babington.[75]

Babington had, at a twenty years' purchase, by Letters Patent, 27 July 1558, in fee simple, for £3008.15s.8d, been granted the Manor by Queen Mary. The chatter at the Inn may well have been about the absentee landlord, his relationship with his two major tenants, Anthony Daston and Baldwyn Sheldon, and the good income Babington received from the Broadway lands.

Elizabeth predeceased her second husband Thomas, around the time the Inn finally passed to William Sambache II, on his coming of age in 1568/9. When William, took possession of the Inn, his stepfather, Thomas, then also returned to Chastleton with his son Edward.

In 1584, Edward, (William's half brother), married William's wife's younger sister Ursula Severne. When Thomas's first grandson was born, around 1586, and Thomas Oakley made a will. In his will he described himself as a yeoman. He was one of six who farmed 675 acres in Chastleton, land belonging to Robert Catesby, the English conspirator.[76] Thomas died in 1602.

13 May 1578, ten years after taking the reigns in the Inn, aged 31, William II married sixteen-year-old Jane Severne. By marrying Jane, the family gained connections with the Sheldon family. Jane's mother was Christian Sheldon a daughter of Baldwyn Sheldon, the late Lord of the Manor. One of her nephews was the current Lord of the Manor in Broadway and her grandfather owned land in Shrawley, near Droitwich. In the forty-six plus years, since his grandfather

---

75. Harleian Manuscripts in the British Museum. Manerium de Bradwey in Com. Wigorn, percella Poffeffionium nuper Monafterij de Perfhore. ratyd 15 die Julij 1558 for William Babington Efq.
76. The Gunpowder Plot.

Thomas White had run the Inn, in 1532, much had changed in the village.

In 1573 - 4, Anne Daston, the widow of William Babington's main tenant, Anthony Daston, living at Broadway's 'Greate Farme,' Bury End, had purchased the farm and lands her husband had tenanted, from Sir William Babington's grandson, also called William; she had purchased the farm, including a dove-house, two gardens and 2,960 acres thus becoming Broadway's largest landowner.

The following year Babington's grandson had deeded the Lordship to Broadway's second largest tenant, Ralph (known as Rafe) Sheldon, son of Baldwyn Sheldon, and the husband of his daughter Elizabeth, his son-in-law, William Childe of Pensax.

Thomas Habington,[77] a relative of Babington, a recorder of history, often referred to as Worcestershire's first historian, knew Broadway well. In his writings, he tells more of the distribution. It was, in Habington's eyes, the dividing of the Babington Manor, previously owned by the Crown, between two families.

When the Abbey at Pershore was ruinated and the coate of the Monastery divided, the glory of thys town was fyrst distributed in towe and nowe last into three partes, yet all tyll of late closed upp in the family of Sheldon, for Mr Baldwin Sheldon a braunche of thys house purchased the manor of Brodeway[78] which yet remaynethe in hys issewe; and Anne daughter of William Sheldon of Beoley, fyrst the wyfe of Frauncis Sauage, of Elmley Castle, and of Anthony Daston

---

77. Habington, (1560-1627) who wrote a Survey of Worcestershire, was an embroiled in the Babington plot to affect the escape of Mary Queen of Scots in 1586, his elder brother was executed for treason. Thomas and his younger brother Richard were held for six years in the Tower of London, on his release he returned to Worcestershire.
78. Baldwyn died in 1548, the purchase was in 1575, the phrase remained in his issue is key.

mistress of Bradeway's greate farme, after shee had survivinge both her husbandes in a longe induringe wydowhood, with thys and other her ample possessyons mayntayned a post of admirable hospitality concludinge in death, leafte thys farme equally between her towe sonnes Walter and Anthony Sauage.[79]

The phrase by Habington *'yet all <u>tyll of late</u> closed upp in the family of Sheldon'* referenced by Habington to Walter Savage's sale of part of his inheritance in 1627,[80] to *'Sir Thomas Couentree (Coventry) Knight Baron of Alesboroughe, Lord Keeper of the* Greate *Seale'* [81]

In 1578, the same year in which William II married Jane another branch of the Sheldon family, Rafe, purchased the lordship and the remaining Broadway land. Either by design, to make a good profit or because he had overextended himself, he had sold off a good number of plots; *'he conveyghed sundry landes to Richard Strech, Phillip Gardiner, John Harrys, Thomas Severne, Nicholas Blackie, John Hodges, Nicholas Hobdaie, John Sambage, Robert and Thomas Ligon, Robert Hodges, Thomas Strech, William Ligon after he sold a house and land to Nicholas Blaby, the husband of his sister Jane.'*

'Thys it seemethe increased the number of ffree-houlders in Bradewey.'[82]

---

79. Thomas Habington, p 107, *'A Survey of Worcestershire Part I'* Oxford, The Worcestershire Historical Society, 1895.

80. Anne Daston died in 1619. It is thought to be part of an inheritance from Ann, and to include tithes, but requires further research.

81. Thomas Habington, p 108, *'A Survey of Worcestershire Part I'* Oxford, The Worcestershire Historical Society, 1895.

82. Thomas Habington, p 107 *'A Survey of Worcestershire Part I'* Oxford, The Worcestershire Historical Society, 1895.

This multiplying of yeomen, as a direct result of Rafe Sheldon's conveyances, gave rise to a sudden expansion of Elizabethan homesteads on the main street and additional wealth in the village.

Quite likely the Inn also prospered during this expansionary phase, though these changes in ownership within the village little affected those less fortunate, those concerned with cloth: weavers, and finishers including fullers, tuckers, shearers, and dyers or the peasantry and farmers who worked the land and common lands.

For the peasantry, and farmers, daily labour, using the ancient method, the plough, and oxen, was hard, especially on the steeper slopes.[83] Those connected with grazing their animals, weaving and cloth, were increasingly struggling economically; the export trade had difficulties, there was a downturn in the cloth industry and a brief resurgence of plague in 1590 hindered movement around the country.

William Sambache II and his wife Jane, based on the surname Sambache, over a period of 35 years, appear to have born twelve children.[84] However, there was a second family named Sambach in Broadway. When added to the family tree, most Sambach references give rise to the proposition that one branch of the family dropped the last letter, from the 16th century onwards. Whilst is does not change the number of William and Jane's children it might explain why some references erroneously claim Jane had twenty-six children, in thirty-five years!

---

83. The drainage afforded by ridge and furrow works to this day; sheep and cattle can be found, especially on wet days, showing a preference for the ridges' drier tops. The ridge and furrow and the steepness can be fully appreciated when walking the route, in the summer, from the upper area of the High Street, beneath the bypass, to Farncombe Estate.
84. Parish records.

Their life at the Inn was probably easier than previous generations, William, and Jane Sambache, had connections, some land, and a large family to share the workload associated with running an inn.

By 1598, given the size of the family, with twelve children only one of whom had married and probably left home: six boys, four of which were teenagers and five girls under twelve, the property was assuredly the *'two burgages and one half burgage, used as one dwelling house or Inn, and one pasture with all houses, barns, stables orchards and gardens.'*

By the end of the 16th century the Inn seems to have three or four areas on the ground floor: a kitchen, parlour, passage, brew house and snug and at least four chambers upstairs, and the use of *'all houses'* to accommodate both family and guests, plus the yard stables, a piggery, outhouses, and barns to the rear as expected with burgage plots.

In 1599, Thomas Habington[85] described the road up Broadway Hill,[86] which passed the White Hart Inn as *'a tedious street in the winter.'* That same year, William Sambache II, now aged fifty-two, was singled out to be distrained along with Anthony Dickens, and Ralph Franklin[87] in a writ to the Sherriff *'for the ill repair of the Broad way, being the highway to London.'*

There is some evidence that earlier Kings, cannily, had originally put the repair of roads in the hands of the church. They understood the

---

85. Thomas Habington, *'A Survey of Worcestershire'* Oxford, The Worcestershire Historical Society, 1895.
86. It appears in part to have been poorly made-up and been a ten horses' route on a winter's day.
87. Whilst there are no supporting documents, as the repair of roads was a responsibility of the parish, it may have been that William and his colleagues, were parish councillors (*parish overseers*) in the village, at that time.

importance to the Church of the highways being kept in good repair, it eased the transport of fleece, and other goods. But in 1555, after the dissolution of the monasteries, parliament passed the first statutory regulated legislation related to roads. The legislation set out specific details of parish statute labour which was to be used to maintain them. It was a particularly unfair system particularly for parishes such as Broadway with long busy roads running through them. The local Justices of the Peace oversaw the legislation. There are many examples of the Worcester Quarter Sessions starting to get tough on parishes in the mid-17th Century.

At some point, in the reign of Elizabeth I, the Inn was renamed the Swan. The Swan was the favoured heraldic badge of Edward III, and when Henry IV married Mary de Bohun, the Bohun Swan became part of his heraldry. It was favoured as a heraldic badge by Henry V, and VI but dropped until it was incorporated into the heraldry of Elizabeth I, (r 1558-1603).

Several Years after Jane's death, aged 52, in 1613, the Inn changed hands. Having such a large family must have created difficulties; it might have been easier to sell rather than decide which family member should inherit. After the sale, William, lived on a further sixteen years and died aged eighty-three, in 1630.

Chapter 8

1620 to 1642
The Treavis family flourish in the reign of James I and Charles I

In 1620, seven years, after the death of his wife Jane, William Sambache II sold the Inn to John Treavis.

Hissy, in his book,[88] written in 1891, considered the purchase to be earlier.

'It appears that as far back as 1549 the White Harte here was in possession of one John Treavis.' 'Given the date 1620 over the doorway, we (Hissy) *concluded that this must have been an earlier building possibly pulled down to make room for the present structure. The landlord, (1891) however appeared to think otherwise, and considered that the date 1620 related only to the doorway as being added at that time.'*

The landlord was right, Hissy visited Broadway infrequently, and his conclusions were at odds with the date of John Treavis' s death, 1641. John was seventy-four when he died so would not have been alive in 1549. 1620 is the date John and his wife Ursula Treavis took ownership.

Some suggest Hissy's reference to 1549 related to John Treavis' father, also called John, but this does not fit to evidence of ownership by Thomas White in 1549. The matter is resolved in a

---

88. James John Hissey, p 101, *'Across England in a Dog-cart'*, London Richard Bentley, 1891.

White Hart sale deed[89] 1683, which refers to the purchase of the Inn from William Sambache II and his son Walter,[90] by John Treavis, 29 November 1620, for £182.4s.

The property is described as two burgages and one half burgage, 70-foot in width,[91] used as one dwelling house or Inn called or known by the sign of the Swan, and one pasture with all houses, barns, stables orchards and gardens.

Sydney Russell, owner of the Lygon Arms in the early 20th century, was sent papers suggesting a John Traves,[92] a wealthy London merchant, a member of the London Vintners Company, was the Innkeeper's father. These papers were said to support John Traves' will referring to a debt owed to him, due to his provisioning the army in Ireland during the nine-year war against the English, 1593-1603. It was suggested to Sydney Russell that when settled, this debt yielded the funds to enable the son, John Traves, to buy the Inn in 1620. Whilst the papers passed to Sydney Russell seem to be lost, John Traves 1604 will is accessible. The tale is interesting but research into the will of John Traves, of the London Vintners Company, does not indicate any connection between the Traves of London, and the Treavis family in Broadway. We are still no wiser as to the date John Treavis came to Broadway, or if indeed his father had any prior connections with Broadway.

---

89. 29 November 1620, Worcestershire Archives and Archaeology Service, BA3464/1
90. No record has been found that confirms William had a son named Walter, his nephew, his brother John's son was called Walter.
91. A measurement that corresponds with the Lygon frontage at that time.
92. Spellings were less consistent in the 17th century.

Where the funds, for the purchase the Inn came from remains the subject of speculation. What is clear is that the new purchaser John Treavis had sufficient funds to purchase the Inn from William Sambache and oversee major improvements.

The Broadway John Treavis, circa 1600, married Ursula Wells, the twenty-two-year-old, daughter of Thomas Wells or Welles, a Badsey farmer. Parish Records confirm her baptism date as 15 March 1578[93] but there is no marriage record.

John Treavis's will, dated 11 May 1641, confirms John and Ursula had a large family; five daughters: Mary born 1613, Ann, Phillippa and Elizabeth born between 1612 and 1616, and a daughter Jane born 1609 who died in infancy. Their sons were Thomas, John, William born 1609, Robert, Mathew, and Gilbert.[94]

In the 20th century, in the eastern section of the Inn, workmen found a wooden apple-scoop carved AN TREAVIS. They also found carved initials HB and AB 1648, above an entrance to a chamber hinting the doorway may have led to married quarters. Ann Treves[95] married Thomas Baldwine in 1647. HB could have been carved to commemorate the birth of a first child, or his chosen initials.

---

93. Ancestry – One record says Broadway and one Badsey, but the year is the same on both.
94. The names of John's children and his wife are confirmed in his will: six sons Thomas, Gilbert, John, William, Robert, and Matthew and four daughters Elizabeth, Mary, Anne, and Phillipa, all save Jane who may have died in infancy.
95. Spelling in the parish records.

In addition, during renovations, when layers of paint were removed from the mullions in a bedroom, named bedroom 3 in 1904, the initials TT were found over carved dates, 1620 and 1624. It is suggested that the initials were carved by Thomas Treavis, one of John's sons.

John and Ursula, the new owners, almost immediately, on completion of the purchase deeds, instigated significant changes to the original building. Very visible today, distinctively Gothic, is the fine, carved, stone Jacobean entrance, with its unusually large carved spandrels. Typical of Jacobean work, the Ionic pilasters, architrave, strap-carved frieze, and bold cornice is surmounted by the scrolled and fretted finials. The ornamental frieze bears the name of John and his wife Ursula and the date of the acquisition of the Inn, 1620, across the top.

Two additional ground floor rooms were added east and west, which enabled additional upstairs chambers on both the first and second floor.

Two new staircases were added. The staircase which gave access to upper chambers to the west of the Inglenook, (now the Hotel's reception) was initially external. This was now brought into the building, though later its position was changed to that now rising from the boot room. In the passageway from the entrance to the newly added parlour a wider Elizabethan staircase enabled a grand assent to the Best Room, later called the Cromwell Room, and room 3.

In the extension to the west two ground floor rooms were added. Over the years they have had several roles. The first additional room, now the Saddle Room behind the reception, is a sitting room entered through a reset 16th century Tudor arched doorway. Its moulded chimney piece is said to have come from Merton Priory, near Wimbledon. Around 1680 this room was the Inn's bar area, for part of the 20th century it was a gift shop.

1915
Reset external arched Tudor doorway looking into the Saddle Room

2024
The Saddle Room

The second room was a small open sitting room, beyond the Saddle Room, which was also be approached through an old yard door. This room, also repurposed many times, was a kitchen, a small buttery, then a *'smoke room'* where guests enjoyed *'baccy'* in their clay pipes, and a tap room.

The old entrance from the yard to the small room now the Boot Room

The kitchen, buttery, smoke room, tap room, sitting room, now Boot Room

There used to be a range in the fireplace, and additional cooking implements above the mantel.

On the eastern side of the Inn, in addition to the new parlour, changes also included a brew house, and store and pantry next to the Elizabethan stairs.

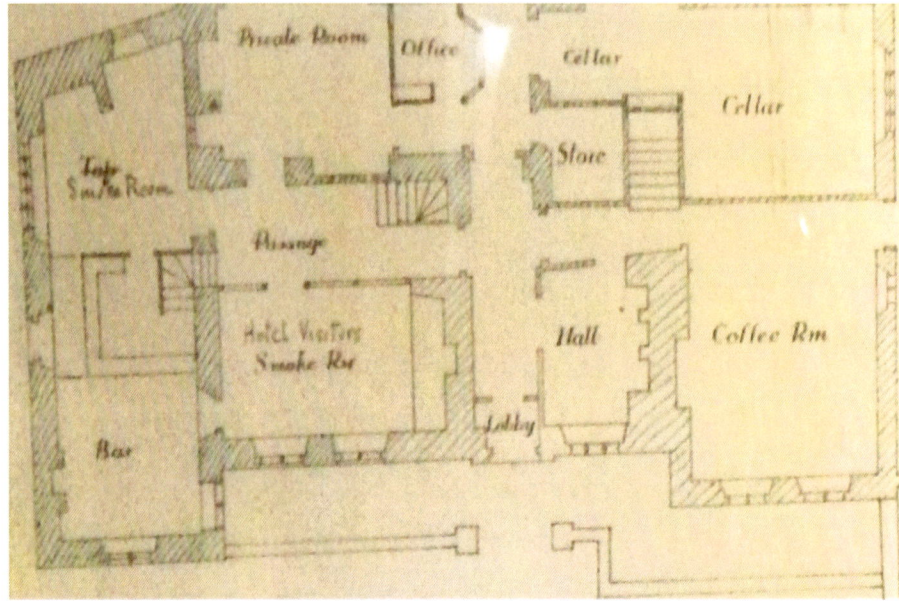

Taken from a 1904 survey – ignoring the names- it illustrates the layout of the Inn after the Treavis' 17th century improvements. It shows the two additional rooms to the west: the Bar now the Saddle Room, and Smoke/Tap Room now the Boot Room. The staircase, next to the Smoke/Tap Room has since been repositioned. The front ground floor room to the east, which has been a parlour, kitchen, dining, and coffee room, and is now part of the entrance to the Great Hall. The cellar area in the 17th century was a brew house and is now a passage linking the Russell Room to the Great Hall and the Tapestry Room. An extra floor and expansion into the dormers added two stories and further bedchambers.

Around eight extra chambers were added on the first and second floors, all fitted with mullion windows. Those in the roof, the dormer rooms, on the second floor were used for guests and in part, at the rear, as servants' quarters.

Along the passage to the Great Hall, carved on a curved wooden lintel is the apt phrase *'Now good digestion wants on appetite and health on both.'*

The 17th century changes initiated by Treavis were considerable. They completely changed the Inn from a small affair to one of grandeur, both through the widening of the Inn and the addition of high floors, coupled with the tall new chimneys. Internally elegance, enrichment both in the fabric of the building and the furnishings appear to have been the order of the day.

The whole, significantly changed the skyline of Broadway's main street; the impact of the new building was almost monumental. When completed the new building must assuredly have impressed the villagers.

Comparative pictures below, though neither are dated 1620, demonstrate the impact of additional floors, dormers and grouped diagonal chimneys.

By the end of the improvements the number of chambers in the Inn had increased from four to twelve.

A large chamber, two storeys high, accessed via the rear staircases from the small sitting room, was one of Treavis' most ornately decorated rooms. Its name, the Great Chamber, is carved on a plaque on its door. Internally the room is open to the apex of the timber roof, one which shows a good deal of reconstruction, and reuse. It looks out on to main street and the western passageway. The room boasted a fine stone fireplace, enhanced by its mantelpiece, which is today a more modest affair.

In 1641, though unevidenced, John Treavis is reputed to have spent his last days in the Great Chamber,[96] which suggests the Great Chamber and adjacent little chamber, were his and Ursula's sitting room (now the bathroom) and bedroom. The Treavis' were a large family, it is possible until their children left home, they chose their chambers to be together on the second floor in the main building, now rooms 8, 10, 11, 12, 17 and 20. By 1680 these rooms were used for guests and one servant's quarters.

One chamber in the Inn was embellished to become the finest room in the house. Situated on the first floor, approached by the original Elizabethan staircase, Treavis added a beautiful early 17th century plaster ceiling, which bears a resemblance to the ceiling at Aston Hall in Warwickshire and a carved decorative frieze of a delicate interlacing strapwork design to enhance the walls. A delightful small, mullioned Oriel 'bay' window looked out on to a garden.

---

96. Alison Ridley and Curtis Garfield, p 59, 'The Story of the Lygon Arms' Burgess, Abingdon, Oxfordshire

Treavis's Best Room later renamed the Cromwell Room

The fireplace, which was splendidly enhanced with an arched Tudor head, flanked by Corinthian pilasters, decorated with strap carvings in low relief, showcases Elizabethan craftmanship at its best. The pair of Elizabethan cast iron fire dogs and fire back dated 1632, added at the time, still sit in the fireplace.

In 1633, as in 1532 when Thomas White is listed as number 25 in Broadway's Parish register, John Treavis' obligation to the Church and the maintenance of its walls is recorded against the number 25.

Two of John and Ursula's sons, William, and Mathew, left home to build up business interests connected to Livery companies in London. William became a member of the Grocers Company and Mathew was a citizen of London and Member of the Salter Company. Records of their sons Gilbert, John or Robert have not yet materialised. Thomas, who appears to have been John and Ursula's eldest son, does not appear to have married.

All the children, as they grew up would have, in one way or another, been involved with the running of the Inn between 1620 and 1641 when John Treavis (Travise) died. Their daughters, all have marriage records apart from Phillipa.

When John Treavis died, he was buried at St Eadburgha's Church where, in the centre of the chancel, on the floor, is an inscribed, plain, memorial brass plaque which records his death.

Here lyeth buried ye body, of John Treavis who deceased ye 27 May, An Dni 1641. Aged 74.

A rubbing of the church's brass plate is prominently displayed, in the lobby of the small sitting room, the Boot Room, beyond the Saddle Room next to the western staircase leading to the upper two floors.

In his will, dated 11 May, just before he died, John left half the Inn and furniture to his wife Ursula providing she was a widow, and the other half to his son Thomas. On Ursula's death the whole was to pass Thomas, and on his death to John, then William, then Robert and finally Mathew, who seems to have been his youngest son.[97]

From 1641 until 1651, Ursula Treavis ran the Inn supported by her eldest son Thomas, until his death in 1649, and possibly his sister Ann, until her marriage to Thomas Baldwine, in 1647. The carvings previously mentioned suggest the married couple lived at the Inn.

There may also have been support from the family based in London if they were not caught up in the machinations of the English Civil War 1642-1651. This is a period where family loyalties could be split in two. Perhaps those living in London where their trade was carried out had to walk the parliamentary line, whilst family members in Royalist Worcestershire wished the King to succeed. We may never know but historic references show the White Hart Inn and Broadway were very soon thrust into the practical consequences of the Civil War.

---

97. John Trevis 1605 PROB- 11-188-174 National Archives

Chapter 9

Autumn 1642 – Autumn 1651
Roundheads and Royalists
A challenge for the Treavis Family at the White Hart

The English Civil War[98] was a series of armed conflicts and political machinations between Queen Elizabeth I's cousin, Charles I, and his Royalists supporters, with their courtly appearance, long ringlets, and flamboyant hats and the English Parliament, Parliamentarians, named Roundheads by the Royalists to reflect their short haircuts. London's apprentices,[99] who actively demonstrated their support for Parliament in the months before the fighting began, also had short, cropped hair or shaved heads.

There were three parts to the English Civil War. In the first 1642 to 1646, Charles I fought the Parliamentarians for control of England. Troops, from both sides passed through or by Broadway, on the London Road, between Worcester and Oxford many times. The Parliamentarians won.

The second part February to August 1647, featured wide-spread conspiracies, including the Broadway Plot:

---

98. Rushworth, John (1612/1690) *'Historical collections of private passages of state: weighty matters in law. Remarkable proceedings in five Parliaments. Beginning the sixteenth year of King James, anno 1618. And ending the fifth year of King Charles, anno 1629 Charles I, King of England, 1600-1649. His Majesties declaration to all his loving subjects, of the causes which moved him to dissolve the last parliament, March 10. 1628,'* James Astwood, 1682.
99. John Rushworth, pp. 614-619 *'Historical Collections of Private Passages of State: Volume 6, 1645-47,'* London, 1722. British History Online http://www.british-history.ac.uk/rushworth-papers/vol 6.

'From its position there were few places in Worcestershire that had seen more of the war and were better suited for the rendezvous of troops than Broadway.'[100]

This second phase ultimately led to the trial and execution of Charles I, early 1649, the exile of Charles II and the establishment of the Commonwealth of England.

In the third and final conflict, Cromwell invaded Scotland, and Charles II invaded England, August 1651, but few rallied to the Royalist cause. Cromwell finally defeated both Scots and Royalists at the Battle of Worcester, 3 September 1651, Charles II was one of the few that escaped.

Over the centuries much has been made of the belligerent's leaders, Oliver Cromwell, and Charles I, resting at the White Hart Inn. It is equally important to understand the impact of the manoeuvres between 1642 and 1646 on the village of Broadway during the first Civil War, inevitably the Inn was engaged with both sides in some way and Broadway's role in the plot of 1647.

Charles I's support was strong in Worcestershire villages such as Broadway and the surrounding countryside; many of the local squires were Royalists, as was much of previously Catholic Worcestershire.

There was no permanent army when the Civil War started in 1642, individuals made great sacrifices to raise the regiments to fight for

---

100. Willis Bund, J. W. (John William), (1843-1928) p.199 *'The Civil War in Worcestershire, 1642-1646, and the Scotch invasion of 1651.'* London: Simpkin, Marshall, Hamilton, Kent, 1905.

the King. As with other villages in England loyal to Charles I's cause, Broadway would have been pressed into contributing to the cost of the King's regiments.

'WORCESTERSHIRE
Since the civil warr in this kingdome, these regiments have been raysed out of this county, pro Reg e: which consists onely of 150 od parish churches.'

'Sir James Hamilton, about May 1643, raysed three regiments. One of horse 400 or thereabouts, one of ffote near 1,000, one of dragoons, all at the charges of the county. These captaynes were under him of this county:

Of Horse
Captain John Blunt, of Soddington, son to Sir Walter Blunt.
Captain William Welch.
Captain Colt.' [101]

The provisioners of the troops organising billeting, any bolt hole: stable, farm, farm building, or church floor, also supplying vitals and water for horses and men on the move, would have been integral contributors to the campaign.

Local people were pressured to make up shortfalls. Sound loyal supporters would have been encouraged to hide provisions in strategic places on their property. Horse regiments always needed good water and fodder.

---

101. Richard Symonds (a Royalist Soldier) p.11-12 *'Diary of the Marches of the Royal Army, April 10, 1644 - February 11, 1645,'* the Campden Society, 1838-1901, London Longmans, Green, 1859.

The leaders and officers of both armies would, of necessity, have dealt with the White Hart, the key hostelry, on Broadway's main street, with its big posting yard, many stables, and horses. Some of the troops, both officers, foot soldiers and dragoons, must have supped at the Inn.

Ursula Treavis and local members of her family would have had to be discrete diplomats on many occasions. They were dealing with opposing armies, and England's most powerful commanders. At another level, inevitably they would have had to manage local conflicts, caused by the troops passing through, drawn to the liquor, unable to maintain discipline.

It is likely the parliamentarian troops dealt with local villagers harshly, for they too needed provisions, and knew the local people, by and large, supported the Royalists.

There are passages in Symmonds dairy where he captures the complaints of the local people to Charles I that *'the enemy was a plundering… and they desired ayde.'*[102]

The scale of the regiments passing through Broadway is hard to imagine.

'Colonel Samuel Sandys, of Ombersley, four myles from Worcester, about the same time raysed three regiments; one of horse, one of foot, one of dragoons,[103] all at his own charge. He has 3,000s per annum.'[104]

---

102. Richard Symonds p. 48, *'Diary of the Marches of the Royal Army, April 10, 1644 - February 11, 1645,'* the Campden Society, 1838-1901, London Longmans, Green, 1859.
103. Horsemen.
104. Richard Symonds p.12, *'Diary of the Marches of the Royal Army, April 10, 1644 - February 11, 1645,',* the Campden Society, 1838-1901, London Longmans, Green, 1859.

'His horse consisted of between 6 or 700.

Mr John Sandys, his unckle, captain-leift.
Mr Windsor Hickman, leift colonel.
Capt. Savage of this county, (a local Broadway family).
Captain Langston.

One regiment of foot was about 1,000.
Captain William Sandys, his unckle.
Captain Frederick Windsor.'
Captain Fr. Moore of this county. (related to Savage)
Captain Heling......

Colonel Sandys gave up his regiment of ffoot to Knotsworth, who was now Governor of Evesham, of the county of Warwick, about Aprill, when Prince Rupert was here.'[105]

Not everyone was a loyal supporter of Charles; the King's taxes on cloth merchants were ill-advised. They encouraged those linked to weaving and cloth, particularly in the towns, such as Evesham, to back the Parliamentarians.

In addition, as in any war that necessitated armaments and vast expenses, the King was creative in raising funds for his war chest. There is a reference to a few Broadway residents being fined for not paying an honorarium for an imposed knighthood: William

105. Richard Symonds p.12, *'Diary of the Marches of the Royal Army, April 10, 1644 - February 11, 1645,'*, the Campden Society, 1838-1901, London Longmans, Green, 1859.

Sambadge (Sambache?) of Broadwaie, Esquire 14 shillings, William Stevens 10 shillings, William Stevens Jun. 10 shillings. [106]

Charles I and his troops passed through or near Broadway many times, as did the parliamentarians, there are references in one diary or another of the time. On other occasions the references to Broadway were captured in more substantial records,[107] even the papers of the House of Commons.[108]

Mid-1642 both sides began to arm, following Charles I's failed invasion of Parliament to arrest five of its members. By the time Charles had raised the royal standard in Nottingham, August 1642, his forces controlled much of the Midlands.

- 16 September 1642, *'Charles left Evesham, rested for some hours at Broadway, but pushed on in the evening.'*[109] The White Hart is a strong candidate for the King to have rested on this occasion.

Some historians suggest the King would have rested in grander houses, not country inns. References in the original manuscript of

---

106. John Noake, p317, *Notes and Queries for Worcestershire, 1856,* London, Longman - a list of Worcester gentlemen fined by King Charles I for not taking the order of Knighthood; extracted from the " *Book of Compositions for not taking the Order of Knighthood at the Coronation of King Charles* I. 1630—1632.
107. John Rushworth, VII., p. 974. *'Perfect Occurrences, January 21 — 2S, 1647,'* Henry Walker (cleric). Perfect Occurrences was a weekly newspaper which became the semi-official mouth piece of Parliament in 1647.
108. D Browne, *'Historical Collections of Private Passages of State: Volume 7,'* 1647-48. *Originally published by, London, 1721. Proceedings in Parliament February 28, 1647.*
109. Willis Bund, J. W. (John William), 1843-1928, p.103, *'The Civil War in Worcestershire, 1642-1646, and the Scotch invasion of 1651,'* London: Simpkin, Marshall, Hamilton, Kent, 1905.

Richard Symonds' Diary of the Marches of the Royal Army,[110] confirm that in the early days of his marches he did stay in the houses of Lords and the wealthy, but later by necessity he took rest where he could: in a farmhouse, country inn, poor house, even in the fields *'This night wee lay in the wett field without any provision. Wee made this march, from four of the clock in the morning to one next night, without any bayte or rendezvous.'* [111]

In 1643, Charles moved his court and military headquarters to Oxford, and continued throughout 1643 to have the advantage, resulting in the Parliamentarian deciding to ally with the Scots, whom Charles had been fighting since 1637. Prince Rupert's papers[112] refer to the idea of Charles I's push on to London as being useless. *'He was therefore forced to fall back on the old plan of conquering the country piecemeal, town by town, village by village; and accordingly.'* [113]

'10 August (1643) he (The King with 30,000 men) laid siege to Gloucester where he battled with Massey,[114] then governor of Gloucester'[115]

---

110. This Diary of the English Civil War is the only first-hand account by a participant on the King's side who was not an officer. The diarist, Richard Symonds, was a royal lifeguard man for the crucial two years of 1644-5.

111. Richard Symonds, p.28, *'Diary of the Marches of the Royal Army, April 10, 1644 - February 11, 1645,'* the Campden Society, 1838-1901, London Longmans, Green, 1859.

112. Prince Rupert (born Dec. 17, 1619, Prague, Bohemia [now Czech Republic]was a talented Royalist commander of the English Civil War). His tactical genius and daring as a cavalry officer brought him many victories early in the war. His favourite Uncle was Charles I. His mother was Elizabeth Stuart.

113. Scott, Eva, p.120, *'Rupert, Prince, Count Palatine, (1619-1682), 'Great Britain -- History Civil War, 1642-1649'* G P Putnam and sons, 1899.

114. Major General Sir Edward Massie a descendent on his mother's side was Rev. Richard Massie Collins, a theologian, a well-known local in Broadway, related to the Collins brothers, butchers, the Lygon Arms neighbours, and antagonist in a legal case of 1906.

115. Scott, Eva, p.120, *'Rupert, Prince, Count Palatine, (1619-1682), Great Britain -- History Civil War, 1642-1649'* G P Putnam and sons, 1899.

Just short of a month the failed siege was over, and the King was forced to retire before Essex arrived at Gloucester. It was around nightfall (Bund suggests 16 September 1643) the King tarried in Broadway.[116] Rupert had mustered his troops on Broadway Down, but, though he waited till nightfall, he received no news from the King who had previously been encamped in Pershore. At last, he set out in person to seek him. *'In the window of a farmhouse, he perceived a light, and, advancing cautiously, he looked in. There sat the King quietly playing at piquet with Lord Percy, while Lord Forth (Commander in Chief) looked on. The Prince burst in upon them, crying indignantly that his men had been in the saddle for hours, and that Essex must be overtaken before he could join with Waller.[117][118] Percy and Forth offered objections, but Rupert carried the day, and dashed of as independently as he had come.[119]*

The following year, in 1644, the Royalist and Parliamentarian armies played *'cat and mouse,'* passing through the village or around Broadway Hill.

Essex and Waller nearly caught Charles in Oxford, but he escaped, marched by Broadway to Evesham, and on to Worcester and Bewdley; the march cost the County of Worcestershire £10,000 from the breaking down of bridges.

---

116. Willis Bund, J. W. (John William), 1843-1928, p.103, *'The Civil War in Worcestershire, 1642-1646, and the Scotch invasion of 1651,'* London: Simpkin, Marshall, Hamilton, Kent, 1905.

117. Sir William Waller was an English soldier and politician, who commanded Parliamentarian armies during the First part of the English Civil War, before relinquishing his commission when the self-denying ordinance was passed by Parliament 3 April 1645, thrown out by the Lords until reformed so it did not forbid re-appointment of the officers. A new model army was brought in.

118. The Earl of Essex, who had captured forty supply waggons, at Tewkesbury, then set off for London.

119. Scott, Eva, p.120, *'Rupert Prince, Count Palatine, Great Britain -- History Civil War, 1642-1649,'* New York : G. P. Putnam's sons, 1899.

- May 1644, Charles I fled to Evesham, and onwards when parliament dispatched the Earl of Essex and Sir William Waller, an extremely effective parliamentary commander, to besiege Oxford.

Massey commented to Brydges, the governor of Warwick *'the enemy is reported to be very strong about Stow, Broadway, Campden, Evesham, Upton, and Tewkesbury, and if he be not drawn off by His Excellency's other forces, your party will be too slender I am afraid.'*[120]

- Monday [121] 3 June 1644, *'The King and his entourage marched to Burford, supped there then nine of the clock, continued his march from Burford over the Cotswold, and by midnight reached Burton upon the Water; where he gave himself, and his wearied troops, more rest and refreshment.'*[122] Interestingly, Waller following Rupert made such haste, that they *'found in Burford some of the straggling soldiers, who out of weariness, or for love of drink, had stayed behind their fellows,'*[123]

Love of drink was just one of the challenges the White Hart Inn had to manage as troops passed through Broadway.

- Wednesday 5 June 1644, *'the King and all his army marched over Cotswold downes and Brodway hills and came to Evesham,*

120. Scott, Eva, p.125, *'Rupert Prince, Count Palatine, Great Britain -- History Civil War, 1642-1649,'*, New York : G. P. Putnam's sons, 1899
121. Sharp eyed critical readers may question the day of the week. Before 1752 the Julian calendar was in use, after this date it was the Gregorian calendar.
122. Clarendon, Edward Hyde, Earl of, (1609-1674), p.453, *'The history of the rebellion and civil wars in England,'* Oxford, University Press, 1839.
123. Clarendon, Edward Hyde, Earl of, (1609-1674), p.454, *'The history of the rebellion and civil wars in England,'* Oxford, University Press, 1839.

his owne garrison, where young Colonel Knotsforth was governour; which was the first night's rest of our army.'[124]

It is clear he continued to Evesham for fear of Waller; this was a sound call.

- 6 June 1644, '*Thursday morning the bridge was pulled up, and Knotsford(sp) commanded to stay till he saw the enemy of whom wee heard (by one of their captaynes who was taken scowting that morning neare Brodway) that Waller was in Brodway with all his army* (10,000 men and 150 horse). *Evesham being slighted.*

  The King marched with all his army to Worcester that night, being twelve myles the worst way. A woody and dursty county. Pershore bridge was pulled downe by our forces, because Waller should not follow, and forty of our men lost. The bridge fell from them into the river.'[125]

  Another source talks of the sudden falling of an arch, killing three or four officers of horse, and about twenty commoners, falling and drowning.[126]

- Friday 7 June 1644, Waller departed from Broadway making his way to Evesham.

124. pp. 244, 255, *Calendar of State Papers Domestic: Charles I, 1644,* ed. William Douglas Hamilton 1888, London, British History Online http://www.british-history.ac.uk/cal-state-papers / domestic / chas1 /1644.'
125. Richard Symonds p.12, '*Diary of the Marches of the Royal Army, April 10, 1644 - February 11, 1645,*', the Campden Society, 1838-1901, London Longmans, Green, 1859.
126. Clarendon, Edward Hyde, Earl of, 1609-1674, p.455, '*The history of the rebellion and civil wars in England,*' Oxford, University Press, 1839.

- Sunday 16 June 1644, 'Sunday, *after Sermon in the forenoone ended in the Cathedral at Worcester, his Majestic about xii of the clock left Worcester and lay that night at Broadway com Gloucester* (was in fact a parish in Worcester) *........ going through Evesholme (*Evesham*). His Majestic lay that night at Mr. Savage, his howse there at Brodway.....*[127]

The Savages of Broadway were staunch Royalists. Walter born 7 September 1628, who inherited the 'Greate Farme' in 1640, aged twelve, would most certainly have had others acting for him in 1644, as he was still to come of age. One of his cousins, Anthony, aged eighteen, was a Captain in the Royalist army; this connection may have led to the King spending the night at the farm in Broadway. It is likely some of the King's officers supped, if not stayed, at the Inn.

- Monday 17 June 1644, *'From Brodway, the King and all his army marched over Cotswold Downes, where Dover's games a were, to Stowe in the Would, six myle. Then that night to Burford in co. Oxon being seven myles further, where his Majestie lay that Munday night at the George Inn in Burford...'*
  [128]

- Wednesday morning 3 July 1644, *'From thence his Majestie with his whole army marched over the Cotswold hills with colours flying, trumpets sounding to Brodway thence on to Evensholme, that night where he lay.'* His troops were quartered at Fladbury[129]

---

127. Richard Symonds p.14, 'Diary of the Marches of the Royal Army, April 10, 1644 - February 11, 1645,', the Campden Society, 1838-1901, London Longmans, Green, 1859.
128. Ibid p.15.
129. Ibid p.25.

- Friday 5 July 1644, *'the King and the army marched from thence* (Fladbury) *through Brodway, then over the Cotswold neare Shudeley Castle, the seate of the Lord Chandos, from whence the rebells gave us two great shott. That night at one of the clock, the king got to his quarters a poore howse, in Coverley'*[130]

- 13 July 1644, Sir William Waller parliamentarian, spoke to the committee of both Kingdoms, at Towcester and indicated that he thought the King was marching to towards Bristol.

Sir William Waller, whose raids thoroughly depleted the Vale of Evesham Etching 1643 by Pieter Rodermondt- National Portrait Gallery London.

---

130. Richard Symonds, p.28, *'Diary of the Marches of the Royal Army, April 10, 1644 - February 11, 1645,'* Campden Society 1838-1901, London Longmans, Green, 1859.

- However, once over Broadway Hill the King quite suddenly at Sudeley Castle, turned towards Woodstock. Sir William subsequently redirected his march to track the King. From July, for the rest of the year, the battle and skirmish grounds moved to Gloucestershire, Wiltshire, Somerset, Devon, North Cornwall, Devon, Dorset, Wiltshire then back up to Oxford, Charles' winter quarters.

With poor, muddy ill managed roads, frosts, then snow the movement of troops was impossible over winter; this gave time for Broadway to recover but dread the return of the armies in the following year.

1645, the Royalist line of march from Oxford to Worcester was cut by Massey, and the Scottish army that had finally decided to aid Parliament.

- 10 March 1645, Charles I is said to have met Sheldon of Broadway Court in a centre front room of the White Hart.[131] Symonds, in his diaries, puts Charles in Oxford. Other publications suggest they met 10 May 1645.

- Thursday 8 May 1645, *'This morning at one o'clock an alarme waked us, and at daybreak the King marched with his 4 pieces of cannon, 8 boates in carriages, &c. : vizt all manner of ammunition, his troopes of life guard and foot regiment of horse, and part of the regiment of horse, and part of the regiment of Lifeguard in the van, ammunition, &c. next then his Majestie, &c. Earl Northampton in the reare...*[132]

---

131. *Worcester Journal*, 13 January 1894.
132. Richard Symonds, p.165, '*Diary of the Marches of the Royal Army, April 10, 1644 - February 11, 1645,*' Campden Society 1838-1901, London Longmans, Green, 1859.

Neare Stow on the Wold, we joined Prince Rupert's army of horse and foot, eithteen myles.'

- Friday 9 May 1645, *'His Majestic marched to Evesham, where he joyned with the Lord Asteleyes foot, consisting of 3300; in the primeir place was Prince Rupert's regiment of foot, consisting of 500...[133]*

  This day, Grenerall Goring marched into the West with 3,000 horse.

  300 foot taken out of our garrison of Camden; the howse (which was so faire) burnt. * Clarendon confirms the wanton burning of this house.

  The King's troope[134]garrisoned at Child's Wickham in Glouc,.. three myles from Evesham.' With so many the foot soldiers and dragoons to bed down every spare inch of Childswickham's barns, stables, or outhouses must have been requisitioned. It is likely the Kings commanders at Childswickham took advantage of the White Hart Inn's hospitality.

- 9 or 10 May 1645, a number of publications suggest Charles met his local supporters with Sheldon of Broadway Court[135] in one of the Inn's first floor rooms, an oak-panelled room, situated above the old kitchen.[136] Post the 1620, improvements this room was would have been accessed

---

133. Ibid. p 165.
134. Ibid, p. 166. About eight thousand horse and foot. At Evesham he was joined by three thousand foot.
135. If it were so difficult to say if they met with a Sheldon or a Savage, whose mother was a Sheldon.
136. S. B. Russell, *'The Story of an Old English Hostelry,'* Letchworth at the Arden Press.

discretely, from the posting yard, (the Drawing Room and Parlour below had not been built) via an external rear staircase positioned west to east, near the little buttery. Given the number of times Charles I moved between his two greatest strongholds, Worcester, and Oxford with his great armies, and the fact the Kings troops were garrisoned in Childswickham this is entirely possible.

At the battle of Naseby 14 June 1645, the balance tipped decisively in favour of Parliament.

- End December 1645 *'2000 men were advancing from Oxford, they were met on Broadway Hill and driven back to Oxford.'*

- March 1646, *'It may be imagined to what straits the Royalists were reduced when it is said that out of these more than half were "reformado" officers, that is, officers of regiments that had either ceased to exist, from being destroyed or disbanded, or become so reduced in numbers there was no need for such officers. They formed a desperate band of broken men, who had all to gain by plunder and everything to lose by peace.'*[137]

Lord Astley, in the early part of 1646, was the most prominent Royalist leader in Worcestershire. He left Oxford on December 22nd, 1645, to go round the different garrisons in the Midlands, trying to raise an army. His task was a difficult one.

'and not the less so by his extreme want of money.......... Astley attempting anything. He fell back towards Bewdley. On the 5

---

137. Willis Bund, J. W. (John William), 1843-1928, p.176, 'The Civil War in Worcestershire, 1642-1646, and the Scotch invasion of 1651,' London: Simpkin, Marshall, Hamilton, Kent, 1905.

February Chester surrendered. Byron had held out to the last and had to yield to want of fuel and want of food. Horses, dogs, and cats had been eaten, and Byron was unable to do more….. Astley was in dire need of money, so much so that he had to borrow from the corporation of Bridgnorth to pay his personal expenses there.'[138]

Astley was aware of two parliamentary commanders Morgan and Birch, who were waiting for him in Broadway. Charles' army collected in Wales, Herefordshire, and Worcestershire but they were defeated in Stow-on-the-Wold.

- April 1646, after a series of defeats and the siege of Oxford, Charles I escaped (disguised as a servant) and put himself into the hands of the Scottish presbyterian army. He was taken to Newcastle upon Tyne. Nine months of negotiations, followed. The Scots finally arrived at an agreement with the English Parliament; in exchange for £100,000 and the promise of more money in the future, the Scots delivered Charles I to the Parliamentary Commissioners in January 1647. He then surrendered to the Scots.

As far as Worcestershire was concerned the Civil War had ended. However, ……

A second Civil War, to no avail, took place in 1647, it was short lasting a few months. Its was a series of plots to bring about the

---

138. Willis Bund, J. W. (John William), 1843-1928, p. 175, The Civil War in Worcestershire, 1642-1646, and the Scotch invasion of 1651. London: Simpkin, Marshall, Hamilton, Kent, 1905.

King's release or achieve a second rising. The chief of these was the Broadway Plot.[139]

'Money was scarce with the Parliament. They could not pay their troops, and so the men became mutinous. The lesson, the evil lesson, that they had been taught by the example of various places, that if they only mutinied for their pay they would get, if not all, at least some of it, had sunk into the minds of the Gloucester garrison. Acting on it, they thought the best way to get their pay was at once to mutiny. The Royalists took advantage of this discontent. In January 1648, the Presbyterian officers of the Gloucester and other garrisons, took action.'

From its position there were few places in Worcestershire that had seen more of the war and were better suited for the rendezvous of troops than Broadway.'[140]

'Under the Cotswold Hills, on the direct road from Wales to Oxford, near to the spot where the road from Warwick to Gloucester crossed, it was a locality of no small importance. Being on the borders of three Counties it made a most convenient centre. It is, therefore, not surprising that at Broadway those who were discontented with the existing state of things met to consider if it was possible that anything could be done.'

139. Willis Bund, J. W. (John William), 1843-1928, p. 2, *The Civil War in Worcestershire, 1642-1646, and the Scotch invasion of 1651.* London: Simpkin, Marshall, Hamilton, Kent, 1905.
140. Willis Bund, J. W. (John William), 1843-1928, p. 200-201, *'The Civil War in Worcestershire, 1642-1646, and the Scotch invasion of 1651.'* London: Simpkin, Marshall, Hamilton, Kent 1905.

A few days later, the House of Commons, received a hasty communication detailing, from the meeting, the names of eighty officers of several regiments who were discontent with their pay and conditions, and the progress of the war.

- 28 February 1647, *'A letter was read to the House of Commons concerning the plotting of some officers in a dangerous design about Gloucestershire and the shires adjacent. Sent by an eminent person, the copy where of followeth: A council was held at Broadway the greatest part of last week* (A venue for the officer's discussions may have been in the White Hart) *by about 80 officers of Colonel Kempson's, Colonel Ayre's, Colonel Herbert's, and another regiment of foot, and of Colonel Cooke's regiment of horse.'*[141]

The Broadway Plot details access to 300 barrels of powder, Hartlebury Castle and Gloucester were to be the plotters targets. The full details alarmed parliament who feared further hostilities in the Midlands. The authorities took immediate steps to halt any conspiracy: the garrison at Gloucester was changed, the London Road protected at Stow, there was a statement in the House of Commons, and monies were paid to provide for the dissatisfied who were then disbanded.

Parliament had reason to be alarmed; a wide-spread conspiracy was afoot. A movement, a continuance of the Broadway plot, had expanded to Bewdley; men and firearms were to be raised by

---

141. D Browne, *'Historical Collections of Private Passages of State: Volume 7, 1647-48.* London, 1721. Proceedings in Parliament February 28, 1647.

Colonel Dud Dudley,[142] who in 1648, attempted a rising, in Worcestershire. It was suppressed and Dudley was taken prisoner, sent to London, and condemned to die. The morning before his execution he escaped.

For Charles, the second phase ended in house arrest and a failed escape, before he was moved to Hurst Castle at the end of 1648, and thereafter to Windsor Castle. January 1649, the Rump House of Commons indicted him for treason, his trial began on 20 January 1649. 30 January 1649 he was executed and buried at Windsor Castle.

Following the execution, the climax of the English Civil War, the Parliament of Scotland proclaimed his son Charles II King of Scotland, 5 February 1649. and the Parliament troops moved their focus to putting down the Irish.

This was the same year that Thomas Treavis, innkeeper with his mother, son of John Treavis, of the White Hart died.

The Third Civil War started in 1651, a good deal of negotiations and manoeuvres led to Charles II, at the end of July, invading England, and marching through Carlisle on London. He halted at Worcester, awaiting reinforcements from Wales. Cromwell, meanwhile, proceeded down the east coast, and marched across to Evesham, to get between Charles II and London.

---

142. Dudd (Dud) Dudley (1600–1684) the illegitimate son of Edward Sutton, 5th Baron Dudley of Dudley Castle, the fourth of Lord Dudley's eleven children by his 'concubine' Elizabeth, was an English metallurgist, who fought on the Royalist side in the English Civil War as a soldier, military engineer, and supplier of munitions. He was one of the first Englishmen to smelt iron ore using coke.

Cromwell and Fleetwood together had twenty-eight thousand men, and the prospect of more to come by the end of August. Charles II had just over half that number, only sixteen thousand men drawn from forty-six different Scottish regiments and clans, many of whom were exhausted from the march to Worcester and several skirmishes enroute.

27 August 1651, Cromwell advanced on to Worcester, via Evesham after passing though Broadway, about the 26 August. For many centuries writers and artists have celebrated this occasion.

This drawing is one of the 1930's Famous Hostelry Series
By Christopher Clark RI for John Haig & Co Ltd Distillers. Markinch, Fife.

On the 28 August Cromwell was at Moor. On the 29 August he slept at the home of Mr. Symonds,[143] at White Ladies Aston, between Moor and Worcester. He said to have written to London of his suggesting his success, though others write of letters that are full of nervousness concerning the Scottish Army.

On the 30 August Cromwell came to Spetchley, the house of Mr. Justice Berkeley[144], three miles from Worcester, where he is said to have established himself during the subsequent operations.

Despite Charles ll's troops rebuilding Worcester's Fort before the battle and managing to blow up four key bridges, they lost the natural advantage of the River Severn and Teme. The bridge at Upton, ten miles from Worcester, was rebuilt by the Parliamentarians. Thirty-one thousand men, the troops of Cromwell, Fleetwood, and Lambert, came together, mainly at Red Hill and Perry Wood, and reinforcements kept coming in to swell the parliamentary troops. Some were enthusiastic to join and some plainly desired to be on the winning side.

The Parliamentarians attacked from the west, the required materials, and boats were brought to the river by the 1 September, and the troops were within pistol shot by 2 September. At daybreak the action began, Cromwell remained in command at Perry wood, just

---

143. Willis Bund, J. W. (John William), 1843-1928, p. 216, 'The Civil War in Worcestershire, 1642-1646, and the Scotch invasion of 1651.' 1905, London: Simpkin, Marshall, Hamilton, Kent.

144. Other accounts say that Mr. Berkeley burnt the house down sooner than it should be defiled by sheltering a regicide. Oliver Cromwell was not so popular with English people once he gained power. There are many instances of people that supported him denying that they did after the Battle of Worcester. The house may well have been burnt down by royalists.

outside Worcester. By 2 September four bridges across the Severn had been completed, and boats were in place to cross the Teme. [145]

The fierce attack began on the 3 September. Cromwell was victorious, but the total of the wounded was enormous: two thousand royalists were killed, and eight or nine thousand prisoners were taken after the battle. Cromwell's sent a short letter to the Speaker, directly, announcing his victory, which was received in London on 5 September 1651. It is likely Cromwell passed through Broadway on his return to London on 7 September 1651.

Charles II escaped from Worcester to France, via Shoreham in Sussex, 15 October 1651.

The English Civil War, which had started with the first skirmish at Powick Bridge, just outside Worcester, in 1642 ended nine years later with the Battle of Worcester on 3 September 1651. Reflecting on this, the second US President, John Adams, on a visit to Fort Royal Hill (then a Park), with Thomas Jefferson, 3 April 1876, when speaking to local people said, *'Worcester is the ground where liberty was fought.'*[146] Many sites in Worcester: St Martin's Gate, Fort Royal, the Cathedral, the Commandery, the Greyfriars and King Charles House bore witness to the struggle between Royalists and the Parliamentarians. It is written post the battle the winds howled though the cathedral, and the streets were empty for many a year.

At the White Hart, Treavis' best room, was renamed the Cromwell Room and a copy of his famous 'warts and all' portrait was hung next to its seventeenth-century fireplace. It now hangs behind the

---

145. Willis Bund, J. W. (John William), 1843-1928, p. 225-265, 'The Civil War in Worcestershire, 1642-1646, and the Scotch invasion of 1651.' London: Simpkin, Marshall, Hamilton, Kent,1905.
146. He was referring to 2 Sept 1651 when the Essex Militia, in a frenzy of enthusiasm, despite a stubborn resistance, bore down the defenders, entered the Fort Royal and the King's standard was torn down and the blue Parliament flag hoisted on the Fort.

reception. It may well have been placed in the Cromwell Room immediately after the Civil War, as early as the 7 September, as a protection from retribution.

In 1653, following his success, Cromwell became Lord Protector of England. The Protectorate, under
which England, Wales, Scotland, Ireland and associated territories were joined together in the Commonwealth of England and governed by a Lord Protector. It lasted a mere seven years, from 16 December 1653 to 25 May 1659.

On Cromwell's death, 3 September 1658. His eldest son Richard, nicknamed Tumbledown Dick, took on the mantle but was no match for his father, the Puritans had just run out of steam. His unsuccessful reign ended nine months into office, 25 May 1659, leaving Parliament to pick up the pieces. Within a year, they reached out to Charles I's son, Charles II, who arrived back in London on 29 May 1660.

The Restoration Period, (1660 to 1685) began and it seemed all England welcomed the overthrow of Puritan grimness and dreary disapproval of pleasure.

At some point, probably after the Commonwealth,[147] Broadway commissioned, a painted armorial panel of the Royal Arms of Charles I, dated 1641, to hang in St Eadburgha's Church. The panel depicts the crown flanked by the initials 'CR,' 1625-1649 and a cartouche bearing the motto, Dieu et mon Droit.

---

147. During the English Civil War and the interregnum, churches were vandalised by Cromwell's troops, and the Royal Coat of Arms pulled down and destroyed.

Chapter 10

1654 – 1683
Stage Coaching comes to Broadway, absentee ownership

When Ursula died in 1654, she was buried with her husband John at St Eadburgha's Church. After her death, as specified in her husband's will, the Inn was to pass to Thomas, but he had predeceased his mother in 1649. In such circumstances the Inn was then to pass to son John, then William, then Robert and finally Mathew.

We don't have the stories of John, William, and Robert; therefore, we do not know if they were caught up in the Civil War, passed of natural causes, or as was becoming common with second and third sons, they had chosen to make their fortunes in the Americas. We do know Mathew, who had with Richard Hope been the overseers of his father's will, appears from 1654 to take over the administration of his father's estate, but due to other business affairs was an absentee landlord. Richard Hope became a family member; he married John Treavis' daughter Elizabeth in 1637.

There is some evidence around 1658 that Mathew was not only busy in the city but was connected to the tobacco trade in Virginia and that William's son, Thomas, Mathew's nephew, had emigrated to Virginia.[148] Maybe, it was this family connection that led to the Inn having a smoke room quite early in the history of tobacco.

---

148. A court case and genealogical records.

In 1657 Charles II commissioned the mapmaker John Ogilby[149] Esq (1600-1676) to survey and produce the first road atlas of England and Wales. From these surveys followed plans for coaching routes, organised in stages,[150] between major towns and cities, necessitating accommodation and hospitality along the way.

The onset of coaching in England, introduced after the invention and perfection of springs,[151] had been set back by the Civil War[152] but with Charles II taking up residence in Whitehall in 1660, implying a promise of stability, there had been a sudden, substantial expansion of travel around the Country.

Shortly after Ogilby started on his 100 maps, the route from London to Worcester and on to Aberystwyth (Aberistwith), was defined; it was a route which went through Broadway. Broadway Hill, one of the highest points in the Cotswolds, has a long pull up rising over 1.7 miles, from 656 feet to 912 feet. The incline at this time was said to be 12% in some places.

---

149. John Ogilby, a 66-year-old Irishman when he arrived in London, after a colourful career turned to map making, having lost his considerable fortune in the 1641 uprising by Irish Catholics. In London, he found a market for the curious, making grand maps of the world and continents such as Africa, Asia, and America.

150. Stagecoaches were so named as each a segment or 'stage' on a planned journey, roughly 10 to 15 miles, was determined by the distance before the horses needed to be changed. These were not mail coaches; mail coaches developed in the 18th Century.

151. In the 15th century, a wheelwright in a Hungarian village called Kocs had devised a larger, more comfortable carriage incorporating leaf steel spring suspension. Then, in 1564, William Boonen, a Dutchman, presented a coach to Queen Elizabeth I which had innovative Dutch springs. Edicts and laws, during Elizabeth's reign, (1558 – 1603) encouraged inns, and accommodation provision to reduce safety concerns, linked to robbers and vagabonds, on routes between settlements.

152. Coaching had been a potential game changer in England since before the Civil War when investment in the technology of springs and their perfection on the continent made it a potentially acceptable form of transport. The first fare-paying royal patent for a short stagecoach route, ran from Edinburgh to Leith around 1610, however the Civil War made travelling a risky business and put a stop on most of the development of the industry whilst the war raged on.

Such plans for a coaching route through Broadway implied economic expansion for any Innholder connected with the business of providing hospitality on such routes.

The steep incline on Broadway Hill implied trade linked to stabling, and the provision of horses would expand. This was to be a fortunate development, which would lead to the emergence of a new merchant class at a time when sheep farming, and wool, despite several unsustainable laws,[153] was in decline.[154]

When Ogilby surveyed Broadway in 1660, he wrote *'Broadway is 'a well-built town of 5 furlongs length[155] affording several good inns for accommodation,'[156]* One of those inns could have been the White Hart but for some reason the White Hart was not deemed sufficiently appropriate to serve the new route.

---

153. The Cappers Act of 1571, pp. 885–886, *'Statutes of the Realm: volume 5'*: 1628–80, passed by Parliament required all male commoners over 6 years of age to wear a cap of wool to go to church, and the Burying in Woollen Acts 1666–80 were Acts of the Parliament of England (which required the dead, except plague victims and the destitute, to be buried in pure English woollen shrouds to the exclusion of any foreign textiles. p. 598, *'Statutes of the Realm: volume 5:'* 1666–80. Both were ways of promoting the domestic wool industry.

154. The increasing size of flocks in Europe were dramatically impacting exports, the Iberian Peninsula's merino sheep's more delicate 'fluffy' wool became preferred to sturdy and worsted Cotswold fabrics, and new materials, such as linen and cotton, from the Americas were reducing wool's value. Additionally, with a burgeoning urban population, domestically the market was more interested in the meat production.

155. It is roughly a kilometre from the green to the Elizabethan Houses, in the upper part of the High Street - measured.

156. John Ogilby, p.2, *'His Majesty's Cosmographer, and Master of His Majesty's revels in the kingdom of Ireland. BRITANNIA, Volume I or an Illustration of the Kingdom of England and Dominion of Wales thereof.' 1 LONDON, 1675.*Printed by the Author at his House in White-Fryers.

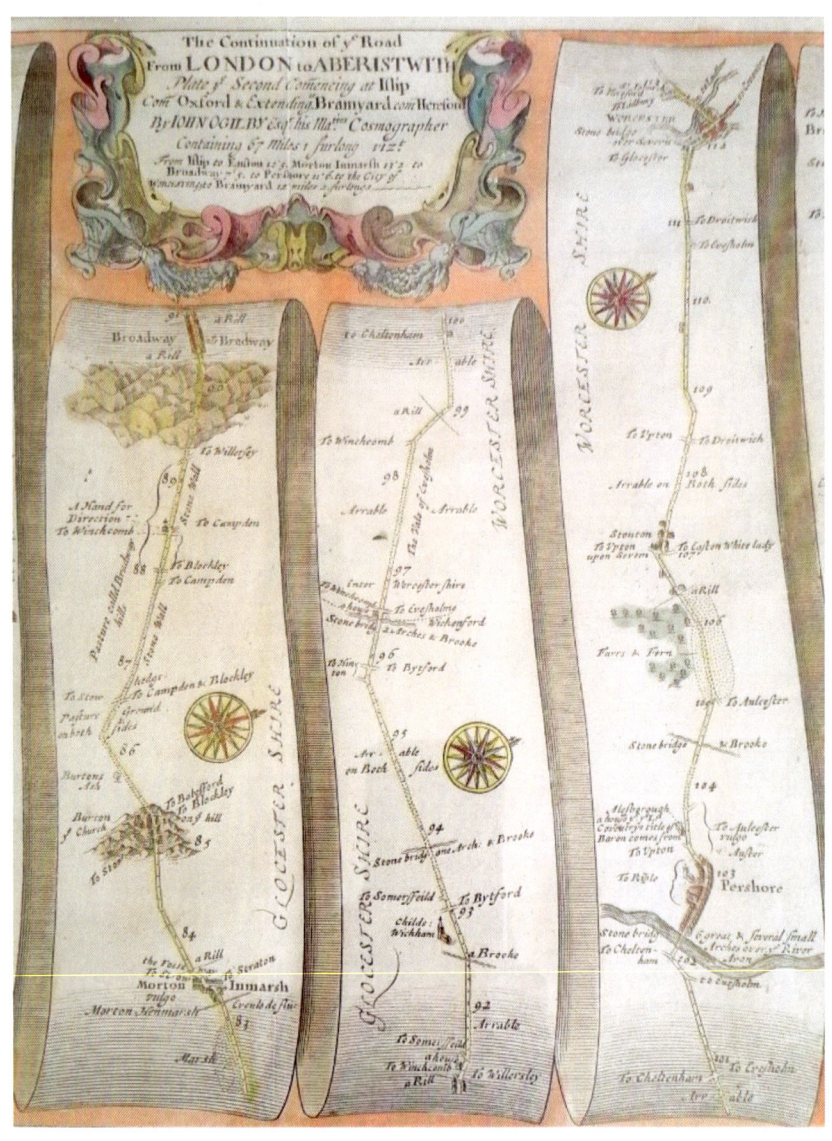

One section of John Ogilby's 1675 map: Continuation of y'Road From LONDON to ABERISTWITH plate of Second - Commencing at Islip Com Oxford, and Extending Bramyard com Hereford, Containing 67 miles 1 furlong.

The 1675 route, *thus reckoned, from* Aberistwith to London was a total of 199 miles, and varied little from the 1722 route: *'From Aberistwith to Riodergowy 28, to Ithon? River 9, to Prestain 13, to Leominster 13, to Bramyard 11, to Worcester 12, to Pershore 9, to Broadway 12, to Mortin in Marsh 7, to Easton 13, to Islip 12, to Wheatly Bridge 8, to Tetworth 4, to Wickham 12, to Beaconfield 5, to Uxbridge 8, to Acton 10, to London 8, which is the Metropolis or principal City of Great Britain.* '[157]

Perhaps, in 1660, Mathew, or his son John running the Inn did not or could not support the idea. Innkeepers who supplied horses for the letter riders, (such as the White Hart) often despised the new-fangled coaches.[158]

To a degree this was not surprising, as in the early days, it was a complicated business. Extra horses were needed for the long pull up Broadway Hill, fully laden, six might be required. In poor muddy conditions passengers had to walk alongside the coach as they went up the hill to reduce to reduce its weight. Pricing was deliberately set to keep the classes apart for fear of disease and discomfort. There was one price for inside the coach, and a lesser price on the box or the roof, where you or the rear guard might, and some did, freeze to death enroute.

---

157. William Stow. p.137, *'Remarks on London being an exact survey of the cities of London and Westminster, borough of Southwark, and the suburbs and liberties contiguous to them…. places to which penny post letters and parcels are carried, with lists of fairs and markets… to what inns flying coaches, waggons and carriers come, and the days they go out…. keys, wharfs, and plying places on the river Thames… description of the great and crossroads from one city and eminent town to another, in England and Wales… the rates of coachmen[sic], chairmen, carmen and watermen…'* London, T Norris and H Tracey, 1722.
158. Charles G. Harper, p. 3, 'The Holyhead Road Vol 1, The Mail-Coach Road to Dublin,' Chapman, and Hall, 1902.

Horses harnessed to a late 17th century stagecoach ©Doug Eyre

The condition of most roads was treacherous. During cold or wet weather, coach travel could be impossible, even hazardous. Overloading was a regular risk, and accidents were frequent. To add danger to danger, seeing an opportunity, robbers took advantage of the coach's slow speeds. It is hardly surprising that before embarking on a journey, passengers were encouraged to put their affairs in order, make a will and pray hard.

The White Hart was overlooked. It did not become the provider of accommodation for these early stage coaches, as a much smaller building than today, though greatly expanded and refurnished in 1620, it had been an Inn for around 130 years, perhaps even longer. It would have been well used, perhaps a little abused, during the Civil War.

Probably due to its age and condition, it was just not the Inn of choice.

In the end it was the innkeepers further up the street on the south side who, in 1659, to support the Broadway coaching stage on the London to Aberystwyth route, became involved with the construction of a purpose-built Inn, the Angel.[159]

In much the same way as John Treavis's White Hart expanded outwards and skywards in 1620, so the Angel's new building, adjacent to their old Angel Inn[160] rose to dominate Broadway High Street's south side.

Given the buildings size, the Angel Inn must have caused ripples in the village; however, its design, in the older tradition, was appropriate and typical of the district. Its very design respectfully reflected the architecture of the White Hart across the road. Both buildings showed Palladian influences, both had earlier Cotswold gable finials giving the buildings dominating, slightly gothic tones, and both incorporated stone balls.

On the parapet of the bay windows of the Angel are two shields bearing the dates 1659 and 1660 respectively, commemorating, it is thought, the commencement and completion of the building.

---

159. Elizabeth Eyre, 'History of the Angel Inn,' 2022, Vale Press, Willersey available at Broadway Museum and Art Gallery.
160. The Angel Inn is now Broadway Museum and Art Gallery, focussing on Broadway's history.

The Angel Inn new building 1659-1660 now Broadway Museum and Art Gallery - on the south side of the High Street

We can't know if Mathew and based in London, busy with his own business, noted this potential rival and the changes in the village brought about by stage coaching: the sudden appearance of farriers, blacksmiths, accommodation providers and brew houses. His son John, based in Broadway, running the White Hart most certainly did.

Coaching inns came to have a higher status than posting inns, such as the White Hart, so one wonders how Mathew or John viewed this

114

change. It was only much later, in the early 19th century, that the White Hart in addition to stabling and providing horses, and cart or carrier services embraced coaching, and then it was mail coaching.

As for the village, coaching made the main street in Broadway, which was probably even busier than today, dustier and dirtier in the summer and a mire of mud in the winter.

Mathew's will, 16 August 1680, provides evidence that he had before his death given his two sons, John, and Gilbert, a sizable settlement, from his considerable estate, a settlement which, in the case of John, included the White Hart and associated appurtenances.

The will implies John had run the White Hart for a time but on his death, Phillip Hodges, innkeeper had been employed to run it.

'concerning of the devising and settling of all that my messuage tenement or Inn called by the name of the White Hart in Broadway, in the County of Worcester, late in the occupation of Phillip Hodges, after the death of my son.'[161]

We do not know when Mathew's son died but Phillip Hodges, the Innkeeper, came on the scene after John's death, and we do know from a later lease 1683 that Phillip Hodges was in occupation in the Inn in 1670 when Mathew leased the Inn to William Adderley and Joseph and Elisha Biscoe for £154. The lease describes the property as *'being'* of Mathew Treavis suggesting John died around 1670.

The writing of Mathew's will in 1680, seems to have been prompted by Phillip Hodges' death that year. Mary and Katherine Treavis,

---

161. Probate Mathew Treavis PROB 11-368-390.

grandchildren of John and Ursula Treavis thus inherited the reversion, after the death of their brother, John, Gilbert too had some interest in the Inn.

'I give will and devise the same messuage or tenement with the appurtenances and all deeds and evidence touching the same unto my two daughters Mary and Katherine Treavis.'[162]

On his death innkeeper Phillip Hodges inventory, dated 1680, assessed him as having a healthy estate to the value of £347 including grain, horses, livestock, and chattels. This inventory helpfully creates a picture of the White Hart, in the late 17th century:

On the ground floor was a kitchen, little buttery, and a parlour. On the upper three floors, were bedchambers of different quality and the servant's chambers.

Ist Floor

- The Hart Chamber with two beds,
- The Hill Chamber with two beds,
- The Great Chamber with two feather beds,
- The Scholar's Chamber with three beds and flocks,
- The Green Chamber with one feather bed and flock beds,
- The Little Chamber on the first floor with two old beds,
- The Sun Chamber with one bed,

2nd Floor

- The room over the Green Chamber with one feather bed,
- The room over the Hill Chamber with two beds,

162. Probate Mathew Treavis PROB 11-368-390

- The room over the Hart Chamber with two beds

The Attics

Two rooms for servants, also with two beds.

The inventory lists linens, sheets, napkins, brass, and pewter, domestic ware everything you would associate with a good kitchen and accommodation in a suitable number of chambers.

There was a brewhouse with its barrels and malt, and the animals: pigs, sheep, lambs, plus all the agricultural implements of husbandry and, of course, the sign of the Inn and its signpost.

The horses, colts, and saddles detailed in his inventory were presumably for hire, as the White Hart was a posting rather than a coaching Inn hiring out stabling, and a change of horse for riders who were carriers of the mail. [163]

In 1683, on acquiring the Inn, Mathew's daughters Mary and Katherine and their brother Gilbert, conveyed the Inn to Thomas Parry, a dyer of Broadway, for £161 using some of the money to buy out the remaining part of their twenty-year lease, from the tenants, Adderley, and the Biscoe brothers. Susanna Hodges, wife of the late Phillip Hodges was the Inn's landlady. Almost immediately Thomas Parry conveyed the property to Walter Parry, a relation, a dyer from

---

163. Following the civil war, in 1657, the 'Letters Office' renamed the 'Post Office of England' by Act of Parliament, was re-established, and the office of Postmaster-General was defined as having 'the exclusive right of carrying letters and organising the furnishing of post-horses around the Country.

Harrington, Northampton. Again, Susanna Hodges was listed as Innkeeper from 1683 to 1700.[164]

In leasing the property to Adderley and the Biscoe brothers, on John Hodges death in 1680, and then selling to Thomas Parry, in 1683, the Treavis family became detached from the grand rebuilding project of their grandparents in 1620; this is perhaps yet another example of one generation building, another caretaking and the third using the inheritance.

---

164. White Hart Inn deeds, 1620 to 1820, Worcestershire Archives.

Chapter 11

1683-1809
Changes, additional rooms, a scandal, finally the illusive stability

As the White Hart entered the 18th century, it appears not to have 'kept up' with Broadway's rise to the challenge of being a stage for coaches. A lack of leadership seems to have played its part. One wonders how closely Katherine and her siblings, kept an eye on the Inn.

Susanna Hodges was still the Innkeeper, possibly supported by her son Luke and daughter Ann, but advancing years must have affected her management.

John Treavis had bought the Inn in 1620 for roughly £184 pounds. He then heavily invested in improvements, yet Thomas Parry purchased it in 1683 for only £161. Some of this loss could be attributed to the Civil War, between 1620 and 1683 when there was a general loss of asset value[165] across the whole Country; many had lost land or had been required to pay fines because of the upheaval of the Civil War. However, seven years later, 5 April 1700, Francis Phipps, son of the leaseholder of the Angel Inn, across the street, bought it from Walter Parry for even less, £159.

After the death of his parents, John Phipps in 1673, and Thomasin his mother in 1676, Francis had considerable funds at his disposal funds from his share of the inheritance. In 1691, he had also finally been

---

165. National Archives currency convertor identifies the degree to which the buying power of had decreased in the period 1620-1683.

repaid by the Broadway overseers for an old debt which harked back to 1687.

'paid for expenses at the Angel when horses were pressed around the time of King James progress.' [166] [167]

King James II abdication in December 1688, possibly explains why it took so long for the expenses to be repaid.

Interestingly, John Phipps inventory, dated 1673, valued his wealth: his assets, the contents, and yard at the Angel Inn, at four hundred pounds, three shillings and ten pence over three times the purchase price of the White Hart Inn by his son in 1700.

In 1710, the parish recorded, in connection with the earlier agreement linked to the maintenance of St Eadburgha's church walls, the ownership of the White Hart; next to number 25 in the name Francis Phipps, just as it was in 1633 with John Treavis, and 1532 with Thomas White.

Until his death in 1713, Francis Phipps, owned both the Angel and the White Hart. On his death his estate, valued at £700, was left to his nephew Francis Mitchell, son of his sister Ann, and her husband James Mitchell. Francis was identified in his will as

'one who hath for many years lived with me in Broadway my house where John Griffiths, Clerk now dwells and also all that house or home stall called the White Hart being a common Inn situated in

166. Overseers' (Parish Council) accounts, Broadway papers, Worcester County Records.
167. The year before King James abdicated, he made a royal progress to Worcester which finally put Worcestershire back 'on the map' giving closure to its role in the Civil War. Worcester had been the first corporate town in which a mayor proclaimed Charles II at the Restoration.

Broadway now inhabited by John Cormell... and all my yard lands, and all my odd lands and commons in grass and pasture... all tenements and hereditaments whatsoever...'[168]

So, the will confirms John Cormell was the innholder, the landlord running the White Hart Inn in 1713.

The first turnpike road came to Broadway, May 1728,[169] this was an important change for any of its Inns. It ran from the top of Broadway Hill, (later that hillside was named Fish Hill), through Evesham, north of the river to Stonebow Bridge, north of Pershore.[170]

November 1732, Francis Mitchell mortgaged the White Hart for £100 to Sarah Taylor, the daughter of a local barrister William Taylor, recorder of Evesham, who built Middle Hill, a local mansion, between 1720 and 1724. In 1734 he was returned as MP for the borough of Evesham. On marriage Sarah Taylor, became Sarah Corbett.

John Cormell died in 1733, leaving a wife Ann and three daughters, Elizabeth, Mary, and Sarah, all living at the White Hart. Later, in October 1734, Francis Mitchell sold the Inn and *'all its houses and outbuildings'*[171] to John Cormell's his widow Ann, who took on the mortgage held by Sarah Corbett and her husband. In the deeds the

168. Will of Francis Phipps, 15 March 1712, County Records.
169. *The Evesham Roads Act* was passed by both Houses of Parliament, around 150 trustees were appointed.
170. Act of Parliament, The *Evesham Road Act 1728*, showing the list of roads initially turnpiked.
171. WHD 1734, WCRO

White Hart is described as *'the two burgages of John Trevis, being now an Inn.'*[172]

By 1739, Ann had transferred the Inn into the names of her daughters, retaining a life interest for herself. She then borrowed fifty-one pounds from John Purser (who was to marry her daughter Mary). Elizabeth married William Touch, and left Broadway. Sisters, Mary, and Sarah remained with their mother. Sarah appears not to have married.

Shortly before Ann's death, in 1740, she arranged a second mortgage against the Inn, of two hundred and twenty pounds, twelve shillings and six pence, with a local landowner, Isaac Averill. Ann used part of the new mortgage amount to pay off Sarah Corbett's £100 mortgage. When Anne died intestate; the ownership of the Inn, mortgaged with Issac Averill passed to her daughters Elizabeth, Mary and their husbands, William, and John and respectively, and Sarah.

The landlord in 1757 is thought to have been Anthony Stratton.[173]

In 1761 when Isaac Averill died the outstanding mortgage was transferred to a John Rickets. Rickets deeded the mortgage to Daniel Clemens in return for a loan of one hundred and sixty-two pounds and twelve shillings. When Rickets could not repay the loan Clemens took possession of the White Hart mortgage.

---

172. S B Russell, *'The Story of an Old English Hostelry,'* Letchworth at the Arden Press,1924.
173. A name on an excise permit found under the floorboards on the second floor.

It is not known when Anthony Stratton left the Inn but in September 1766, Giles Attwood, late butler to Viscount Tracy, the sixth or seventh, left his employ to *'enter upon the White Hart Inn.'*[174]

When Attwood advertised[175] his new position, he mentions:

'he is fitting up the Inn, which has neat post chaise, able horses, and careful drivers.'

In a newspaper advertisement, January 1776, Attwood mentions a thirty-year repairing lease into which he had entered, and which had twenty-four years to run. This suggests Attwood started as an innkeeper in 1766, but in 1770 purchased the thirty-year repairing lease from the Trust.

14 December the following year, 1767, the Inn was a little busier than usual, despite the time of the year, as the commissioners determining the Award Plan for Willersey,[176] part of the enquiry for Willersey's Inclosure Act, had chosen to meet at the White Hart.[177]

'We the said commissioners, hereunto set our hands this fourteenth day of December in the year of our Lord 1767 at a public meeting of the said commissioners at the house of Giles Attwood known by the name or sign of the White Hart in Broadway in the County of Worcester.'

---

174. Likely to have been the seventh Viscount who in 1766 became Warden (Head of College) of All Soul's College, Oxford. His seat was at Toddington,
175. Oxford Journal 20 September 1766.
176. Willersey village greens, the pond and Willersey quarry were vested in the Lordship, subsequently purchased by the Parish Council.
177. Inclosure Acts, 1604-1914, created legal property rights to land previously held in common in England and Wales, particularly open fields, and common land.

and in their schedule of expenses, we find:

'To Giles Attwood for his bill for entertaining the Commissioners and Proprietors at the White Hart in Broadway, on several Commission days £84 15s 2d.' [178]

Five pounds, five shillings were given to the servants of the Inn.

Disappointingly, for Attwood, all the commissioner meetings and determinations for Broadway, in 1771, were held at a rival Inn, the Bell Inn, (now Picton House) further up Broadway's High Street.

On Broadway's Award Plan legend, plot 11, the White Hart, is in the name of John Purser, husband of Mary Purser, one of Anne Cormell's daughters. This confirms the property and associated land was in Trust. John Purser was acting as family administrator. Clarity around the actual trust deed is lacking. The landowner RH is Richard Hyatt.

---

178. S. B. Russell, p.3-4, *'The Story of an Old English Hostelry, Third Edition'* Letchworth, Arden Press, 1914.

1772, Mr Giles Attwood leaseholder and Innholder, made several improvements to the Inn: part of the posting yard was built over to become an additional large third parlour, which accommodated the increasing number of travellers, and extra stabling was built so the Inn could accommodate over thirty horses.

View from the posting yard: the picture on the left shows the doors to the cellars before the 1772 extension, doors which are now internal, and visible in the Lobby Lounge area. On the right are the new entrance, and new parlour windows. The upper floor came later.

In July 1752, twenty years earlier, ascending Broadway Hill by coach had become safer and easier when the Worcester Quarter Sessions had given its approval to an increase in the number of horses that could be used from the White Hart Inn in Broadway to the top of Fish

Hill from six[179] to ten.[180] The documentation of this permission was one of the first time the new description Fish Hill was used. It predates the name of the old Inn at its top, converted from a summer house around 1771.

There are many suggestions but no definitive answer as to why, locally, the hillside became known as Fish Hill, possibly because,

- fish was a term used for horses bred for speed and agility, linked to horses used for hunting, and hunting took place on Fish Hill,

- historically fish was a collective noun which described a group of horses that were harnessed together to pull a carriage or wagon,
- in the 18th and 19th centuries a fish described a coach that had three seats inside, with the middle seat facing backwards so passengers on this seat sat sideways 'like a cod in a fishmonger's basket,'

- one of the methods of storing fish in the 17th century was the use of cool quarries, and there are quarries on this hillside,

- the hillside is oolite limestone the surface of which looks like fish eggs,

---

179. By charging extra tolls coaches or carts with more than four horses were strongly discouraged by the turnpike trustees. Six horses were the maximum allowed except where the gradient was more than "four Inches in a yard, upon an average" (i.e. 11.1%). The gradient on Broadway Hill was around 12.3%.
180. The hillside immediately facing Broadway was named Fish Hill before 1752.

- or purely because when the horses pulling the coaches got the top, they 'drank like a fish.'

It seems, as the new name came after the arrival of stage coaching, its in some way relates to stage coaching.

By 1772, the Evesham Trustees finally, and very sensibly, decided to significantly modify the old direct, steep gradient route up the Hill. The work was completed by November 1772, most likely to the satisfaction of most of Broadway's residents, not least Mr Attwood. Several bends were constructed, resulting the gradient being reduced from 12.1% to 9%. The new section was named, due to its twisting nature, the Serpentine Road. It was still difficult but at least more manageable.

That same year a new tollhouse, Turnpike cottage.[181] was opened at the top of the village.

Though the Inn appears to have been running successfully at this time, on 15 October 1774, an advertisement in the Oxford Journal highlighted all was not well. There were tensions between two companies running post chaise between Evesham, Broadway, and Oxford. The complainants accused Giles Attwood, of the White Hart, Broadway, Thomas Kirby, of Chapel House, Chipping Norton and John Rogers of the White Hart, Morton in Marsh of running post chaises from each other's houses to the frustration of other innholders and travellers (they were accused of running a cartel).

Four innholders from Bengeworth, Enstone, and Chipping Norton placed an advertisement against this practice, offering to step in

---

181. The Serpentine route was retained until 1998 when Broadway Bypass was built. Turnpike Cottage, now Pike Cottage is the last house on the left-hand side on the old A44, Upper High Street, which now ends in a turning circle and bridle path.

wherever and whenever the public needed.[182] Immediately the accusations were refuted as a falsehood, in another advertisement, by Attwood, Kirby, and Rogers, in the *'Oxford Journal,'* 20 October 1774.

Attwood and his partners through the journal, November 1774[183] thanked the public for their support and made an offer to supply an additional pair of horses, free of charge, at the top of Fish Hill, should they be necessary.

The controversy, however, did not rest there. Again, in the *'Oxford Journal'*[184] Attwood and his colleagues were accused of falsehood, more detailed evidence was given:

- 5 October, a gentleman took a chaise from Enstone to Moreton, Rogers refused to take him to Bengeworth, and would only take him to Attwood at Broadway.
- 9 October, a man came in with his own carriage and asked for horses to take him to Chipping Norton, but Attwood would only take him to Moreton.
- 26 October, William Burlton, recorder of Leicester, and his Lady were enroute to Chipping Norton when the chaise man stopped two miles outside Chipping Norton saying he would lose his job if he went further. The couple were left stranded. Their servants had to go ahead on foot to get fresh horses.

---

182. *'Oxford Journal* '15 October 1774.
183. *'Oxford Journal'* 12 November 1774.
184. *'Oxford Journal'*3 December 1774.

It is not known how long the accusations and counter accusations continued but 12 months later, January 1776,[185] Giles Attwood advertised that the thirty-year repairing lease of the White Hart, Broadway with twenty-four years unexpired was available to let at a low rent. [186]

Attwood advises all the buildings are in good repair, and the Inn has good stabling. Horses, wines and spirits, and household furniture are included in the transaction. He was ready to treat with any person interested in the lease, furniture, post chaise, horses, stock wines or other liquors at fair value.[187]

There is no mention of the views of owners if they knew of it at all. There is no indication that they had in any way required Giles Attwood to leave. There is no doubt an inn's success, to a large degree, rests on its reputation and that of its innkeeper and it seems his reputation was sullied.

6 September 1776, Giles Attwood used the *'Oxford Journal'* to thank the nobility, gentlemen, and tradesmen for the favour they had shown him at the White Hart, Broadway and advised that he had declined business at the White Hart in favour of Christopher Holmes, late of the White Hart, Kinfare, (now pronounced Kinvar)[188] who he was sure would meet public approbation.

Christopher Holmes used the same publication on that same date, 6 September 1776, to advise that he had entered the Inn, hoping those

185. *'Oxford Journal'* 13 January 1776.
186. *'Oxford Journal'* '13 January 1776.
187. Ibid.
188. Just outside Stourbridge.

that had used it before would use it again, and assuring them that the Inn would be as good as ever. The new beginning promised by Attwood, ten years earlier, was now being promised by Holmes.

Two months later, 6 November 1776, Giles Attwood informed his loyal customers that he had purchased the Crown and Cushion Inn in Chipping Norton, which he was furnishing and fitting up. He hoped the favours conferred on him at Broadway would now continue at the Crown and Cushion.

When, in September 1776, Christopher Holmes took over the remaining twenty-four years of the lease as innkeeper, from Giles Attwood, he was recently married, and starting a new life with his wife Martha Knowles. Given the recent history, the troubling business of the cartel, Christopher may well have had many concerns regarding his new responsibilities, and in December 1776, he would have been aware of, and perhaps disturbed by, a spate of horse stealing and daring robberies in the area.

There was such a general disappointment at a lack of prosecutions concerning the horse stealing and robberies, that a fund, based in Chipping Campden, was established to collect monies, presumably to hire protectors and bring the perpetrators to justice. Within 3 months of Christopher Holmes arrival at his public house he was collecting monies from public subscribers, as were other establishments, to be used by communities to hire protectors. [189]

189. 'Oxford Journal' 14 December 1776.

A year later, 1 April 1777, the first of his sons, Theophilus, (meaning Friend of God), named after one of his wife's brothers, was born, followed by a daughter, Harriot, 13 April 1780.

In October 1781, a Court Leet[190] was held at Christopher Holmes's house, commonly known by the sign of the White Hart. This is one of a few records that confirm Broadway's entry-level Court, the old manorial Court, for local disputes, was still being held at the White Hart. It is thought, but not yet proven, that the core part of the Lygon Arms Building may have been used in earlier times to hold manorial court proceedings, and significant ceremonies, before it became an Inn.

By 1783, the Holmes family had enlarged to three, young Christopher Holmes being born 13 June.

March 1786, Sophia Ellison, a grand daughter of Ann Cormell, through Mary and John Purser, married to Charles Ellison, who had become entitled[191] to one quarter share of the Inn, transferred her interest to John Scott, a wine merchant, for £50.00.

It was during Holmes tenure, as innkeeper, that the Hon. John Byng, a notable English diarist, one who travelled on horseback throughout England and Wales, during twelve summers, 1781–1794, visited the White Hart on four separate occasions. [192]

---

190. Court leet, an English criminal court for the punishment of small offenses.
191. Possibly inheriting from her aunt Sarah Cormell, who does not appear to have inherited.
192. John Byng was an Army Officer and Civil Servant, who later became 5th Viscount Torrington and wrote fifteen extant diaries.

His first reference, 23 July 1784, is to the village of Broadway, which *'though in dirty soil, is tolerably built of good stone, contains many decent houses and is larger than many market towns.'[193]* He notes Broadway Hill is long and steep, with an abundance of stone quarries.

Sunday, 12 August 1787, Byng pressed on from Bengeworth, an approach to Evesham and recorded.

'as it was too early for my dinner stop; so kept on to Broadway, in hopes of finding there another inn as good; and did put up in a most comfortable cleanly house, the White Hart, where a delicious loyn of veal was ready to be served, and I was ready for eating it; which I did in ample quantity and had then a super-abundant temptation by an apricot tart.'

'The hay is so good, and everything so neat and the dogs so fat.' [194]

After a ride up to the home of Sir John Cotterell, (Farncombe) to take in the sweeping views to Wales, he returned to the Inn, and borrowed some books off the landlord, before turning in. On this visit too he waxes lyrically about the Inn.

Monday, 13 August

'There cannot be a cleanlier, civiller Inn than this is, which bears all the marks of old gentility, and of having been a manor house: walls very thick, floors oaken and wide, with a profusion of timber, and the remains of much tapestry, for carpeting, whereon was told

193. Hon John Byng, p. 190-191 'The Torrington Diaries, Volume I' London, Eyre and Spottiswoode, 1934.
194. Hon John Byng, p.318, 'The Torrington Diaries, Volume I' London, Eyre and Spottiswoode, 1936.

instructive church history. My bedroom was very large, with black oaken boards, a wrought seiling,[195] a wide cornice, with lofty mantle-piece: in short, I appear'd to be in the grand bedchamber of an old family seat. In the kitchen hung a picture, which appear'd to me the work of a great master, (perhaps of Rubens) but the landlord, having had a hint of its value did not seem inclined to part with it, unless some foolish sum had been offer'd him.'

'Most inns will do during the summer's heat, but there are not ten endurable in the winter, when you come out of London from register stoves, and turkey carpet; tho' the inns now mend in their rooms and stabling, as we here begin to enter a fine fox and hare hunting country, to which many gentlemen resort in winter; nor are their charges unreasonable, as you may perceive by the following bill:

White Hart Broadway

Tea	0.9
A chicken &c.	2.0
Tart(apricot)	0.2
Liquors	2.3
Breakfast	0.9 [196]
	5.11'

---

195. Treavis's Best Bedchamber now the Cromwell Room
196. Hon John Byng, p. 319-320, '*The Torrington Diaries Volume I*,' London, Eyre and Spottiswoode. 1936.

14 June 1790: when writing about an old Inn in another place, Byng refers to *'the finest and oldest I ever slept in was at Broadway Worcestershire.'* [197]

This connection with John Byng, his travels and diaries would later, in the evolution of the Inn, be celebrated in the naming of the Torrington Room, built in the 20th century a supper or function room, from the remodelled garages of built in 1926 (but repurposed as bedrooms in 2018).

1787 Christopher Holmes's land tax assessment is one pound, sixteen shillings, and two pence.

It is not known how Giles Attwood paid the Trust in 1770, or for the repairing lease in 1766, or how Christopher Holmes paid the Trust for the remaining years of lease.

By 1790, fifty years had elapsed since Ann died in 1740. The ownership of the Inn, rested, in part, with new players: Daniel Clemens who had a obtained his benefit when John Rickets had defaulted on his loan, and owned the outstanding mortgage, Sophia Harris, granddaughter of Ann Cormell, daughter of Elizabeth Cormell (Touch), and John Baylis great grandson Ann Cormell, grandson of, Elizabeth Cormell (Touch), and John Scott the wine merchant.

Though Christopher and Martha were now living in the Inn with five children, John having been born 5 Feb 1785, and Charles 6 November 1786, the 1790 Land tax records underline the fact that Holmes is only the innkeeper but that same year, in August, his status changed.

---

197. Hon John Byng, p. 179, *'The Torrington Diaries, Volume 2,'* London, Eyre and Spottiswoode, 1935.

When Daniel Clemens died intestate, through John Purser, now an old gentleman, Christopher, with the help of his wife Matha, and her brothers, bought out all four interested parties: Anne Spencer, the personal representative of Daniel Clements, Sophia Harris and her husband Charles (the married daughter of Elizabeth Touch) and John Baylis and his wife Sarah, (grandson of Elizabeth Touch) and John Scott and wife Lillies (John was the wine merchant).

Martha's brother, John Knowles, paid off Ann Spencer: one hundred and sixty-two pounds and twelve shillings. Martha's brother Theophilus Knowles contributed to the purchase price. When the interested parties had received the sum of £500 in total, for the whole messuage, the Inn, its houses and outbuildings, the deed was put in the names of Theophilus Knowles, John Knowles and Christopher Holmes. Christopher and Martha Holmes now had a secure home for their five growing children, ranging in age from 4 to 13.

Despite the ownership issues of the previous fifty years, the Inn was always more than a highly regarded venue for visitors and village imbibers. As in older days it had a community function: it was where village meetings were held, it was a prime location for the auctioning of land and property, when bankruptcies were announced in the regional newspapers it led to creditor meetings at the Inn on many an occasion.

The innkeeper was required to be a fountain of knowledge on many matters, many an advertisement ended with……. apply to Christopher Holmes, for particulars, apply to …,   ……can be obtained from Christopher Holmes of the White Hart.

2 August 1794, Christopher Holmes, himself, consigned to auction thirty-four acres of arable, meadow and pastureland, in Broadway.

In 1801, Martha's brother, Theophilus Knowles, a gentleman of Burford Shropshire died. His will[198] dated 1795, bequeathed to his nephews Theophilus, Christopher, John, and niece Harriot, the sum of £100, to be paid to each when they became twenty-one. For those children that were underage the responsibility, for the principal and interest, before they came of age, lay with their parents.

Christopher Holmes was already indebted to Theophilius, but any shortfall was now to be paid out of the Estate.

If his wife died additional sums from the Estate would pass to her children. A codicil 16 October 1796 took account of family changes.[199]

Sadly, a year later, in 1802, Christopher Holmes died. His will, 4 January 1800,[200] showed he had left all his lands, hereditaments, and messuage - the Inn, in trust to his wife's brothers to manage, or sell as appropriate. The proceeds of the whole were to provide an annuity to his wife of fifty pounds, the balance to be divided by his children. He left specific additional lump sum legacies to Harriot and John.

The remaining brother, John, together with Martha, his widow, decided to sell the Inn. This finally took place by 1807,[201] when the prospective buyer, an Evesham solicitor, William Phelps, was finally

198. 1801 Theophilus Knowles PROB-11-1364-136 p. 166-167
199. 1801 Theophilus Knowles PROB-11-1364-136 p. 167
200. 1802 PROB-11-1384-360 Christopher Holmes
201. Sydney Russell, 'Birmingham Post.' 24 January 1964.

satisfied that all mortgages and encumbrances, linked to the past, the dealings of the Trust, Cormell, Attwood, and Holmes, had all been cleared.

For most of the 16th and 17th century, there were only a few Inns in the village. As the 18th century progressed coaching brought more and more people to Broadway, to rest before the assent up the serpentine road, up Fish Hill. The number of Inns increased, [202] and a sizable number of house-based ale and beer sellers, maltsters, and cider retailers[203] established themselves, springing up to cash in on the coaching economy.

Despite the reduced asset value of the White Hart, moving into the 18th century, the mortgages, the Innholders that who were not owners, the owners that were absent, it is pleasing to read the diary entries of Byng and know that Christopher and Martha Holmes had steered the ship back on course.

The Inn appears, in most of its dealings, to have continued supplying post horses and the post chaise, which were fast carriages used for a stage, of a certain distance. These vehicles, each a closed body on four wheels, usually carried two to four persons, and were drawn by two or four horses.

In 1752, permission had been granted for ten horses to be used from the White Hart Inn up Fish Hill, but this reference may well have been a general reference to be adhered to by all those in the village

---

202. The Woolpack, The Royal Exchange (The George), the Old Swan Inn, the Bell or Old Bell Inn, the new Bell Inn, the Spinning Wheel, the Crown, and the Boot.
203. The New Swan Inn, The Red Lion, The Fox and Dog, The Farmers Glory, The Coach and Horses, The Malt Shovel, The Dog and Lamb, Milestones, The New Inn, The Kettle, Stone Steps, and the Croft

providing for stage coaches.[204] The White Hart continued to provide good service to the community and guests alike with horses, post chaise and a courier service.[205] The earliest reference to the White Hart Inn providing a service which linked to coaching, mail coaching would be early in the next century.

To end this chapter, of added interest, is that Christophers eldest son Theophilus, who married Mary Ricketts, in Broadway, 30 December 1800 was a distiller, so he may well have collaborated with his father for a brief period.

---

204. The Angel Inn (Broadway Museum and Art Gallery) was known to service stage coaches from 1659 and The Bell Inn (Picton House) from 1788 but the date 1752 suggests earlier.
205. Bell's *Weekly Messenger* 17 January 1808.

Chapter 12

The 19th century: The White Hart Inn becomes the Lygon Arms

When William Phelps, the aforementioned solicitor from Evesham, bought the White Hart, it consisted of a dwelling house, four stables, two coach houses, presumably for the post chaise, one brewhouse, two additional buildings, a number of yards, two gardens, two orchards, two acres of land and common pasture, and all manner of cattle with appurtenances, outhouses etc. The inventory covered all that one might associate with the Inn's self sufficient ways at that time; the Inn would have grown most of its food, produced its own ale, and butchered its own livestock.

The reference to two coach houses, two gardens and two orchards seems to fit well with earlier references to an Inn that was two burgages, brought together.

During Phelps ownership he engaged several landlords/innkeepers. John Startling left early 1814, he later entered upon the Chapel House near Chipping Norton.[206]

In 1814 Broadway seems to have been a sleepy place, as a first-hand account describes:

'a long and straggling, but very curious place, being built entirely of stone, which gives every house an air of the most pleasing antiquity. This place, properly speaking, is called Broadway Street, the church

---

206. '*Hereford Journal*' 13 November 1816.

stands at some distance to the right, and once contained some painted glass, and some monuments of the Sheldons, but these are all in a shattered and dilapidated state. The whole parish, which bears an air of antiquity seemingly unindebted to modern improvement, has yet an air of plenty and comfort, arising from its situation in a good corn district.'[207]

In 1814, Giles Lawrence leased the Inn from Phelps for nine years.[208] It was Lawrence, who in March 1814, organised an inventory of the Inn, identifying the value of its contents as being one thousand, three hundred and five pounds.

These two inventories, the inventory of 1680, and that of 1814, showed little at the Inn had changed structurally between the two dates, save even more stables and one additional large chamber over the third parlour, the large parlour that Giles Attwood had built to accommodate additional travellers.

This new upper large parlour, a Georgian(1714-1830) room was most likely added when Christopher Holmes managed with the help of his brother in laws to purchase the Inn. It featured an Adam fireplace, so named after it was championed by Robert Adam (1728-92) after his Italian tour of 1758. The ceiling was curiously domed as mentioned by Arthur Benson in 1904 (Chapter 14). A door connected this room to the oak pannelled Charles I room's private sitting room. Today this room, the Drawing Room, is a small conference, meeting or dining

---

207. Francis C Laird, *'A Topographical and Historical Description of the County of Worcester ... Illustrated with Fourteen Engravings and a Map,'* Sherwood, Neely, and Jones, George Cowie & Co, 1815.
208. MS 3192/5/102 Acc1930-009/362986 National Archives.

room. The door in the panelling which previoulsy led to the Charles I room and a private dressing room is now closed off.

Though the Inn had the same number of chambers, they had different names reflecting how furnishings had changed: The Chintz Room, The White Room, The Best Bedroom, The Best double-bedded room, The Room over the kitchen, The Back bedroom next to the yard, The First White room, The best double-bedded room, The room over No.3, The Dressing Room, The Men's Room, The Maid's room, The Front Attic, Attic chamber number 2, and The Soldier's Room.

The kitchen had been moved to the little buttery at the rear, now the Boot Room, creating space for parlour number 2, (the front room just before the Great Hall). As well as this new parlour, there were the two other parlours, a wine cellar with a granary over, a second granary, a dairy, additional larders, a back kitchen, and stabling for nine horses.

Moving into the 19th century the number of horses and stables seems to decrease. This may well have been linked to the change from post horses and horses to hire carrying one rider which would have been lighter breeds for faster shorter journeys compared with those used for chaise, or heavier, stronger, sturdy horses such as Percheron and Shire, for carriers and stage coaches and the breeds such as the Norwich Greys, known for their strength, stamina and speed required for mail coaches.

The descriptions of the furnishing imply they were lighter or more distinctive in colour and somewhat plusher then previously: blue and white hangings, linen window curtains, carpeting to a scottish pattern, Kiddermnster carpeting - the very best. Some rooms had looking glasses, dressing tables and drawers. Some chairs had horse hair seats and silk coverings. There was a mahogany elbow chair with a horse hair seat and arms, a handsome four-post bedstead, with hangings and more. The inventory painted a picture of a move towards greater opulence.

During much of the period that the Inn was in the ownership of William Phelps, 1807–1820, as well as carrying out its main business: providing vituals, refreshement, and horses for post chaise, or mail coaches, as in the previous century, it continued to be a property that could accommodate frequent auctions of land, property, household furniture, horses, cattle, hay, timber, wines and/or spirits. It was, as before, a formal meeting place for the handling of bankrupcies now more numerous.[209] Creditors met at the Inn to discuss possible dividends.

Guests and local villagers came and went, however, no story of particular interest or noteriety, connected with the White Hart, has been found.

In the early 19th century, from about 1809 onwards, the honourable Henry Lygon, (1784–1863), of Madresfield, his elder brother, William Lygon (1783-1823) and younger brother Edward Lygon, (1786–1860) chose to spend more time in Broadway. Their father William Lygon, (1747-1816) was one of two representatives for Worcestershire between 1775 and 1806. In 1806 he was raised to

---

209. In 1815, there was a chronic economic depression, the aftershock of the Napoleonic Wars. That same year the Corn Laws of 1815 imposed a tariff on foreign grain, to protect English landowners who grew grain, which created periods of famine and chronic unemployment. The cost of food for working people rose, and British grain, to make it go further, was doctored thus lowering its quality.

the peerage as Lord Beauchamp of Powyke. In 1815 he was further honoured becoming Viscount Elmley and 1st Earl of Beauchamp.

Henry and Edward were British Army soldiers. Both had fought in the Peninsular War, and then Edward had joined Wellington's army in 1812 and distinguished himself at Waterloo.

Their brother William matriculated at Christ Church, Oxford University, in 1801, becoming a Bachelor of Arts in 1804. It is thought their father, the Ist Earl, had quite frequently visited Spring Hill,[210] in Broadway, a model house with every internal and external domestic convenience designed by Capability Brown in 1760 for George Coventry, 6th Earl Coventry.

George Coventry had reflected on the revolving door aspect of Croome Court *'it had always been an Inn and always must remain so.'*[211] Spring Hill was his recreational retreat, effecting privacy and the opportunity to pursue his sporting and horticultural interests.

In 1806, William took over from his father when he went up to the Lords, and became MP for Worcestershire, he was only 24, unmarried, and a keen huntsman. Bailey's monthly magazine of sports and pastimes, first published in 1860, reprinted in 1872, relates in 1808 how Colonel Berkeley, Lord Seagrave, and Earl FitzHardinge, who hunted the Broadway country,[212] regularly, dined

---

210. The house, thought to have been conceived around 1760 and finished around 1763, was arranged around a courtyard.
211. Dr Catherine Gordon, p.131, *'The Coventry's of Croome,'* Phillimore and Co Ltd, 2000.
212. There are one or two references to individuals 'going a hunting' but foxhunting as understood in the 18th century, in the North Cotswolds dates to 1772, when the area was part of the vast hunting ground of the Earls of Berkeley.

and slept at the White Hart Inn, particularly enjoying lamprey and excellent claret.[213] As did other members of the Hunt.

Late 18th century, the hunting of the fox had become became a popular sport.[214] By 1772 the North Cotswolds had become part and parcel of the vast hunting grounds of the Earls of Berkely.[215] To facilitate hunting these vast grounds the first kennels in Broadway had been built, in 1839, by Admiral Maurice Berkeley[216] (who in 1861, became 1st Baron FitzHardinge).[217]

In 1815 a Thomas Phillipps, a young neighbour, living at Middle Hill, ten years William's junior, who had not long completed his degree at University College Oxford, returned to Broadway. Already Thomas's passion for collecting books and manuscripts was evident. Despite the age gap, their fondness of riding out, and pleasurable hunting around Broadway[218] and conviviale company may well have created a friendship.

After the death of their father William, 1st Earl Beauchamp in 1816, William Lygon, his eldest son, in October 1816, followed in his father's footsteps, into the peerage, a position which obliged him to relinquish his Parliamentary seat.

---

213. Lygon Arms Archives.

214. The first recorded evidence of hunting locally was in 1610; it is recorded that William Sheldon the younger was 'goeinge to huntinge the ffoxxe with his hounds.'

215. 'North Cotswold Hunt History' www.northcotswoldhunt.co.uk.

216. The family are said to be the only English family still in existence in England that can trace its ancestors from father to son back to Saxon times.

217. Marion Eason, p. 2, 'The Best Little Hunt in England' Marian Eason Book Empire, Leeds, 2019.

218. Marion Eason, p. 150, 'The Best Little Hunt in England,' Book Empire, Leeds 2019.

His brother Major Henry Beauchamp Lygon, the third son, of the 1st Earl, entered the house of Commons in 1816 to take up his brother William's seat, as Member of Parliament for Worcestershire. Like his brother he was well known in Broadway for his enjoyment of hunting, and the divertisments at the Lygon Arms.

Henry Beauchamp Lygon, 4th Earl Beauchamp, K.C.B. (1784-1863) pencil and watercolour signed: Richard Dighton

In 1818 a great storm was recorded in a number of newspapers: *'On the top of Broadway-hill, Worcestershire, when the mail coach arrived there, the wind and snow were so tremendous, that it became impossible for the coachmen to force the horses on; the consequence was, they became ungovernable in so much as they turned completely round, and the coach was blown over. Happily no serious injury was sustained either by coachman, guard, or passengers; but it was impossible the coach could proceed and a messenger was dispatched for a chaise and four to convey the mail bags on as soon as possible. The coach was left on the road without any hopes of getting it up until the the wind subsided, and the passengers retired to the Fish public-house.'*[219]

The post chaise mentioned may well have come from the White Hart. It was not the first time coaches had been blown over. As usual with mail coaches, the order of priority was to the mail, then the passengers!

Four years after Henry took up his Worcestershire seat, 15 June 1820, William Lygon, 2nd Earl Beauchamp,[220] purchased the White Hart from the solicitor William Phelps for one thousand, five hundred and eighty pounds. His motivation for doing so is unclear. He was a Peer but no longer Worcestershire's MP. Certainly, he enjoyed the hunting locally. He had been elected a Fellow of the Royal Society, in 1810, suggesting he had a curious mind. His neighbour Thomas Phillipps had that very year become a Fellow. A number of letters[221] over a good number of years confirm that there was a good friendship between Phillipps and all of the Lygon brothers, William, Henry and Edward, on most occassions. Perhaps William's friendship

219. *'Caledonian Mercury'* 12 March 1818 – the storm date was 8 March.
220. The Beauchamp ancestral home, Madresfield, situated close to Malvern, was first, specifically, mentioned in a charter dating from 1120. Urse D'Abitot, sheriff of Worcester, 'the bear' who is represented in the old Beauchamp coat of arms spent 40 years at Madresfield. The title Baron Beauchamp was created for William Lygon in 1806 and that of Earl Beauchamp, 1st Baron Beauchamp, in 1815.
221. Emily Tarrant, *'Topographical collections, correspondence, and papers of Sir Thomas Phillipps,'* Bodleian Library, 2019.

with Thomas was intellectually deeper than that of his brothers, despite the nine year age difference; they may have been kindrid spirits in some respects; it is possible the purchase fitted to his love of hunting, and wish to retain such good local friendships.

Thomas Phillips was made baronet of Middle Hill in 1821.

Giles Lawrence appears to have been the innkeeper when the Lygon family, took over in the June 1820. There have been sugestions of an Innkeeper called Stanley but he appears to have been a member of the family managing the Lygon Arms[222] in Chipping Campden.

The innkeeper after Giles Lawrence, was Charles Drury, a local Gloucestershire man, from Weston sub edge, born in 1801.

It has been written that William Lygon promoted Charles Drury, who was his butler, in service at Madresfield Court, to be the Inn's manager. Others suggest that Charles Drury, a faithful Madresfield butler, merely left service to become the Inn's manager. A third suggestion is that Charles was batman[223] to William's brother Henry, who from the moment he entered the British Army, aged 19, and was a commissioned officer, though initially only a cornet.[224] A handwritten note, referred to in one publication, states that General (Edward) Lygon's butler, [225] Charles Drury (referred to as 'Old Mullins'), took over the Inn's management between 1837 and 1840, renaming it to honour his former employer who had settled in

---

222. So named after General Edward Lygon, who in 1830 owned Spring Hill, see Patterson Road references.
223. A soldier assigned to a commissioned officer as a personal servant.
224. A former British cavalry troop rank that signified the lowest level commissioned officer. The name comes from the instrument, which was used by a cornet player in each cavalry group. It fell out of use with the British in 1871 and today its equivalent rank is second lieutenant.
225. Both Henry and Edward became Generals, the former in 1853, the latter in 1854.

Springhill, after Waterloo. This reference is to Edward who had served at Waterloo.

In 1822, a new section of the road up Fish Hill opened, with an improvement on the gradient reducing it from 9% to 8.4%, thus, rendering its assent less problematical. This was good news for the Lygon Arms, from where the mail coach operated. The modifications were only achieved because, in 1821, Sir Thomas Phillipps had offered some of his own land to create the section of road down to the lower hairpin bend, a section which is still in use today. One wonders if a conversation between the Earl and Sir Thomas led to this helpful outcome. It is important to recall this that this feat of engineering was achieved before the days of JCB's, scrapers and dumpers; 35,000 tons of rock and soil, was moved by hand. This was back breaking labour for local workmen,

Sadly William's ownership of the White Hart was short-lived; three years later he died in 1823, at the young age of 40. His second brother John became the 3rd Earl. Through inheritance the Inn passed from William to his brother Major Henry Lygon but there was no immediate name change.

Soon afterwards, in 1824, the Lygon brothers, Major Henry Lygon and Colonel Edward Lygon leased Spring Hill.

From 1823 to 1826 the Inn traded as the White Hart, not the Lygon Arms, with Charles Drury at the helm as Innkeeper.

- On 25 July 1825 a meeting of the Trustees of the Turnpike Road from Broadway to Mickleton met at the White Hart[226] for

226. 'Worcester Journal' 14 July 1825.

the purpose of ordering Toll Gates or side bars to be erected across certain roads in accordance with the Act of Parliament: Colin Lane to Evesham, the road to Wickhamford and Badsey, the road to Saintbury.

- In 1826, a local newspaper recorded particulars of an auction at the White Hart Inn.

- In the eighteeth and last edition, of Paterson's Roads, 1829, published after his death[227] the Inn is recorded as trading under the name of the White Hart. However, the delay in changing the name to the Lygon Arms is most likely due to the time it took, post Paterson's death, for a gentleman called Mogg, to take over the work and publish it.

The permission or request to use the 1st Earl of Beauchamp, William Lygon's old coat of arms seems to have occurred around 1826.[228] By 1828, Drury was using the older Beauchamp coat of arms as his new Inn sign, the one that lives on today, as discussed in chapter 2.

In 1828, Pigot's directory sets out that the Royal Mail[229] ran daily from Worcester, as did the Sovereign, both were accommodated at the Lygon Arms.[230] This reference also, not only confirms the use of

---

227. Paterson, Daniel, 1738-1825; Mogg, Edward, 'Paterson's Roads 1829,' London, Printed for Longman, Orme, Brown, Green, and Longmans.
228. 1826, Paterson's Road states that Spring Hill is the seat of the Hon. Col. Lygon, therefore Edward Lygon
229. *Pigot's 1828 Directory*.
230. The focus of these coaches would have been speed and the timetable, not accommodation for passengers. The Lygon Arms was ideal. It had many good stables. Three other coaches, the Aurora, the Old Fly, and the Telegraph, still went through Broadway, but we do not know from which Inn they ran.

the new sign and change of name but definitively confirms the Lygon Arms is accommodating mail coaching. This was a definate change of policy brought about by the new owner.

The earlier 1818 reference, mentioning the coach on Fish Hill caught up in the storm, only evidenced that mail coaches were already running through Broadway but not that they stopped at the Lygon Arms.

Whether the Inn needed to boost its income by association with the prestigious family and their hunting friends, or Charles Drury had asked to use the name Lygon and sign to thank the Lygon family for their ownership and patronage or the new owner, Henry Lygon, who had been elected MP for Worcestershire,[231] needed to improve his engagement with the local community, so encouraged the use of the name and sign, we may never know.

There is no doubt that the name change would have been valuable to Henry from 1828, as he looked to the next election in 1831. The increasing participation of the English middle classes in politics, from 1815 to 1835, had strengthened the Whig's[232] position in Parliament. They were known to use a national network of newspapers and magazines as well as local clubs to deliver their message. The Lygon's were Tories, any promotion of the Lygon name may have been strategically helpful, especially with an impending election.

---

231. 1816-1832.
232. It was a different time but as a generalisation the Whigs were a party of free trade, anti slavery, moral reforms, pushing for parliamentary reforms which would shift power away from the aristocracy.

Equally, it would become evident over the next century, that patronage by the Lygon family and their friends, played a vital part in the Lygon Arms sustainability. Other inns without such patronage would be far less able to stand up to the winds of change.

In 1830 Colonel Edward Pyndar Lygon, later to achieve the rank of General, purchased Spring Hill House. To commemorate the epic victory at Waterloo he spent the next few years planting a complex collection of spinneys on the hillside at Spring Hill to represent the troop formation at the battle.[233] [234]

In 1833 the Lygon Arms Inn was mentioned 'in connection with an auction of livestock and implements.'[235]

On 26 March 1835 'the tolls arising from several toll gates upon the Broadway and Mickleton turnpike roads' were let to the best bidder at the Lygon Arms Inn,[236]

5 May 1838, a dentist advertised appointments at the Lygon Arms Inn!

In 1840, travelling to London: *The Royal Mail from Worcester called at the Lygon Arms every evening at 8. The fare was 30s. and 16s. The Monarch called at the Bell every evening (Sundays excepted) at half-past 8., and the Sovereign calls at the Lygon's Arms every morning (Sund. excepted) at half-past 10. The fare was the same as the mail.*

233. Dorothy Stroud, p.60. 'Capability Brown' London, Faber, 1975.
234. Dr Catherine Gordon, p.84, 'The Coventry's of Croome' Chichester, Phillimore, and Co Ltd, 2000.
235. 'Worcester Journal, '13 April 1833.
236. 'Gloucestershire Chronicle,' 11 April 1835.

Travelling To Worcester: *The Royal Mail from London called at the Lygon's Arms every morning at a quarter past 6. The fare was 10s. and 5s.; the Sovereign called a quarter past 4 in the afternoon; and the Monarch called at the Bell every morning at half-past 6, they went through Evesham and Pershore.*[237]

Helpfully[238] by 1841 the authorities in England and Wales had started to collect census data. The 1841 census identified the head of the household at the Lygon Arms Inn, (written as The Lyganbury Inn) as Charles Drury aged thirty-nine. His wife Jane was slightly older, aged forty-one. They had a daughter, Ann, in her twenties and a ten-month-old son, Charles, born 6 September 1840. It is unclear if the remaining five people in the census, whose ages ranged from nineteen to fifties, were visitors or servants.

With the Lygon family name over the door, their patronage and that of their friends Drury was more confident that, given the coming of the railways and the cessation of coaching, the Inn could ride out the impending economic decline.

As early as January 1843 it had been recommended that Broadway had a railway station but there was a condition *'that Sir Thomas*

---

237. Joseph Bentley, p 63, 'Bentley's history, guide, and alphabetical and classified directory, of the borough of Evesham; of the market towns of Pershore, Shipston-upon-Stour, and Upton-upon-Severn, and the villages of Broadway and Great Malvern,' and an history and alphabetical directory of seventy-eight parishes in the county south of the city of Worcester ... forming vol. III of Bentley's history, directory, and statistics of Worcestershire, 'Bull and Turner, Birmingham, 1840.

238. Unhelpfully, a further fifty-one people, unconnected with the nine residents at the Lygon Arms on the day of the census Inn, were recorded against the location 'Lyganbury Inn.' Their occupations range from butcher, to maltster, cordwainer and boot maker to carpenter and labourers and their dependants thus suggesting the enumerator used Lyganbury Inn (misspelt) as a generic location.

Winnington, Bart, as Lord of the Manor[239]*, granted the requisite land for that purpose* [240] *to the county.'* Disappointingly for both the economy and wellbeing of the village, he refused. Broadway was not to get its station until 1904.

Disastrously mid-19th century the introduction of the railways in Britain reduced the passing trade upon which Broadway relied.

In 1845, the public was respectfully informed of arrangements being concluded with his lordship, the Postmaster General *'A New ROYAL MAIL service will commence on Sunday, 19 inst. leaving the Star Office, Worcester, every Evening at Half-past Six via Pershore, Evesham, Chipping Norton, and Woodstock to Oxford to meet the Mail Train on the Great Western Railway.'* [241]

Two hundred years earlier, mid-17th century, Broadway's geography, and a planned new stage-coach route had brought new opportunities, growth, and wealth to Broadway. Overnight the foci of the village had shifted to meet the needs of a new clientele, from accommodation to a wide range of ancillary trades. As fast as the

---

239. Sir Francis Winnington 5th Baronet sold 400 acres of Broadway's 3360 acres, mainly West End Farm and Peasebrook, and the title Lord of the Manor in 1886. Records say it had been in his family for 70-80 years. The Lordship itself is a curious title having been taken up by Sheldon after Babington who purchased the land from Queen Mary in 1558 sold him a smaller part of his land in 1573/4. Anthony Daston's widow purchased 2960 acres through Babington's sale. Habington, who knew Broadway well tells of the distribution. The history of the Lordship still requires research as the statement re the length of ownership of the Manor by Sir Francis is at odds with that outlined elsewhere. Remnants of the Manor of Broadway and the Lordship of the Manor were acquired by the Broadway Trust in January 1985.
240. *'Worcester Journal'* 5 January 1843.
241. *'Worcestershire Chronicle'* Wednesday, 22 January 1845.

business of coaching had grown, so too had the population of Broadway.

Now, mid-19th century, the village was about to slowly wane, due to the introduction of the railways to Worcestershire, railways that would bypass Broadway.

Charles, Jane, and their eldest son Charles Richardson who ran the Inn would have to navigate and survive this new challenge; Ann had left home. There were three female servants and three visitors on the day of the 1851 census.

When the railway finally came to Evesham in 1856, the decline of the trades accelerated, and Broadway's population began to shrink, and with it the local National School intake. It was a decline that would, in time, be compounded by the agricultural depression of 1870.

This very abandonment turned Broadway into a rural backwater. Those with a cushion may have managed but the circumstances of villagers such as John Wheatley, a hostler who looked after the horses at the Lygon, and his wife, a laundress, changed; he followed the route of many skilled men becoming an agricultural labourer. His neighbour, Francis Collett, the blacksmith carried on his business until 1861 but by 1891 there were no wheelwrights on Broadway's High Street. It is not until 1901 that we see their return in any number. Of the six inns in 1840, only two remained in 1899 but one smaller inn the New Inn and one Hotel, the Coach and Horses opened later.

Some villagers left to find work elsewhere, but others hung on, through to the next generation, such as the Kemp family who took over the blacksmith opposite the Lygon Arms between 1851 and 1861; their children chose watchmaking as a profession.

It is little wonder that the census of 1861 shows Drury, who is still managing the Inn on behalf of the Lygon family, had taken to letting part of the Inn to Henry and Lucretia Robert, and their young family of five children. The census refers to Drury not as an innkeeper but merely as a victualler, a person selling alcohol, however, the Inn still employed two young female servants, in their twenties.

Drury hung on through the challenging times but unsurprisingly on the death of Henry Lygon in 1863, his son, Earl Frederick, put the Lygon Arms up for auction:

Lot 14, 16 October 1867: The Sale of the Estate of Rt Hon Earl Beauchamp in the occupation of Mr Charles Drury: Entrance Hall, Commercial Room, Sitting room, Bar, Smoke room, Parlour, Kitchen and two Cellars, a large Dining room, six Bedrooms, and attics. Externally there is a Brewhouse, a Granary, a capital double Coach Houses, a Harness room, Saddle Room, Loose Boxes, and Stables affording accommodation for upwards of forty hunters and other horses.

Lot 15, in that same auction, was freehold land in the occupation of Mr Charles Drury, seven acres fronting the road from Willersey to Broadway, bounded by the lands of A Savage, T Averill, R Long and Mrs Payne. Charles Drury it appears was cashing in this asset, to add to other assets so that he had the necessary funds to purchase Lot 14.[242]

---

242. 'Worcestershire Chronicle,' 16 October 1867.

Given that the introduction of the railway had made mail coaches redundant, purchasing the Lygon Arms in 1867 would have been a gamble. The enormity of his venture is reflected in two quotes, which underline the degree to which Broadway was gracefully spiralling into a decline:

During the good old coaching days Broadway was a place of considerable note, having been one of the 'stages' on the road to Oxford and London but since the introduction of the 'rail' into the Country it has lost much of its briskness, and has settled down into a very quiet place, many of its chief inns being closed.[243]

No credible person of small means will come to reside here, and most of the better houses are occupied by almost solitary widows and old maids and batchelors; the farmhouses by labourers or baliffs.[244]

But Drury was fortunate, to a large extent, that he had family members to support him. From 1866, his eldest son Charles Richardson Drury, traded as a wine merchant and brewer, in a portion of the premises, rent-free.

'Old Mullins,'[245] with his knowledge and experience of running the Inn had seen an opportunity, and assuredly based his decision on the continued patronage of both the Lygon family and the Hunt, especially from the end of October to the end of April. Then some guests would stay for periods during the game season from October to the end of January, and there would be summer visitors.

---

243. *'Billings 1855 Worcester Directory.'*
244. Derek Parsons, p. 86, *'Broadway, a village history'* The Cornmill Press, 1996.
245. A rumoured nickname – he was 66 when he became owner, and his wife Jane was 67 years old.

The Cotswold Hunt was formed in 1858[246] and then split into two in 1867, when it was finally agreed that the North of the Cotswold country needed a separate pack to hunt it efficiently, therefore, in 1868 the North Cotswold Hunt was established. Most of the hounds had been gifted by Baron FitzHardinge, with the 9th Earl Coventry, of Croome Court, maintaining the pack at his own expense, and then opening the sport to a small field of local gentry and farmers.

When The 9th Earl felt his seat at Croome Court, near Pershore, was too far, from Broadway, his health necessitated re-opening the vacant Spring Hill house. From there he conducted his hunting operations until, in 1873, he stepped down to found his own Croome Hunt in 1874. The local landowners and businessmen agreed to continue, thus creating a subscription pack.

---

246. At the time, there was much concern about the railways amongst hunting folk. How would the hounds not be struck down? How could straight runs ever be had again? Over time their fears subsided.

Etching - 9th Earl of Coventry with the Countess of Coventry 1873 – a founder of the North Cotswold Hunt 1867/8 by William Henry Hamilton Trood (1848-1899)

When Drury purchased the Lygon Arms, in 1867, he would have known of the impending subdivision of the Earl of Berkley's Hunt. He was astute to the possibility of the patronage of the Lygons and the Coventrys and their friends; accommodating their meetings and balls was most possibly with good luck a substantial part of his 'business plan'.

Luck was on his side, shortly after his purchase, the Lygon Arms did become a regular meeting point for the North Cotswold Hunt. The hunting tradition, whereby the Lygon Arms provided the Stirrup Cup at the North Cotswold Hunt opening meet each November, began and continued well into the 20th century.

Once Drury had elevated his status, by becoming an owner, he further developed his ideas to ensure the Inn's profitability. In 1869, Charles undertook the building of an Assembly Room, for entertainments: hunt gatherings, balls, and musical evenings.

This building was not sympathetically designed to complement the historic main building, but rather erected to a very tight timescale and on a limited budget, around £238 10s 10d, a low quote from a local agent Christopher French Hensley, a land and engineering surveyor.[247] The build was probably a local family affair, as the men in the Hensley families, descended from stonemasons, were stonemasons bricklayers and carpenters and the young nephews, were labourers.

AN OLD COACHING INN, LYGON ARMS, BROADWAY

On the far right the brick built assembly rooms,'a gigantic brick box, required to achieve the greatest cubic capacity, at the lowest cost...almost impossible to use in the summer.[248]

247. 1871 England and Wales Census
248. Gordon Russell, p.72.'*Designer's Trade Autobiography of Gordon Russell,*' George Allen, and Unwin Ltd London 1968

Now entertainments could take place such as Hunt Balls,[249] and amateur dramatics – farces and burlesque were popular.[250] After a North Cotswold Puppy show the Master of the North Cotswold Hunt invited fifty-four guests, including the Earl Coventry, one of the judges, to lunch,[251] a meeting of the British Archaeological Association at Evesham had a jolly outing to Broadway and a sumptuous lunch at the Lygon Arms.[252]

In a declining economic environment, against all odds, the Lygon Arms began to flourish; slowly the number of its staff and clientele increased. Had it not been for Charles Drury's resolve, and sheer determination the Lygon Arms Inn might have followed the decline of other inns in Broadway. At the height of the coaching era, it is said there were 23 inns, ale houses and beer sellers along Broadway's High Street, by the end of the century there were very few.

The 1871 census paints a picture of Charles, 69, and Jane, 70, at the Inn with three servants but no visitors, but as it was a Sunday in April, it gives no clear indication of their viability. His son, Charles Richardson, married to Laura, lived across the road from the Inn, in the old vicarage on the main street, (now Broadway Deli), with their six sons aged between two and nine.

From the diaries of Robert Newton Chadwick, a keen huntsman, and subsequent purchaser of Farncombe Estate, we are reassured that

249. '*Evesham Journal,*' 15 November 1873.
250. '*Worcester Journal,*' 23 January 1875.
251. Worcester Journal, 10 July 1875.
252. Worcester Journal, 21 August 1875.

upon visiting the Lygon Arms in March 1872 he found it *'a very comfortable old place'*[253]

The 1873 census of landowners, owning more than 1 acre, shows Charles Drury in addition to running the Inn owned forty-two acres of land. It is not clear whether this was the father or the son; in a later census, his eldest son was recorded as being a farmer. However, later accounts suggest the father had a better grasp of business than the son. The asset suggests the father was not only doing well but also setting some monies aside to build up reserves in the form of land.

In theory, Charles Richardson should have been a good candidate to inherit and make a go of the Inn, Sadly this would prove to be a wrong assumption.

In 1874, Charles Drury retired from the business to Farnham House, gifting the property estimated to be worth £5,000 net to his eldest son, Charles Richardson Drury. In consideration of this gift, Charles Richardson paid his father an annuity of £200 per annum, which continued till his father's death in 1879.[254]

The Inn he took over from his father was now a much larger place, with significantly more stables at the rear, many specifically for hunters. allthough it did not include the the next owners considerable 20th century acquisitions.

---

253. Barbara Cookson, p15, *'Robert Newton Chadwick,'* Spring Campden & District Historical and Archaeological Society, 2012.
254. *'Worcestershire Chronicle,'* Saturday 15 July 1893.

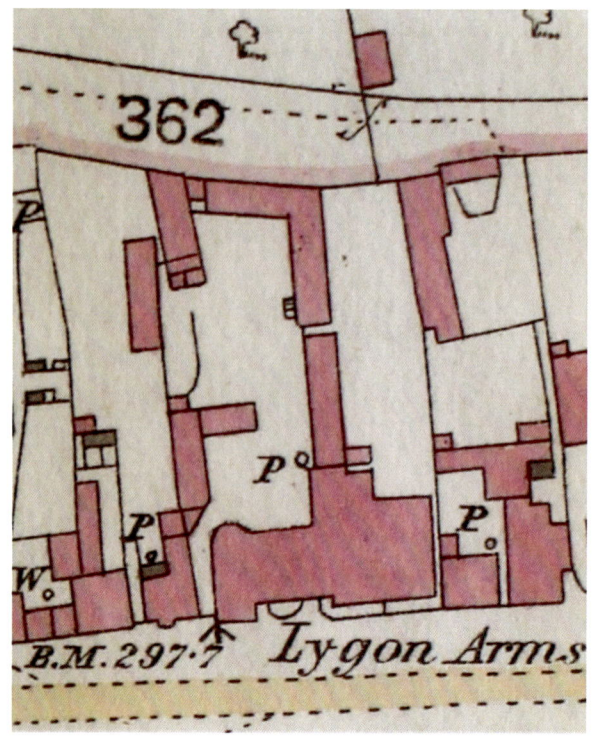

1880 map showing the Lygon Arms estate on the High Street located between the Back Lane and the High Street, which shows the Assembly room extension to the east above the letters 'on' of the word Lygon. The pink areas at the rear are stables

Disappointingly, after receiving the property from his father, Charles Richardson, immediately mortgaged it, and from an account in the newspaper of his bankruptcy in 1893, seems constantly to have used the Inn to borrow money.

On his death, in 1879, Charles Drury senior, left the sum of £46 13s 6p.[255] Probate was granted in 1881. That year's census showed Charles Richardson still dwelt at the old vicarage with his wife Laura and their seven sons. Two of the older boys, William and Arthur worked with their father as wine merchants, the other five were still students.

In 1881 we have a glimpse of Broadway's recovery from the transformational change brought about by the railways

'We turned our steps southwards to Broadway, which of recent years has had an invasion from America. But the great broad street of substantial Tudor and Jacobean houses deserves all the praise that has been lavished upon it.' [256]

It is surprising to learn how early in the development of tourism Broadway had been *'discovered.'*

'We were there before it had particularly attracted Jonathan's eye, and after a fortnight's fare of bread, cheese, eggs, and bacon (the usual fare of a walking tour), we alighted upon a princely pigeon pie at the "Lygon Arms." Under such circumstances one naturally grows enthusiastic; but even if the fine old hostelry had offered as cold a reception as that at Stilton, we could not but help feeling kindly disposed towards so stately a roadside inn. Like the "Bell" at Stilton, it is stone-built, with mullioned windows and pointed gables; but here there is a fine carved doorway, which gives it an air of grandeur. There are roomy corridors within, leading by stout oak doors to roomier apartments, some oak panelled, and others with moulded

---

255. £47 in 1881 is equivalent in purchasing power to about £7,161.87 today per the CPI inflation calculator Office for National Statistics.
256. Alan Fea, p.85, *'Nooks and Corners of Old England,'* 1908, New York, Charles Scribner's, and Sons. Comment also published in the Antiquary in 1881.

ceilings and carved stone fireplaces. One of these is known as "Cromwell's room," and one ought to be called "Charles' room"[257] also, for during the Civil Wars the martyr king slept there on more than one occasion. The wide oak staircase with its deep-set window on the first landing, reminds one of the staircases leading out of the great hall of Haddon.'

By 1887 it was rare to see coaches pulling up at the Inn, save for those Charles Richardson drove himself. He was known to be a fine whip and used to drive a coach and four regularly once a week to Cheltenham well into the nineties.[258] He was a fine horseman and an expert fisherman.

Charles Richardson Drury outside the Lygon on the box of the coach, to the left, with four of his seven sons – Assembly Hall to the right.

In the 1891 census,[259] Charles Richardson is described as a hotelkeeper, landlord of the Lygon Arms Inn and a farmer. His sons,

---

257. There may not have been a room so named at this time.
258. S. B. Russell, *'The Story of an Old English Hostelry,'* Letchworth at the Arden Press,1924.
259. Sunday 5 April 1891.

Arthur, Hugh, and Percy worked at the Inn. His eldest son Charles S Drury was working as a jockey at a racing stable, in Bourton on the Hill. There is no mention of William, Frank, and Roland. On the day of the census, there were seven borders, two visitors, two servants and one barmaid at the Inn. He appears to have been a well-liked genial host

In 1891 Hissey writes about the Lygon Arms in glowing terms: *'one of the finest and most interesting old coaching inns imaginable, and but little altered or spoilt.'* [260]

His references to the landlord were equally effusive.

'The landlord too was an ideal one, in true sympathy with his romantic surroundings. Seeing the great interest, we took in his delightful old-time Inn, he kindly showed us all over it, and fortunate indeed is the chance that has given to such a rare old building a proprietor who so highly prizes its possession.'[261]

Hissey is a valuable source of information concerning the renovations that had taken place at the Inn: half-timber stairways[262] behind plasterwork on top of ancient panelling, oaken doors, mouldings, spandrels, a frieze, and the addition of exquisite antique furniture. He noted that even though the Inn was no longer in the hands of the Lygon family, it still retained its armorial signboard displaying the heraldic coat of that family, with their motto, *Ex Fide Fortis*.

The sentiments of Fea and Hissy were supported royally in 1893 within a book which waxed lyrically about Broadway and the Lygon,

260. J.J. Hissey, p 126, *'Across England in a Dogcart,'* London, R. Bentley & Son, 1891.
261. J.J. Hissey, p 99, *'Across England in a Dog Cart,',* London, R. Bentley & son, 1891.
262. Probably the hidden staircase in the inglenook.

*'The very look of the place is to the lover of history an inspiration;
Here, one Saturday in the March of 1645, came Charles I; and here,
one night just before the battle of Worcester, in the September of
1651, slept Oliver Cromwell. The room occupied by the latter worthy
is still indicated .... At my behest, the courteous and gentle hostess
promised to have dinner ready in a little while; a good, plain dinner of
roast mutton, green peas, and new potatoes'*[263]

However, all was not as calm as it seemed to these men. Charles
Richardson's situation: either his way of life - for he had a large
family and expensive tastes, or poor management - still we recall he
ran a business in his earlier days without paying rent to his father, or
his lofty ambitions outstripped the reality of the current market.
Matters came to a head in 1893.

On 30 March one of his creditors presented a bankruptcy petition
against him, on the grounds that he had made an assignment for the
benefit of his creditors, and that he had given notice to them that he
had or was about to suspend payment of his debts. In May 1893,
Charles Richardson became officially bankrupt. On 14 July 1893, the
first meeting of his creditors was held at the Lygon Arms. Charles
Richardson admitted that he had been borrowing money at high
rates of interest for six or seven years.

Finally, a trustee was appointed. The official receiver's observations
stated upwards of £2,400 of his present unsecured debts was due to
loans, plus interest. His deficiency account showed that 12 months
before he had a surplus of upwards of £300, but during that period
he had accrued £180 in interest, plus £190 for law costs, valuers, and
accountant's charges.

---

263. Rev. James S Stone DD, p. 24-25, *'Over the Hills to Broadway,'* Philadelphia, Porter, and
Coates 1893.

During the proceedings, it was revealed that his wife was the bookkeeper, and he, Charles Richardson knew extraordinarily little about the books. He constantly claimed he knew little of his affairs. His accounting books were incomplete. [264]

He claimed he lived rent-free at the Inn, yet the census showed he lived with his family at the vicarage across the way. In addition the debtor, Charles Richardson, was sending posting orders (orders for horses) meant for the Lygon to his son who was setting up a posting business elsewhere in the village.

Over time the full extent of his problems became clear: in early ventures, his father had bailed him out, and when he took over the Lygon Arms. After his father's retirement he had resorted to money lenders. He had failed to keep track of his business matters. In summary the conclusion of the proceedings was that this was a case of 'the *Honest Fool and the Money lenders.'*[265]

Throughout 1893, despite the legal proceedings and his difficulties, the Inn continued to provide hospitality and arranged dinners and balls.

On 18 January 1894, the famous old hostelry, with its historical associations, renowned throughout England and across many parts of America, was offered for sale by order of the mortgagees. Despite a large assembly, of interested parties, bidding only reached £2,100 so the property was withdrawn.

---

264. '*Worcestershire Chronicle,'* p.7, Saturday 15 July 1893.
265. '*Worcestershire Chronicle,'* p.7, Saturday 30 September 1893.

Charles Richardson continued to involve himself with the Inn until 1894 when Frances Lane was given permission to take it over by the courts.

In his book, Hissy offers us evidence as to the next chapter in the history of Broadway and the Lygon Arms. He refers to a colony of artists that had recently come to Broadway:

'not far from the Grange stands a substantial stone-built barn. This has been converted into a grand studio; for certain fortunate artists have discovered Broadway, and besides converting a barn into a studio, have, I believe, converted an old farmhouse into a delightful country abode.' [266]

As one era in the village ended another opened. William Morris (1834-1896) the renowned textile artist, poet, artist, novelist, and conservationist was already familiar with Broadway and its environs and would establish roots in the area.

Broadway's very tranquillity drew the American artist Frank Millett, and his artistic and writer friends, to live, stay and work in Broadway. The village's offer of large houses, available at low rents was an added reason; nothing is more helpful to an artist than space to work, to store paintings and if so inclined, to host like-minded fellow artists and friends.

So it was that Broadway became the rural idyll for this group of artists and creatives at the end of the 19th century. The Lygon Arms played a bit part during this period which lasted until 1912 when the leader of the colony, Frank Millet, died in the tragedy that was the sinking of the Titanic, which put an end to the colony.

---

266. J.J. Hissey, p. 104, *'Across England in a Dogcart,'* London, R. Bentley & son, 1891.

Chapter 13

1885–1912
Patronage of the Lygon Arms by members of Broadway's Artistic Colony

Artists and writers were drawn to Broadway at the end of the 19th century.

The seeds of this artistic colony were planted as early as the summer of 1877 when William Morris spent the first of several summers at Broadway Tower, with his good friends Edward Burne-Jones and Gabriel Dante Rossetti. Broadway's reputation as a rural idyll had already leaked out to a good number of Morris' connections.

Morris, at the time, fleeing the increasing industrialisation of urban England, was heavily championing rural tranquility. In Broadway and similar Cotswold villages, he was able to see for himself the consequences of these villages being sidelined due to the decline of coaching, their deteriorating splendour, and the slow decline of their fabric.

The Tower was an ideal base with breathtaking views. Said to have been the brainchild of Capability (Lancelot) Brown, designed by James Wyatt,[267] the *'castle'* folly had begun in 1794 and been completed for Earl Coventry around 1797-8. It was from Broadway Tower that Morris addressed the letter that gave rise to the Society for the Protection of Ancient Buildings.

---

267. Dr Catherine Gordon, p.131, *'The Coventry's of Croome,'* Phillimore and Co Ltd, 2000.

Though later, this quote sums up both the decline and new possibilities:

'Let us then imagine ourselves at Broadway, in Worcestershire and at the "Lygon Arms" there. The village, still somewhat remote from railways, was once an important place on the London and Worcester Road, and its long, three-quarter-mile street is really as broad as its name implies; but since the disappearance of the coaches it has ceased to be the busy stage it once was, and has become, in the familiar ironic way of fortune, a haven of rest and quiet for those who are weary of the busy world; a home of artists amid the apple-orchards of the Vale of Evesham; a slumberous place of old gabled houses, with mullioned and transomed windows and old-time vanities of architectural enrichment; for this is a district of fine building-stone, and the old craftsmen were not slow to take advantage of their material, in the artistic sort.'[268]

In 1885, the beauty and tranquility of Broadway, coupled with the low rental cost of its fine homes and Inns, now lying empty, teased Frank Davis Millet, (1848-1912), the American academic classical painter, sculptor, and writer, to bring his family to settle at Farnham House, near the Green.

Frank and his wife Elizabeth, 'Lily,' became the nucleus of an artistic colony. That year Edwin Austin Abbey also visited. In the gardens of Farnham House John Singer Sargent started work on what was to become one of his most celebrated famous paintings: *Carnation Lily, Lily, Rose.* During one visit Sargent incurred a head wound that

---

268. Charles G Harper, p. 2. *'The Old Inns of Old England Vol II, '* London, Chapman, and Hall, 1906.

reopened due to a second knock, so spent time in Broadway recovering and in September 1885, for a short period, took up residence at the Lygon Arms.

In the summer of 1886 Millet returned to live in Russell House. Later he and Abbey jointly acquired it to better accommodate their numerous friends.

Members of this enchanted artistic colony: J.S. Sargent, Henry James, Frank Millet, Mary Anderson, a famous American Actress, and her husband Mr Antonio Navarro, Robert Hitchens, Alfred Parsons, J. M. Barrie, E.A. Abbey, Phil May, Vaughan Williams, Elgar, the Bancrofts, were all seen in Broadway, and many visited the Lygon.

After years of inward decline this bohemianism gave the village a unique atmosphere, bringing to it art, literature, and music, as well as a connection with the outside world. It was just what Broadway needed.

Millet and Abbey set up a studio in the ruined farmhouse on the grange which had once belonged to the Abbey in Pershore and is now referred to as Abbot's Grange. This building adjacent to Russell house had for several years from around 1820 to just before 1875, served as Broadway's workhouse.

Supported by Morris, as the advocate for the protection of ancient buildings, Millet began to restore the run-down farmhouse.

Mary Anderson, (1859-1940) of famed beauty and voice, and her husband, arrived in Broadway shortly after they had lost their first child. To stave off her melancholy, her doctor had ordered outings on the Malvern hills and riding, a favourite pastime. Mary was keen to go beyond Bredon Hill, to explore and show her husband Tony, the Broadway that she and her brother Joe knew, having previously been a guest of Millets and Abbey.

The couple accompanied by Mary's sister Blanche, were smitten with the village. Despite offers of accommodation, they chose to take rooms at the Lygon Arms,[269] not at all perturbed by its age or crooked floors. That one visit was sufficient for the Navarro's to fall in love with its charms and become Broadwayites.

Mary and her husband, Antonio de Navarro stayed at the Lygon[270] until the following spring during which time a number of people visited them including Maude Valerie White, (1855-1937) the French-born English composer and successful songwriter of the Victorian period.

They then rented Court Farm, in the upper part of the High Street from Lieutenant Frederick Charles Northcote Hall, of Crawley. Maude rented the house next door, Bell Farm, from the same gentleman.[271]

Whilst their new house, Court Farm, was being adapted to their needs, they left the Lygon to take up residence at Millet's house, as the Millets were away in New York.

15 August 1890, on the completion of the house, the couple moved into Court Farm. Soon afterwards, the Duke of Norfolk, a frequent visitor to the Lygon Arms,[272] visited Court Farm. He was to be one of many visitors.

---

269. She was reputedly the model for the heroine of E.F. Benson's popular "Lucia" stories.
270. Mary Anderson, p 14, 56, 'A Few More Memories' 1936'. London, Hutchinson, and Co.
271.1900 rate books.
272. Mary Anderson, p 59, 'A Few More Memories,' London, Hutchinson, and Co, 1936.

Mary and her husband, no strangers to the artistic greats of the day, embraced Broadway's artistic crowd. Their own visitor's book includes Edwin Abbey, Cecil Aldin, Fred Barnard – illustrator of Dickens novels, James Barrie, Arthur Benson, Robert Browning, Conan Doyle, Edward Elgar, E. W. Hornung - the author, Victor Hugo, Henry James, Claude Monet, Alfred Parsons, Bernard Partridge, E. T. Reed, John Singer Sargent, George Bernard Shaw, Walter Sickert – Whistler's pupil, Robert Louis Stevenson, Lawrence Alma Tadema and Whistler.[273]

For most of 1893 Charles Richardson Drury soldiered on during his bankruptcy proceedings, though from the appointment of the official receiver he was not involved in the management. Any parties, entertainments, dinners, and well-known visitors were still very welcome.

In 1894, Court Farm was purchased; it and Russell House, were probably the most visited houses in Broadway. Some visitors stayed and one, Walter Sickert (1860-1942) the Bavarian-born British painter and printmaker, fell in love, with a chambermaid from the Lygon Arms. The outcome of this encounter is not known.

One famous member of the colony, James Barrie, the novelist, and playwright, had started a cricket team, which included literary figures such as Arthur Conan Doyle, creator of Sherlock Holmes, several members of Punch magazine, and the novelist A.E.W. Mason, best remembered for The Four Feathers, a 1902 adventure novel.

The visiting cricket team were known as the Allahakbarries.

---

273. Mary Anderson de Navarro, 'A Few More Memories,' Hutchinson & Co Ltd, 1936.

In 1897, after playing a local team led by Mary Anderson, the parties retired to the Lygon Arms for a fine dinner.

Over 35 years, from 1877 to 1912, the coterie that was Broadway's Art Colony became an integral part of Broadway: *"these 'dragonflies" of culture, English, French, American delighted and amused, came, and went, enjoyed, and were refreshed by Broadway. There were japes, larks, dressings up, painting, theatre, circus and music, cricket matches, drinking. The locals then as the locals now took it all in their stride.'*[274]

This quote rather nicely reflects the lack of tension between the residents and the artists colony but from 1891 even more 'excursionists' had begun to come to Broadway, and sometimes in groups!

This was good for the Lygon Arms, the owners minded not if it was the beauty, the tranquillity of Broadway or even colony of well-known artists who were increasing trade.

Consternation how the artis who came for tranquillity might be viewing the excursionists was however being discussed elsewhere.

'the beautiful Broadway district is becoming better known though there is little chance of the railway invading the village, the artists who season after season take up their residences under the hill from which such splendid views are obtained will hardly think the charm of the place is increased by the frequent appearance of pleasure parties.

---

274. Attributed to the writer Edmund Gosse. He described great larks as a young artist in fancy dress was chased up the village street, while the locals looked on impassively. 'Whatever we do or say or wear or sing,' Gosse concluded, 'they only say, them Americans is out again.'

Let it be hoped however that they are not selfish and will not less esteem the delights of the neighbourhood because so many non-residents share the enjoyment in the fashion of excursions.'[275]

Again, the village was walking that tricky balancing line. Just in the same way it had balanced stage coaches and sheep, as the wool industry slipped into decline, so now it was debating the balance between trade and tranquillity.

A life drawing dated 1902, drawn sympathetically, humorously, and reasonably accurately, by Phil May (1868-1903),[276] a colony member, often seen propping up the bar at the Lygon Arms, depicts this challenge.

Set outside the Lygon Arms, it is entitled a 'Quiet Village.

'May, the cartoonist of 'Guttersnipe' drawings, and Punch magazine, reflects the changes the village is experiencing: the old is mingling with the new, motorised vehicles are vying for high street space with horses, carts, and carriers, rurality challenged by this new phenomenon 'tourism' yet not named as such.

---

275. Crowquill's Jottings, *'Worcester Journal,'* 27 June 1891.
276. Phil May died at the early age of thirty-nine, of tuberculosis, a condition he suffered from since childhood.

Drawn by Philip William May caricaturist, and political satirist for Punch.

Despite the patronage of the early members of the Artist's colony, the efforts of Mary Anderson her entertainments, musical evenings, and the patronage of the Hunt, sadly by the end of the 19th century the Lygon Arms had become a much-reduced Hotel and beer house.

Exactly when the Inn was purchased after the 1893 bankruptcy is unclear but on 2 June 1894 Frances Lane, thought to have been a relative of Charles Richardson Drury, applied to the courts for the Lygon Arms to be transferred to her.

The Hotel opened under her management on 12 July 1894. Robert and John Cordell, the sons of John Cordell, a draper, of 66 High Street, Bromsgrove, who had run the Golden Cross Hotel, 60 High Street, Bromsgrove until 1890,[277] then the Angel Inn, 143 Regent Street, Leamington,[278] moved to Broadway to take up the running of the Lygon Arms, for its owner, sometime after March 1894.[279]

Three sources refer to the brothers differently as licenced victuallers, landlords, or proprietors: two newspaper articles that reported the Evesham petty sessions appointment of licence holders and the report of another stay at the Lygon Arms in 1896 by Mary Anderson.

Charles Richardson Drury remained in Broadway until 1898 then moved to Cheltenham, where he died aged sixty, in August 1900.

The 1901 census clarifies Robert Cordell, a widower, and his brother John Cordell aged 55 ran the Hotel, with the assistance of a Hotel manageress Charlotte Jones, and three female servants. The brothers may have purchased the Inn, from Frances Lane, or been landlords, licensed victuallers, who worked for her, most likely the latter as they continued to manage the Hotel when it was later purchased by

---

277. The 1884 and 1888 'Kelly's Directories for Bromsgrove.'
278. 'The Leamington Spa Courier,' 20 December 1890.
279. The Angel - A licence was transferred from Robert Cordell to John Hopper Jeffery – 'The Leamington Spa Courier,' 10 March 1894.

Samuel Allsopp & Sons, one of the largest breweries operating out of Burton upon Trent.

Allsopp's new ownership was promoted as a hopeful new start in Bentley's Business directory of 1899.

'The Hotel has lately come under new proprietorship management, and nothing has been left undone to meet the views of Tourists and Commercial Gentlemen with regard to comfort. Apartments, ensuite for Families, Carriages for Hire, Good Accommodation for Hunting Gentlemen. R Cordell Proprietor.'[280]

Hindsight has proven the proprietor, who wrote the entry in the Directory, was optimistic. Samuel Allsopp & Sons, by the 1900's was a poor guardian of the Lygon's heritage; it was itself lurching from crisis to crisis.

There is, however, as always, a positive aspect to many stories of decline. The beneficial aspect of the brewery's ownership was that one of their agency managers, responsible for inspecting public houses, previously a bank clerk in London, working for businesses involved with Hotels, Sidney Bolton Russell, was a man with a vision. He had a notion to restore the property to make the perfect English inn.

The Inn was *'purchased by the great unwieldy brewing firm of Allsopp, but in 1903 was sold again to the present resident proprietor.'* [281]

---

280. *'Bentley's Business directory'* of 1899.
281. Charles G Harper, p. 4. *'The Old Inns of Old England Vol II'* London Chapman and Hall, 1906.

Chapter 14

1903 – 1907
Sydney Bolton Russell the first few years
First steps in reviving a declining Beer House

At the outset of the 20th century, Sydney Bolton Russell read about the Lygon Arms in a book called *Across England in a Dog Cart,* by J. J. Hissey. He was intrigued by the Lygon Arms description and its rural situation. Coincidentally, as it happened, the Inn was owned by his employers, the brewers Samuel Allsopp, and Sons, of Burton on Trent where he worked as an agency manager.[282]

Born in 1866, the second of four children by his father's third wife, Ellen, Sydney as a young man endured a degree of hardship. Withdrawn from school at the age of fourteen, when his father died, he had set to earning a few shillings a week in a coal merchant's office. Some years later, aged seventeen, he joined the London and Country Bank,[283] as a clerk earning £150 a year, barely enough to ask Elizabeth Shefford to marry.

At the time of the birth of his first son Sydney Gordon, 20 May 1892, he was supplementing his income from the bank, to build up reserves, by keeping books for several small firms, who were the

---

282. Jeremy Myerson, '*Gordon Russell Designer of Furniture 1892-1992*' Broadway, The Gordon Russell Trust, 1992.
283. Now the National Westminster Bank.

bank's customers. These banking contacts would prove of immense value later in his life.[284]

Aged thirty-five, in the words of his son, Gordon, he escaped from the bank and accepted the position of agency manager at Samuel Allsopp & Sons. His role included inspecting public houses. One of the premises he inspected was the Lygon Arms, the very Inn he had read about in Hissy's book.

Despite it languishing as a beer house, with unoccupied rooms, charmed by the oak ceilings, deeply recessed mullions with leaded lights, timber framed corridors, moulded, richly carved, oak doorways, and huge fireplaces he immediately recognised its potential.

Additionally, somewhere in the back of his mind, he must have noted that, at long last, Broadway was to get a railway halt. Great Western Railway was finally going to construct the Stratford to Cheltenham line, one which would bring the railway to Broadway.

Sydney was not blind to the emergence of a new era: the dawn of the motor car and motor tourism; there was little doubt Broadway was about to become more accessible. Whist the Lygon had stabling for forty horses, that was history, increasingly there was tremendous interest in the horseless carriage; Birmingham and Coventry were not far away.[285]

His report to management urging the firm not to treat the Lygon Arms as an ordinary Inn but to respect it for its architecture and

---

284. Gordon Russell, 'Designer's Trade Autobiography of Gordon Russell,' George Allen, and Unwin Ltd London, 1968.
285. 'Birmingham Post,' 24 January 1964.

location went unheeded. The brewery would not, could not, support a rescue of the old Inn. Like many companies, they were suffering financial difficulties after the Boer War.[286] Sydney was convinced that he could.

In 1903, with the backing of one of his old banking clients, R.C Drew, a man with interests in Hotels, he bought out Allsopp and Sons, purchasing the Lygon Arms, for £6,000.[287]

With few assets, a modest income and family responsibilities, Sydney faced a monumental task. He had no experience of running an Inn or a Hotel but was a determined man with a mission; to bring the Lygon Arms back to life.

On 26 January 1904, aged 38, he moved to the Lygon Arms; it was his wife's birthday, the family would follow later. The family, including three small boys, Sydney Gordon Russell, known as Gordon, born 1892, Donald George Shefford Russell, who would be known as Don, born 1894, and Richard Drew Russell, born 1903 just six weeks old, who would be known as Dick, had been living at Askew Cottage, Repton, Derbyshire. Within a week he had moved them to Broadway.

The Lygon Arms was not a welcoming place for a family, particularly for a newborn baby. Undaunted Sydney set about making his vision a reality.

---

286. Many of Allsopp's public houses had been bought at ruinously unreasonable prices around the time of the Boer War. Valuations appear to have been based on sales and sales had been rigged by the licensees.
287. Gordon Russell, *'Designer's Trade Autobiography of Gordon Russell.'* George Allen and Unwin Ltd London 1968.

1904 Sydney Bolton Russell, his wife Elizabeth and their three children - courtesy Gordon Russell Museum

On that first day in February, when they arrived, Elizabeth and the boys found the Inn tired, run-down, and shabby, a ramble of a place, in a sorry state. The good old oak and mahogany furniture had vanished, along with its Sheffield plate and glass. In the cellar, there was only a depleted bin of Madeira.[288] The dirty wallpaper was garish, the kitchen filthy and everywhere there was an atmosphere of stale beer and tobacco. The stunning Jacobean doorway had been thickly painted and all the fireplaces in the property, save that in the Charles I room, had been blocked up.

---

288. S.B. Russell, '*The Story of an Old English Hostelry,* 'Letchworth at the Arden Press, *1924.*

The staff were untrained, the back premises squalid, and there were untidy dens inhabited by members of staff referred to as 'The Boots' or 'The Ostler.' Everywhere bell pulls hissed and rustled.

A Glory hole said to have been used for smoking bacon, went up through two floors. A Bogey Hole, with doors in odd places in the wall, led to the attics. There were stables with haylofts, and all sorts of bedrooms, each different from the other.[289] Everything needed repairing from the pigsties to the cottages for the staff.

On the plus side, there was still the Charles I room, with its original 17th century oak panelling, its simple arched-headed fireplace with a fine fireback, and the original wainscot on the walls. This was the room where Charles I was said to have met his local supporters. Then there was the room that Oliver Cromwell was rumoured to have slept in before the battle of Worcester in 1651.

From day one, Sydney was determined that the ugly brick 1869 Assembly Hall, to the east of the building, was doomed. It simply had to go but funds and planning was needed.

By 27 February 1904 Sydney Russell[290] had been granted the licence from Robert Cordell the old landlord.[291] There had been tensions between Sydney and Robert initially, a hearing on 13 February had been postponed, however, when Robert had found himself a new position these all melted away.

289. Gordon Russell, p, 29. 'Designer's Trade Autobiography of Gordon Russell.' George Allen and Unwin Ltd London 1968.
290. 'Evesham Standard & West Midland Observer,' 27 February 1904.
291. 'Evesham Journal,' 30 January 1904.

In 1904, Robert Cordell became the licensee of the Lion Hotel, Wyle-Cop, Shrewsbury.[292]

Sydney's *'mission impossible'* impacted heavily on his family. Their living quarters were miserable, and money was a problem, by all accounts the first few years were a struggle.

Never one to be downhearted, little by little, he began to rescue the building, improve the Inn's reputation, rebadge its offer, and bring in more trade.

To support the restoration, from the day Sydney took ownership, for one or two days a week he had commuted to London, taking on the role of sole receiver in lunacy for a large estate, and administering a good deal of property in London. He became managing director of the headland Hotel in Newquay, and others in Bournemouth and Swanage.[293]

Whilst he was away in London, Elizabeth kept an eye on the day-to-day operations, in particular supervising in the kitchen and the guest's dinners. The two older boys were weekly borders at school in Chipping Campden, but still had tasks to complete at the weekend.

When Sydney returned from London at the end of each week, each family member was questioned on the Inn's operations and its progress. His excursions to London were to last to 1909, and little did the family know the whole project would take twenty years.

292. *'Evesham Standard & West Midland Observer,'* 13 February 1904.
293/294. Gordon Russell, *'Designer's Trade Autobiography of Gordon Russell.'* George Allen and Unwin Ltd London 1968.

Apart from mending, cleaning, ensuring the right permissions were in place, Sydney's priority first was a great survey of the property, every section, and every area was to be inspected.

The Survey showed there were only fifteen bedrooms and two rooms for the servants, most rooms were stale, uninviting, and the communal areas were no better.

Immediately, the old wallpaper and matchboard were stripped away, the rotten old Victorian sash windows were removed,[294] and the original Elizabethan rooms were carefully restored.

A very ugly stove, painted in two shades of brown, was removed from the Cromwell Room.

Unbelievably, in many areas fine old timber and beams had been plastered over and needed to be returned to their original state. Using his own hands, Sydney undertook much of the work himself as it saved hard-earned cash. Restoring the essential character of the Inn was always the focus.

As the good oak and mahogany furniture had vanished into thin air before Sydney and the family arrived, and the remaining unsightly furniture had been removed. He set about acquiring furniture, which while not exactly belonging to the Inn, was at least from the 17th century.

By the end of 1904 Sydney had established a joiners' workshop, a loft over the wash house that became a coach house at the entrance to

---

294. S.B.R thought that the sash windows may have been put in to avoid the window tax. p. 4, The story of an Old English Hostelry Third Edition. This maybe but the window tax was introduced in 1696-1851, a period when the Inn was smaller than today, the number of sash windows was not large, sash windows, a Georgian innovation, may have seemed 'modern'.

the Inn's yard, to make repairs to the house and to repair any existing or acquired pieces of *'antique'* furniture.

Gordon's sketch of the first workshop 1904

Two or three men, and Jim Turner, a Snowshill man, an ex-carpenter to the Middle Hill Estate, repaired the old furniture and would mentor Gordon and Don, when they popped in, outside of school times.

Not long afterwards, a metal workshop was established to address the difficulty of acquiring the appropriate antique hinges and lock plates for the furniture repairs, the smithy was now pounding out a variety of gates and grills for customers as, well as the Hotel.

Where he could Sydney retained the historic elements of the Inn, inevitably some of the past had to be swept away, one bathroom to ten bedrooms was hardly acceptable; in keeping with the times two more bathrooms were added.[295]

Renovations in 1904: the replacement of the sash windows on the left. On the right, the photograph captures the west wall of the 1869, ivy-covered, single-storey Assembly Hall.

From the outset Sydney made a favourable impression on those who met him; the same year he took over the Inn, there is a reference to the Lygon Arms in the diaries of Arthur Benson,[296] the essayist, who following an accident had given up Alpine climbing and devoted his vacations to discovering his own country by bicycle. From 1897 to

295. *'Birmingham Post'* 24 January 1964.
296. Edward Frederic Benson, Arthur's younger brother, also visited Broadway. In his 1920 novel 'Queen Lucia,' Broadway appears as the peaceful Elizabethan village of 'Riseholme' and the Lygon Arms as 'The Ambermere Arms.' Benson introduces the reader to Mrs. Emmeline (Lucia) Lucas, Queen of Riseholme High Society.

1925 he kept a diary, amounting to five million words. His Cotswold's holiday in 1904 began,

'Being warmly welcomed at the Lygon Arms, Broadway, by a nice landlord, a gentlemanly young man interested in antiques – anxious to restore his house.'
'We have got a perfectly enchanting, panelled room, full of china, to sit in. Out of this opens my bedroom, about thirty feet long, with a huge white dome in the ceiling, painted with orange stars: a piano, etc.' 'The Cromwell room has a fine stone fireplace and a plaster ceiling. He slept here before or after some battle.' (Cromwell spent the eve of the battle of Worcester here. By dinner-time next day, the civil war was over).[297]

The gentlemanly young man Arthur Benson referred to, who had the vision to rescue the old building from decades of dereliction, was Sidney Bolton Russell.

Along with the Lygon Arms, Broadway needed to modernise so Sydney, pragmatically, found time to be a Broadway Parish Councillor, to help to resolve local issues such as Broadway's gas or water supply, or the age-old problem of litter on the green. Broadway's gasworks were small and inefficient, so much so that from time to time a chap ran around the village advising to the locals that gas would be shut off at 9 pm. In a dry year, water ran short in the village. It was through Sydney's persistent efforts that a small tank was installed as an emergency measure. He also became a member of Evesham Rural District Council, Winchcombe Rural District Council. and the Archaeological Society.[298]

---

297. Athur Benson, *'Edwardian Excursions 1898-1904,'* London, John Murray Publishers, 1981.
298. *'Evesham Standard & West Midland Observer'* - Saturday 11 June 1938.

Chapter 15

1904-1907
The entrepreneurial owner Sydney Bolton Russell

Regardless of all the pressures of the day, and the pressures were considerable, Sydney always found time to be with his family for Sunday lunch and have a glass of wine from 'Mr Osborne's' bin.

Always on the lookout for funds, Sydney snapped up whatever initiatives he could. Some projects were successful others were not.

Initially, he became responsible for the Post Office mail contact. Post horses and coaching carrying mail belonged to a different era. By 1904, the Post Office in the UK was responsible for the delivery of mail and parcels throughout the country. The mail contract was an agreement between the Post Office and Sydney to transport mail and parcels from Evesham to Broadway.

There was no requirement to take the mail from Broadway to Evesham as it was collected from post boxes. Boxes for collection had been rolled out from 1852 onwards. Such an arrangement was more of a carrier service, between Evesham and the Post Office, in Broadway opposite the Inn, than a delivery service for individuals.

The agreement between Sydney and the Post Office would have set out exactly which way route the fly took to get to Evesham and back, the frequency of service and the amount to be paid to Sydney.

Most likely the whip that Sydney employed was an army pensioner.

The fly, a quick horse drawn vehicle, such as that used to pick up the mail

The contract did not last long, as the mail was predicably late on too many occasions when the Lygon's whip arrived at Evesham to pick it up. Sydney did not do anything by halves, he expected others to run their business as efficiently as he did.

Then Broadway's railway station, the section of the line from Broadway to Honeybourne, opened, on 1 August 1904.[299] Dray loads of people from the surrounding villages came to witness its opening ceremony. Almost immediately Sydney recognised another opportunity.

Now the High Street was to be disturbed by the horse-drawn four-wheeler station fly, belonging to the Lygon Arms, piled high with luggage, as it lumbered backwards and forwards to the station.[300]

---

299. The section from Broadway to Toddington opened 1 December 1904.
300. Sid Knight, *'Cotswold Lad,'* London, Aldine Press Letchworth for Phoenix House, 1960.

1 August 1904, the opening of the railway station

Some projects progressed almost too well. Initially, purely by accident, another business opportunity came Sydney's way, as part of the process of upgrading the Lygon from a beer house to a cross between a Hotel and a Country House.

From the day he took over the Inn, Sydney worked tirelessly to turn it into a Hotel and find the specific furnishing for each room, using personally chosen antiques.

With the help of his sons, he bought all sorts of old and rare antiques:
furniture, glass, china, and pewter from a wide range of local and regional auction houses. These needed to be stored before they were repaired by Jim Turner and his colleagues or made fit for the Hotel. Repairs, if needed, were carried out in the workshop over the coach house, in the yard.

To store the items before the repairs were made, he needed clean, dry, accessible space. The answer was in a neighbouring property to the east. He rented room in Spencer House, off the owner John Spencer.[301]

A photograph dated 1899 of the Lygon Arms, Spencer House with its awning and the 'Old House' to its right.

When bidding or buying pieces sometimes lots contained items not suitable for the Hotel, and these need to be moved on. The room in Spencer House acted as both a store and small showroom allowing him to sell the items he did not want. Initially the rented showroom in Spencer House did the job.

---

301. S. B. Russell, *'Story of an Old English Hostelry,'* Letchworth, Arden Press.

This source of 'spare' antiques coincided with guests being so delighted with the furnishings and the ambiance in their rooms and the public areas at the Hotel that they wanted to recreate the same environs in their own homes. Unexpectedly, mid-to late 1904, Broadway gained a new attraction, not just the Hotel, but a reliable source of antiques available for sale.

This new venture expanded so much faster than Sydney ever anticipated. Very soon, increasingly, old antiques or parts of antiques were making their way to and from the Lygon, via the rented space in Spencer House. The volume of items being handled increased to the point that the whole of Spencer House was needed, both to sort out which of the antiques should be retained and which resold, then display the antiques to be sold, as in a showroom.

Instead, of renting one room, to accommodate Sydney's antique finds, including those to be improved, the whole of Spencer House was required. Luckily, for Sydney the whole house was available for rent and able to be turned into showrooms.

At this point in the development of the Hotel, selling antiques at a profit was desirable but this unexpected surge in demand created a dilemma, how would he replace the antiques when he had sold them?

Ever resourceful he had a brainwave; why not establish a small business for that very purpose? When well-heeled clientele purchased a repaired individual piece, could the workshop create copies for sale. Sydney soon became inundated with requests to sell both newly restored and recreated *'antiques.'*

This new line of business required a much larger workshop. Sydney decided on a building on an adjacent plot that he had acquired when he took over the Lygon Arms in 1904, the *'Old House'* and one of its outbuildings that he named the Lygon Cottage would fit the bill. Sydney described the *'Old House'* as 'adjoining the Inn,' having quaint rooms,[302] and the rear of the building as being *'purely Elizabethan.'*

The Lygon Cottage workshop supported the new antique business in all its forms and the *'old House'* was used as the showrooms for several years.

The second workshop, 1907

A drawing by Gordon Russell 1907

The will of Stephen White III, dated 1815, confirms the name of the neighbouring freehold messuage: *'the Old House.'* It described his property as a malthouse, stable, limehouse, pigscott, and yard garden, another three retail premises, and an adjoining freehold parcel of land, measuring five acres or thereabouts, thought to

---

302. S. B. Russell, p 37, 'The Story of an Old English Hostelry,' Letchworth at the Arden Press 1914.

194

include the 4 acres, 1 perch and 3 roods shown on the 1771 award plan. This description fits to various plans.

The earliest found record of the *'Old House'* associated it with Stephen White, (circa 1677-1726) who became a plasterer. The 1771 enclosure award plan identified his son, Stephen (1716-1781), as owner of the property, outbuildings and 4 acres of land across Back Lane. His grandson Stephen White III, (1748-1815),[303] was a maltster in 1795. The 1801 the rate book refers to a house and malthouse. Sydney wrote *'During the coaching days it formed part of the Inn and had a Brew house, which has been pulled down since.'*[304]

The main house with its little cellar in the court (*still accessible today*) passed Stephen White IV, (1797–1865) a maltster, beer seller and baker. He may well have collaborated with the innkeepers of the White Hart/Lygon Arms. When Stephen IV retired to live with his daughter in Leamington Spa, his son John lived in the house for a while then let it to a saddler and harness maker. In 1894, the *'Old House'* including the building fronting the High Street, was bought by a retired fishmonger, Mr King for his family for £355.00. In 1901 the property was sold by the powers of the mortgagees and purchased by a Mr Jewsbury, then to Sydney Russell.

The picture below, circa 1850, shows an eastern gable, over the original entrance to the *'Old House.'* An 18th century property was built on the *'Old House'*'s Garden but was incorporated into the house by 1880.[305]

---

303. Broadway Parish marriage record 1795.
304. S. B. Russell, 'The Story of an Old English Hostelry' Letchworth at the Arden Press, 1914.
305. Various census records show boarders, including Lygon staff, rented rooms in the front part of the building. It may at one time have been a beer house.

A painting circa 1880, showing
Assembly Rooms behind trees,
Spencer House with its awning,
building on 'the Old House's'
garden, and eastern gable.

The Award plan 1771 – the long building.
running north south, coloured red,
identified SW, Stephen White

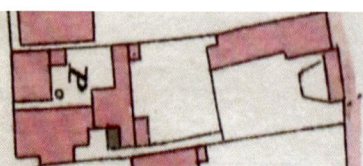

Lygon Cottage[306] is on Back Lane -1880

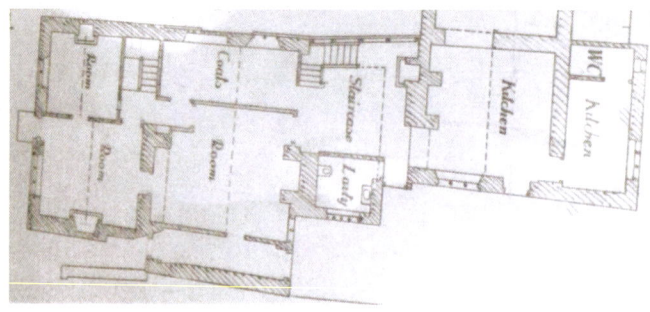

1904 Internal plan of the 'Old House' at the High Street end of the plot

---

306. Sydney was rather free with the name. When he moved his showroom to Low Farm, a photograph of Low Farm was titled The Lygon Cottage. Presumably, this was to give the customers some level of continuity.

Chapter 16

1905 to 1909
New challenges, running the Hotel, refining the antiques arm of the business, planning and expanding

Just as the Lygon Arms was overcoming its initial challenges, in 1905, a new problem emerged. Messrs John and Mr Bert Collins, both butchers from King's Heath, Birmingham, and farmers in Yardley, snapped up an ailing butchery business in Broadway from a family named Bunn.[307] The shop itself was the front section of a large property known as Aldington House.

In addition to the large retail shop, it had numerous other rooms, and outbuildings and accommodation behind the shop, large offices, and domestic rooms on three floors.

There was a slaughterhouse, garages, storeroom, stables, and a lairage where the cattle, sheep, and pigs rested on their way to the slaughterhouse. The whole, including the front shop area, (today, Hayman Joyce, an estate agent's business), and small parcels of land, extended all the way to Back Lane.

The businesses' most important asset was its slaughterhouse. John's son William immediately expanded it, slaughtering pigs for the London market.[308]

---

307. The reference to Bunn by Rev R.J.M Collins is unclear. E Loxton butchers went into liquidation in 1901. There were, however, several branches of the Bunn family, descended from William and Mary Bunn (Foster), an Evesham lass. The father, three sons and a grandson were all involved in the butchery trade in different owned or rented premises on the High Street.
308. Rev R.J.M. Collins, *'Collins in the Cotswolds,'* printed by E P Lowe Ltd.

A slaughterhouse next to an Inn would never be ideal. Apart from odour, the squeal of pigs anticipating their demise, was particularly off-putting to the Lygon customers. This was a very tricky situation that would have to be managed, which it was. However, it was almost seventy-five years before the ideal solution was found, and the problems finally resolved.

The Ordnance Survey maps of 1884-5 and 1902 confirm the land north of back lane, which is now in the ownership of the Lygon, was 1905 four different parallel parcels of land, with different owners. The parcels were mostly planted as orchards. One parcel, which was one acre, three perches and three roods in total, in Richard Hyatt's[309] ownership in 1771, was purchased by Sydney Russell as early as 1905 from one of Hyatt's inheritors.

By the end of 1905 Sydney had acquired all four parcels, roughly five acres of land, across Back Lane to establish the much-needed gardens, including kitchen gardens and orchards for the benefit of the Hotel.

Whilst all the renovations were going on, where possible, visitors were still catered for. There were marriage breakfasts,[310] concerts,[311] Hunt meetings,[312] frequent auctions of property, livestock and grains, and the annual January Broadway Hunt Ball, held in the Assembly rooms, which was Broadway's most prestigious event of the year.[313]

---

309. 'Evesham Standard,' 5 September 1908 – report of an ownership dispute in Broadway
310. 'Evesham Standard,' 12 September 1905.
311. 'Evesham Standard,' 3 November 1906.
312. 'Evesham Standard,' 2 March 1907.
313. 'Evesham Standard,' 30 December 1905, 6 January 1906.

As the routines of the Inn continued, already, thanks to the artist colony, and accessibility, the fame of the village was spreading to the Continent and America.

In 1907, at just sixteen, his eldest son Gordon was privileged to have joined his Uncle Joe, a ship's captain, on a trip to South America. On his return he joined the family business working his way up in the office, roasting coffee, bottling fruit, typing up menus, designing advertisements and letterheads, being as helpful as he could.

Gordon was, however, somewhat was drawn to his father's embryonic, multi-faceted antiques business, so he helped by marking up the antique stock. In doing so he acquired a good deal of knowledge about glass, eventually designing a few pieces himself.[314]

In 1907, a large bay window was added to the 18th century Georgian visitors' drawing room, on the first floor, which looked out over the remaining, yet still spacious, old posting yard.

314. Gordon Russell 'Designer's Trade, Autobiography of Gordon Russell,' George Allen, and Unwin Ltd London 1968.

2023 External view of the Drawing Room showing the brick extension of 1790 added after the posting yard was covered over 1772, to create what is today the Lobby Louge. The bay gable was added to the Drawing Room in 1907. The meaning of the curious symbol on the front of the Drawing Room gable remains a mystery.

Today, the view from the Drawing Room Bay window, past the magnificent feature chestnut tree, looks out on the individual gardens that enhance each of the courtyard's individually named open plan suites.

In the summer, an area below the window becomes a Courtyard dining area.

Outside the enhanced Drawing Room, cabinets used to display fine examples of blue and white Worcester porcelain. Today around the

Hotel, particularly in Russell Room, there are still feature blue china vases and collections of plates sympathetically displayed.

Fine china generously given to Sydney by Mr Antonio de Navarro was displayed in the Charles I room.[315]

It was Sydney's interest in antiques, which led to his further interest in china, which eventually expanded into an arm of his antique business, the sales and export of china and glass; this was yet another string to Sydney's bow.

The extent of Sydney's transformation of the Inn into a Hotel was fully recognised in writings of the period.

'The house has during the last few years been gradually brought back to its ancient state, and the neglect that befell, on the withdrawal of the road-traffic, repaired. But not merely neglect had injured it. A gas-lamp and bracket had at the same time been fixed to the doorway, defacing the stonework, and where alterations of this kind had not taken place, injury of another sort arose from the greater part of the Inn being unoccupied and the rest degraded to little above the condition of an ale-house.' [316]

'The whole house is a full legacy. Latter days it has been carefully 'restored' and so fitted out with modern-ancient features by Warings, and some really old articles of furniture, purchased here, there, and everywhere, that in course of time posterity may agree to consider the whole house full a legacy, as it stands, of the old domestic

315. S B Russell, *'The Story of an Old English Hostelry,'* Letchworth at the Arden Press.
316. Charles G Harper, p. 7. *'The Old Inns of Old England Vol II,'* London Chapman and Hall, 1906.

economy of the inn-keeping of the sixteenth, the seventeenth, and the eighteenth centuries.' [317]

Jim Turner must be recognised as the man with the skills, who enabled much of the transformation, through the work of the antiques workshop. Whilst the guests loved buying the restored or copy antiques, after a couple of years those adorning the Hotel, itself were no longer for sale.

Even though the restored and copy antiques sales helped finance the Hotel's renovations, and was a terrific opportunity, this was no simple business, there were many aspects to it: the finding of the antiques, cataloguing, the repair or copying. Viewing arrangements had to be made; nobility, gentry and well-known collectors were now on the guest list. Sydney sometimes needed to sketch out an example to send to a prospective buyer and then there might be the packing of the most delicate pieces glass or china, and of course, records needed to be kept.

Encouraged by a local man, Edward Arnold, Sydney started to collect 17th to 19th century glass, including a 'Yard of Ale.' To inform his purchases he referred to a copy of 'Hartshorne's Old English Glasses,' published in 1897, by the antiquarian Albert Hartshorne.[318]

A small selection of Sydney's glasses collection is now displayed in cabinets outside the Drawing Room, at the top of the Elizabethan stairs.

---

317. Charles G Harper, p. 244. *'The Old Inns of Old England Vol II'* London Chapman and Hall, 1906.
318. the first attempt at a classification of 18th century drinking vessels in England, from early times to the end of the eighteenth century.

Having foreseen the increased trade, the motor car would bring, in 1908 Sydney, bought himself a small de Dion car,[319] thus joining in the increasing numbers of horseless carriages on the roads of Worcestershire. He was developing a lifelong interest in motor cars, which would lead him to build friendships with those of a similar passion, such as Henry Ford, and Lord Montagu. He began to increasingly consider the motor car, as he formulated plans for further development.

It would be foolish to imply that Sydney Russell's early years in the village were all plain sailing. He was a canny man and must have realised he was just an 'outsider.' Many Broadway residents had spent their whole lives in the village. Many had 'corporate' memories going back to the end of the first quarter of the 19th century, as illustrated during a land ownership dispute, about rights on a small piece of land on back lane, which led to a County Court action[320] that Sydney brought against the Collins brothers, in 1908.

Sydney wanted to stop his neighbours, the Collins Brothers, asserting their perceived rights. It centred on the furtive night-time movements of piles of manure by the Collins brothers, on to Sydney's land, only to be put back, where the manure belonged, by the Inn's staff during the day. Eventually enough was enough.

The amusing story played out at the Court House, usefully teased out information that it unpicked, in part, the ownership and usage of Back Lane previously known as Back Way or colloquially as 'The Back.'

Resident after resident gave evidence during the proceedings. As expected, in a village, loyalties, were divided, however, Sydney did

319. *'Birmingham Post,'* 24 January 1964.
320. *'Evesham Standard,'* Saturday September 5th, 1908.

make his point, he obtained his injunction and damages of five shillings.

On another occasion, minutes of the parish council demonstrate the tension between Sydney and some of his fellow councillors who seemed not to appreciate the pressures on his time and his aversion to time wasting.

One byproduct of Sydney's antique business and passions was their influence on his eldest son Gordon, who had attended school in Chipping Campden and in his own right become interested in local crafts and the Guild and School of Handicrafts[321] brought from London to Chipping Campden, in 1902, by C R Ashbee (1863-1942) the English architect and designer, a prime mover of the Arts and Crafts movement. The movement took its craft ethic from the works of John Ruskin and its co-operative structure from the socialism of William Morris.

Like his father, Gordon had vision and talent. These were halcyon days when he learned quickly through observation and engagement with local designers, building up a real understanding of design and appreciating how an object constructed was vital to producing precise design.

---

321. The Guild of Handicraft specialised in metalworking, producing jewellery and enamels, hand-wrought copper, wrought ironwork, and furniture. The Guild operated as a co-operative. Its stated aim was to set a higher standard of craftsmanship, and in so doing, to protect the status of the craftsman. The school attached to the Guild taught crafts.

Chapter 17

1909-1914
Sydney Russell tackles the difficult matter of the Assembly Rooms

Finally, early in 1909, the question of Charles Drury's 1869 brick-built Assembly rooms had to be addressed. It had originally been a practical addition to house the prestigious Annual Ball of the North Cotswold Hunt, and much needed to improve the Inn's finances, but thirty-nine years later it was clearly a huge, ugly, brick building, thrust against the east wall, of the Inn blocking windows on the first floor and light on the ground floor.

Again Sydney knew from the start that whatever he did he this was going to be very complicated.

Already in 1904, quietly, he had acquired the plot and dwellings to the east of Spencer House, 'the Old House' and its outbuildings one of which at that time he called the Lygon Cottage. He later used the name for another property further down the street. Acquiring the 'Old House' in 1904, was a shrewd move to ensure the Lygon Arms could grow and prosper in years to come but in terms of the replacement of the Assembly Hall it turned out to have been an essential decision.

Using the skills of a local architect Mr Bateman, and the advice of a London architect, Sir Aston Webb, a guest at the Hotel, a design for a new hall was agreed upon.

It was Sir Aston Webb, designer of the Queen Victoria Memorial, in front of Buckingham Palace, who hit upon the solution to the knotty detail of the lack space to accommodate the new hall. He simply suggested it be repositioned and built parallel to the street, rather than at right angles as before with the Assembly Hall. This was a stroke of genius, achieving more space, and allowing the retention of a secluded rear garden.

This design, however, required the acquisition of the immediate neighbour to the east, Spencer House, in much the same way that when the Assembly Hall was built in 1869, part of the old garden to the east of the Inn, and old garden walls had been used, thus taking away the view from the oriel window in the Cromwell Room.

Until his suicide, in 1846, Spencer House had been owned, and run by Thomas Spencer, Master Draper.[322] The property was inherited by his son John. The business was continued by his widow Mary, her daughter Mary Ann, and her niece Mary Ann White. Around 1861 Mary and her daughter moved to new premises,[323] while Mary Ann White continued the Draper's business at Spencer House. Her aunt rejoined her around 1871. For the period 1881 to 1901, Mary Ann White, 56, was still running a Draper's business. She was probably doing so when Sydney rented a room for his antique storage and sales business.

Renting the whole house, circa 1905 seems to have coincided with Mary Ann White's desire to retire. It is also seeming fortunate that when Sydney's wished to acquire the building, in 1909, the timing coincided with and John Spencer's wish to sell.

On 10 June 1909, just before the pulling down of the Assembly Room and Spencer House, as a final push to maximise sales and help finance the Great Hall project, a sale of items such as fine oak

---

322. 1841, p.10, England, and Wales Census.
323. The 1861 census shows Mary, and her daughter occupied a premise further to the east of the Lygon Arms. Mary Anne Whie was next door. Both shops were Drapers.

dressers, a beautifully carved old linen chest, a mahogany pedestal writing desk, a mahogany four poster bedstead, several oak gate-legged table grandfather clocks, ornaments, oil paintings, china, and other effects, was announced.[324]

With Sydney's canny experience of selling, these effects were well-priced.

And now that his showroom in Spencer House was to be demolished, taking advantage of the antiquity of *'the Old House,'* and its rooms, Sydney, always the pragmatist, turned it into showrooms.

The build was now able to commence. It was conducted by Messrs Espley and Co. The gallery and panelling were constructed in the Lygon Cottage. Workshop.

As the Great Hall's build moved towards completion the next challenge was to seamlessly weave the eastern element of the new Great Hall into this 'simply Elizabethan' *'Old House'* building.

There were two staircases to the upper rooms in *'the Old House,'* but a new access to the upper floors was sorely needed. Very skilfully, a reclaimed staircase, circa 1665, was removed from a roofless house in Shropshire, and introduced during the building of the Great Hall. It now enabled guests to access to the minstrel gallery and the upper areas of to the Old House/Lygon Cottage. The whole really was 'joined at the hip.'

---

324. *'Gloucestershire Echo,'* 10 June 1909.

The 1665 stairs added by Sydney Russell around 1910 to access the newly created first floor in the 'Old House' to the East

Large double doors opened out from the Great Hall onto a delightful, paved courtyard and formal gardens.

By 1910, the build, all fifty-six feet long and twenty-four feet wide, a mix of dining room and ballroom, had risen in place of the Assembly Hall and Spencer's House.

Stunning features of the Great Hall, completed in 1910, included the oak floor, an imposing barrel-vaulted ceiling, with plaster bands in low relief, by the Birmingham Guilds.

The Great Hall's fine fireplace was rescued from a dilapidated Tudor house near Abbey Church at Winchcombe along with a Sussex fireback with the arms of Hyde, Earl of Rochester.

A 17th century fine oak minstrel's gallery which overlooked the Great Hall was added at the eastern end.

The almost completed Great Hall in 1910

The South wall above the panelling was designed to carry the shields of the Earl of Gainsborough, Earl de la Warr, the Duke of Portland, HRH the Prince of Wales, Lord Montagu of Beaulieu, the Bishop of Worcester, and Sir James Stirling; they were all painted under the guidance of Reverend E. E. Dorling.[325]

---

325. Edward Earle Dorling (1863-1943) was a priest of the Church of England, archaeologist, historian, and notable writer on heraldry. It is not evidenced that he painted them.

The new hall not only fitted the proportions of the Hotel, but it was also, as before, available as a new dining and venue for the North Cotswold Hunt's annual ball.

The integration of the old and new was an amazing feat, both in design and in sympathetic artisanry.

The *'Old House'* internally and externally is indeed very old, some parts especially the roof trusses appeared to be medieval. Its entrance, originally from the   door alley to the east (now Keil Close) and the features of its largest room are reminiscent of a late medieval Hall House, even though the original house has been extended.

Rear Gable End the 'Old House'

An internal picture of *'The Old House'* 1904, courtesy Gordon Russell Museum.

The 'Old House's ' northerly gable

The northerly rear gable is embellished with rose carvings on a curved section, and carved figures, possibly grotesques. There are two diamond plaques, each supporting an initial. R to the east and S to the west, but no date. These are thought to refer to Russell and Sons in the same way that the 1926 extension bears the initials R and S, 1926.

Details of the end gable and grotesques

A Gordon Russell's drawing dated 1914 shows how the *Old House'* and the Great Hall build were painstakingly woven together around 1910. The long middle section of the dwelling as it stood in 1910 only has upper windows.

The courtyard showing the integration of the Great Hall and the 'Old House,' 1910

Post the 1914 a floor was added to create two storeys facilitating six bedrooms: 45 and 46 on the Ground Floor and 40, 42, 43 and 44 on the first floor.

Additionally extra windows were added to give light to the ground floor.

The complex roof trusses are no longer visible from the ground floor but are visible from a landing area used to access guest bedrooms 40, 42, 43 and 44.

In 2016, partition walls were added on the landing to create an en-suite to bedroom 43. If the partition walls and the landing floor were removed, the original and complex vaulted ceiling of the reception hall in the *'Old House,'* would be visible.

A section of the roof structure of the medival hall in the 'Old House' area

Two downstairs bedrooms, which were created from the lower floor of the largest room in the *'Old House,'* 45 and 46, were previously known as the Broadway suite, and accessed from the cocktail bar at the rear of the Great Hall. For a period, during Cheltenham Festivals, these rooms were renowned for accommodating J. P. McManus, the Irish businessman and racehorse owner, who on occasions, it was rumoured, entertained the Queen mother; certainly, the locals noting the discretely armed royal protection officers, taking their break at the Horse and Hound Inn, supported that conclusion.

Over the years the old building would have undergone many changes. Timber-framed vernacular houses with large rooms, and steep roofs, were often thatched, which slates or tiles would later have replaced. Structural timbers infilled with wattle[326] [327] would have been repaired many times over the life of such a building. In the 16th century, bricks were more widely used for smaller houses, and brick infill, or 'noggin,' slowly replaced the wattle and daub as walls fell into disrepair. The 17th century saw the peak of the repurposing and converting halls, or hall houses to houses with chimneys. Stronger walls were added upstairs, shutters became glass windows. On occasions the rooms upstairs were used for malting or the storage of grain.

Gordon loved architecture and inherited his father's passion for buildings. Watching the craftsmen build the Great Hall, bringing large blocks of stone to be sawn on site from the quarry on heavy horse-drawn drays, watching them work the slates for the roof, mix mortar, learning the workman's skill and the various old building terms, just embedded this passion, a passion that also focussed on crafts.

---

326. The poles would be interwoven with slender branches -withes, or reeds, then daub, clay, mud, animal dung and a binder such as straw or horsehair made up the infill.
327. Though not the most rigid material, wattle and daub accommodated even the most severe structural movement in a way other infills usually did not. Its properties, lightweight but not flimsy, its weight not dissimilar to bricks, provided better insulation and security than brick.

Influenced by Katherine Adams, one of England's finest book binders, who set up business at Eadburgha Bindery, 69 High Street, he developed an interest in leatherwork, calligraphy, and printing. He learnt to cut goose quills, write on paper and parchment, and use gold leaf, trying his hand on notices for the Inn. Later he joined a life class in Campden in the company of Paul Woodroffe, who had a stained-glass studio, along with J.C.M. Shepard, who worked in it, Will Hart woodcarver, George Hart, Silversmith, Alec Miller sculptor and Fred Griggs the etcher. It must have been marvellous to be in the company of all those craftsmen.

Chapter 18

1910-1914
The days of excursionists leading to further expansion

When the Great Hall project was behind him Sydney, had time to concentrate on his another of his passions, the motor car and how it would influence his business. He had always been convinced that the motorcar, and Broadway as a motoring centre, would finally put an end to the village's inflicted isolation.

Touring, a new craze, was bringing increasing numbers of visitors to Broadway, along with guests to the Lygon Arms; he saw that it could be a game-changer in terms of all-year-round visitors.

Sydney made friends with another car enthusiast, Lord Montagu of Beaulieu, who generously spread the word about the Lygon.

'Mr Russell has wisely grasped the fact that a new species of tourist is now using the roads, one who is not pleased with the somewhat coarse fare of the farmer's ordinary, and who equally doesn't like that type of messy cooking termed by many English Hotel keeper's French.'

'He has realised that visitors arriving in cars costing £500 to £1000, each are likely to appreciate good wine and like to drink something better than; gooseberry bottled in the village or neighbouring town….

'In the course of time other inns will doubtless arise which will imitate Mr Russell's efforts, but it is unlikely that any will surpass the pioneer of the hostelry of the future.'[328]

By 1911, with the increasing number of guests, and diners, it was obvious that new kitchen facilities were required, the answer was to let go of the old 19th century stabling and repurpose them to create both kitchens and bedrooms. The work was carried out by Espley and Sons, to a design of Mr C.E. Bateman.

On the ground floor the old stables very quickly morphed into a large kitchen, a stewards' room, staff room, pantries, and larders.

On the first floor a central corridor was created off which there were nine additional single bedrooms and two bathrooms.

The courtyard and formal gardens, accessed from the Great Hall, were retained to the east, behind the new wing.

Rumour has it the rooms over the 1911 kitchens certainly overcame any concerns about lack central heating and were a nightmare in the summer.

---

328. Lord Montagu of Beaulieu a well-known authority on transport, member of the House of Lords, a good friend to Sydney Russell, *'1910 July edition of the Car Magazine'*

Five coped gables – the 1911 new accommodation and kitchen wing to the east of the Courtyard – now the Russell Room and refurbished ensuite bedrooms

That same year, on the other side of the posting yard, alongside the yards' horse boxes, almost opposite the new kitchen and bedroom wing, a large modern lock-up garage was added, forty-seven feet by twenty-seven feet, with cement floor and modern accessories.

Here was the juxtaposition of the old ways and the new; the horse boxes were available at moderate prices, for hunters, horses, and carriages, whilst other Hotel visitors could have their cars washed and filled up with petrol and oils.

A 1911 aerial view of buildings showing the new garage in the old posting yard, on the site previously of a brewhouse, store and stables

Even as the dust was settling on this venture, Sydney was starting to plan a whole wing with four large lock-up garages, various offices, on the ground floor, ten cubicle rooms for the owner's chauffeurs above, and dormitories for women staff.

To that very end in 1913, Sydney purchased a property on the west of the Inn, that had been, very briefly, circa 1861 – 1871, the Stanley families' beer house, the Baker's Arms.[329] Later in 1911, it had been a boarding house, amongst its boarders had been the Lygon's Arms porter and its chauffer!

The Old Bakers Arms-1861-1871–now the Tavern

Work on a new project on the west side of the yard had just started when war broke out. Sydney could not have anticipated that by the time the war was over, the social fabric of England would have changed, and the needs of his clients would have altered.

---

329. Around 1871, the Stanley family ran the beer house, the Baker's Arms, from Church Street (Bannits).

After World War I the property for a time became the premises of the Capital and County, Broadway's first bank.

1913 was a time when Sydney's son Gordon, having successfully helped launch the '*Old House*' as a showroom for antiques acquired or created, was just beginning to get to know the dealers, and expanding his own business based on the buying and selling of antiques.

Neither Gordon nor his brother Don, knew that they would return changed men – none of the service men that volunteered to serve their country in 1914 or were conscripted did.

As the clock struck midnight at the dawn of 1914, Elizabeth and Sydney reflected on their successes and challenges over the ten years, from 1904 – 1914. So much had gone well. That year they were hoping for a good summer. Summer was the busiest and most lucrative time of their time of the year.

Just before the season started, they published their '*en Pension*' terms: three guineas a week in the winter, three and a half in the spring and autumn, four guineas in the summer months.

In the summer a one-night stay in a single room was six shillings and in double rooms nine shillings, rates were less in the winter. Breakfast and luncheon were two shillings and sixpence, afternoon tea one shilling and three pence and dinner three shillings and sixpence. Meals were served at 9.00 am, 1 pm, 4 pm, and 7.30 pm except on Sundays.

Cakes, jams, marmalade, etc were all made on the premises and fruit and vegetables were grown in the garden.

Chapter 19

1914-1918
The Lygon Hotel during the Great War and its impact on its evolution

Across the land, the Great War, 1914-18, impacted upon every family. The Lygon was no exception, it touched Sydney's older sons Gordon and Don, porters, waiters, and gardeners alike; Dick, Sydney's youngest was still a scholar, in Cheltenham.

War began 28 July 1914, on the run up to the busiest month, August, for the Lygon.

All building work ceased, though true to form Sydney continued planning. High on his list was an increase in the lounge areas, the addition of a smoking room, and yet more bedroom accommodation.

He would plan to move these projects forward when it was next possible.

In the first years of World War I, more than 170 men of Broadway, approximately 20% of the village's male population, voluntarily enlisted. It is interesting to note that the village of Broadway had a higher-than-average enlistment rate.[330] With the introduction of conscription in 1916, that number rose to more than 300.[331]

When the war started, 22 September 1914, for Gordon who went off to Worcester to enlist in the Worcestershire Regiment as a private, only to find himself ordered about by an old soldier who had a few months earlier been day porter at the Lygon and was now a corporal. He was 22 years old.

The autumn of 1914 was spent in billets in Worcester with no khaki uniform or rifles. At Christmas he was sent to Maldon in Essex with a draft for the 1st/8th Battalion. By Christmas he had a uniform and a rifle, then after more home service, on 31 March 1915, his regiment embarked at Folkestone on SS Invicta and arrived at Boulogne the following day.

The battalion then headed north into Belgium and gained their first experience of life in the trenches at Ploegsteert Wood, where on 21 July 1915 Gordon was promoted to lance corporal.

In September 1915, the battalion returned to France and took part in the Battle of Loos, which began on 25 September.

Donald, who had listed his occupation as Hotel manager, enlisted 12 December 2015. He was19 years old. He was immediately placed into the Army Reserve until he was mobilised on 2 February 1916 and posted to the 3rd/8th Battalion.

---

330. At the beginning of 1914 the British Army had a reported strength of 710,000 men including reserves, of which around 80,000 were professional soldiers ready for war. By the end of the First World War almost 25 percent of the total male population of the United Kingdom of Great Britain and Ireland had joined up, over five million men. Of these, 2.67 million joined as volunteers and 2.77 million as conscripts (those that volunteered after conscription was introduced would most likely have been conscripted anyway).
331. Of these 48 were killed in action or died shortly afterwards.

1914 - Gordon and Donald Russell

He was promoted to lance corporal on 19 August 1916 and on 1 September he returned to the 7th Battalion, where he was promoted to lance sergeant the following day.

In 1917 he joined Number 13 Officer Cadet Battalion at Newmarket but was soon admitted to hospital with measles. He was discharged from hospital on 6 March 1917 and returned to his officer training.

On 9 November it was reported that he was "on the heavy side but has the right qualities and will make a good instructor".

Back in Broadway, Sydney, and Elizabeth, kept the Inn running with a skeleton staff, but the bar had to close. Both worked tirelessly to support the war effort, in any way they could.

In addition to keeping the Inn as a going concern, Sydney and Elizabeth provided convalescent respite at the Hotel for serviceman.

The Hotel was busy, the days were long. Making do and mending, holding everything together was exhausting and took its toll.

By 1915, both Sydney and Elizabeth realised they needed a break from the Hotel. Just before the war Sydney had purchased three cottages in Snowshill, now he turned his attention to their conversion and improvement, despite the call on manpower, and the challenges in respect of materials.

Gordon recalled commenting on the plans from the trenches in France.

Two projects, Tower Close, Snowshill, and a stone laundry desperately need by the Hotel, both designed by Batemen, went ahead.

In 1916, Sydney purchased the Sand Farm, closer to the green, not far from Lygon Arms.[332] The whole property, limestone ashlar with a Welsh slate roof, comprised of a main house, two storeys with attics and three bays, two smaller eighteen century dwellings, and numerous outbuildings. More importantly, at the time, it came with seventy acres. Though a good many of these acres would have been tenanted and supporting the war effort, they gave him access to meat, fruit, vegetables, eggs, butter, and milk. Sydney was committed way before his time to buying British and local produce, though sadly, due to shortages of sugar, not jam.

Just as with the Lygon Ams in 1904, he organised men, who though not young enough to go to war, retained their skills. His team from

---

332. Russell& Sons, penultimate page, *'The Lygon Arms, Broadway,'* London, The Arden Press, 1919.

the Lygon Workshop tackled most aspects of the work, at the newly acquired property including the panelling and added a one-bay two-storey porch with hipped roof, a particular feature of the building. I

In addition to being able to move forward and carefully repair and alter the buildings he had just acquired; he saw the real value of keeping the old crafts going even at this challenging time.

The running of the Hotel, the war effort, and this new venture were taxing Sydney, as was his decision to remain as an active member of the parish council. There was no doubt that Sydney was stretching himself to the limit, such that in 1916, the driven visionary, with an impassioned eye for detail and quality, unfortunately, suffered a small stroke.

To add to the families' personal difficulties, nationally food security became even more of an issue, indeed it impacted every aspect of life across the country. The Hotel was fortunate in that it had reserves from the vegetable gardens but now the management had to take a personal hand in the buying of essential produce; rationing, even for guests, was about to become the order of the day.

In December 1916, the first attempt at rationing was made with an order restricting meals in Hotels and restaurants. In 1917 food prices had doubled with only two- or three-months supply in the Country.

In November 1917, the meat control order became law and their neighbour's slaughterhouse was duly registered by Evesham Rural District Council. Wider rationing came in February 1918. In the July cards were issued, and the Hotel along with everyone else had to register with a local butcher or grocer.

The guests, by 1918, were a mixture of remaining locals, convalescents, those visiting on war business and a few remaining business clients.

One visit from Walter Hines, the American ambassador to the UK (1913-1918) did not go as well as one would have expected. Being a privileged American, used to a degree of modernity, he was not enamored of the crooked floors and the ups and downs of the Lygon's many corridors. The charm of the age and heritage of the Lygon Arms was lost on this one American.[333]

Both boys, saw a good deal of the action.

Donald was commissioned on 30 April 1918 and posted to the 7th Battalion, Worcestershire Regiment as a second lieutenant. He arrived in France on 22 June 1918 and like his brother went on to Belgium where in August he was wounded at Locon, in the Lys Valley, in Belgium. His discharge from the army came in 1919.[334]

Gordon, after four years of trench warfare was discharged 15 January 1915, as a subaltern, with a Military Cross for distinguished service.

They returned to Broadway, as most men who survived, changed men, who had grown up very quickly, grateful to have survived, bursting with innovative ideas.

333. Mary Anderson de Navarro, 'A Few More Memories,' Hutchinson & Co Ltd 1936.
334. Chipping Campden School WWI records, of old boys.

Chapter 20

1919 – 1938
Between the Wars

War and major disasters always create an atmosphere where matters change at lightening speed, in such circumstances cultural changes that were once unthinkable, gain acceptance. It was no different in 1919.

January 1919, on demobilisation, Don and Gordon came home to Broadway.

Initially, on their return a partnership was formed. Instead of S B Russell it was Russell & Sons (proprietors), including Sydney, his wife, Gordon, and Don; Dick was too young to be included. After a while, the early ideas of how Sydney and his eldest sons[335] would work together fell by the wayside, and increasingly Gordon and Don started to follow their own paths.

The war had altered the boys; they understood how society had radically changed. Their father had set out to create a Country House environment for a specific section of the leisure society, specifically pre-war. Gordon and Don understood that post-war the Inn had to serve all travellers, not just those who dressed for dinner, and that the lock up garages that served those with skilled and trusted

---

335. Dick was still away at architectural college.

chauffeurs would, post war, be serving those that drove their own cars.

Building on their war experiences, where they had developed empathy with the needs of working men, they encouraged the opening of more areas of the Hotel for the locals to enjoy. This was a risk, what remained of the upper classes did not always welcome the company of the hoi-polloi who could put the Lygon's reputation in peril. Gordon and Donald saw their roles as balancing modernisers, to encourage the right sort of locals whilst discouraging those drunken louts that might pour onto the High Street at 'turning out' time.[336] Sympathy for soldiers who might be experiencing PTSD was not on the agenda at this time.

However, with Gordon and Don's input in the running of the Inn, increasingly modern touches appeared: extra bathrooms, some central heating, and even electricity!

The question of electric light had first arisen during the war, 12 March 2015, a group of petitioners in the village had asked the parish council, at its meeting to consider the matter of electric lighting in Broadway. Mr Williams and Mr Russell had proposed the matter be discussed with the District Council to see what steps would be necessary to instigate electric lighting locally. The petitioners were also asked to investigate the matter further. Not long afterwards the first local electric light plant was installed, and a man called Grant was taken on to run it.

336. Sid Knight, *Cotswold Lad,* London, Aldine Press Letchworth for Phoenix House, 1960.

In 1913, Before Gordon left for the front, the Lygon's workshop employed six skilled men: a joiner, cabinet maker, metal worker etc plus two masons, and a painter. Post war it was being run by Jim Turner and his youngest son, Sid, who was only fourteen. On Don and Gordon's return the staff began to get back to its old numbers, and the antiques that had been languishing for the past five years were fished out; work began again.

Though the antiques business and the overseeing of the maintenance of the Inn were revitalised, Gordon's army record book of 1917 had described him as a designer of furniture. It was never going to be long before his passion, his ambition to design furniture, would take over and steer him in this direction.

Gordon already had technical skills, and as a decorated officer, he had gained experience, in man management; both these skills had enabled him on his return to set up a new workshop behind the Hotel and to employ skilled cabinet makers, to produce furniture influenced by the Arts and Crafts style.

Going one step further he now looked to marry his sound knowledge of old furniture with all the possibilities that the machine age offered. Soon the more modern pieces were being displayed and more importantly sold. As early as 1920 Gordon began to exhibit his designs, winning several prestigious awards.

In October 1919, a property previously owned by a butcher George Charlwood Bunn and his wife Catherine Julia, and passed to Julia when George died, came up for sale January 1920. The partners purchased it. The house, Low Farm, (now Russell's Restaurant) was to be Gordon's showroom for his new venture, *'modern furniture.'*

In time the estate of Sands Farm acquired in 1916 by Sydney, and that of Low Farm would enable Russell and Sons to have sufficient land, and buildings to renovate, to accommodate the development of a furniture factory, showrooms, and offices. all of which would become part of Russell Workshops Ltd. Of particular interest was a Great Barn behind the properties.

Up to this point guests at the Hotel had been gently reminded to visit the Hotel's antique showroom, in its ideal setting *'the Old House'* after Spencer House had been demolished to make way for the Great Hall. Guests had been able to acquire or delight in the pewter, china, old furniture, and glass. All at reasonable prices. It was stressed by the management that great care was taken in packing, for those travelling overseas or long distances. All aspects of the business, as always, stressed personal service.

After the purchase Gordon moved his showrooms from *'the Old House,'* to Low Farm, enabling him to renovate *'the Old House,'* which he described as *'a small house, with a back part thought to be 16th or 17th century, which was rather dark, and a front extension of the early 19th century which meant it had no front garden,'*[337] prior to his wedding to in the summer of 1921,

During the refurbishment, in 1921, he had found a copper token[338] issued from Broadway, stamped Michael Russell Broadway 1677, leading him to believe a Michael Russell may have lived in the *'Old House.'*

---

337. Gordon Russell *'Designer's Trade, Autobiography of Gordon Russell,'* London, George Allen, and Unwin Ltd, 1968.
338 During late seventeenth century, such coins were struck for local use by people standing to mitigate the shortage of coin caused by hoarding before the era of banking.

Both boys married that summer. Donald married Effie Bowker Rowlinson, the youngest of nine from a family in Cheshire, at Buckland Parish Church.

Gordon married Toni Denning, a couple of months later, 8 August, at St Martins in the Fields Church, London.

Gordon and Toni lived in the *'Old House'* until 1924, when the lack of a garden did become a problem, after their second son was born, so they chose to build their own house, Kingscombe, near Dover's Hill, above Chipping Campden.

Donald and Effie lived at the Hotel.

In 1921, the Sydney pragmatic and thrifty as ever, for continuities sake and to ensure marketing material, advertisements and press coverage was not wasted, changed the name of Sands Farm to the Lygon Cottage!

LYGON COTTAGE

Sands Farm circa 1923, purchased 1916, took the name Lygon Cottage from the buildings at the rear of the 'Old House,' but focussed on selling Gordon's 'modern' furniture

235

Whilst Gordon was changing direction, moving increasingly into the design and production of modern furniture, Don occasionally covered as antique buyer. He kept an eye on necessary maintenance, but neither maintenance nor antiques were his natural habitat.

With his inherited love of English food and country hospitality, Don, was well suited to the task of managing the Lygon Arms. Finally, realising he had to let go, Sydney, and favoured Don his middle son to manage the Hotel. Given his new freedoms Don set about rebuilding the kitchens and in an inspirational move, in tune with his clientele's tastes, dismissing the comments of Lord Montagu ten years earlier, and his father, despatched a local boy to France to train as a chef. He understood he had to keep prices keen but insisted on increasing the intrinsic quality and service in the restaurant.

For the staff he knew post-war, accommodation was an issue. To attract competent staff, he commissioned Bateman to design a solution, The delightful, thatched brick and part weather board building was built across the lane.

Orchard Cottage, the original 1920's purpose-built staff accommodation

Nearly twenty years had passed, and Sydney supported by his sons had made many more alterations than he could ever have envisaged were necessary. Despite enlargement and renovation and appropriate modernisation, he had managed to preserve and protect a great deal of the original details of the buildings that had been incorporates into the whole or modified within the original dwellings.

Cecil Aldin (1870-1935), artist, illustrator, frequent visitor to Broadway, and the Broadway colony summed up how its many visitors and residents' felt about the Hotel. He pointed out that the guest list has been star studded, as far back as the White Hart, that by 1921 the furnishings were an antiquary's dream, the bill of fare top quality, and the service beyond reproach.. it is excellent value.'[339]

'To me, the Inn is Broadway. It's feeling of bigness makes it look like a parent to the wide, streeted village with its background of purple hills.' [340]

The Lygon was praised, with affection, for its *'Creature comforts... nooks and corners most carefully tended and preserved.* [341]

In the winter, you sit in front of large open fireplaces free from draughts and well-lit, a thing that cannot always be said of many of these chimney corners where I am bound to admit, you usually get your feet scorched and the back of your neck frozen or find yourself unable to see to read when sitting by the fire on account of inadequate lighting arrangements. At the Lygon Arms, all this has been altered; central heating and electric light, both unobtrusively hidden, save you from cold and darkness, while the old-world effect

339. *'Financial Times'* -late 1970's
340. Cecil Charles Aldin, p.106, *'Old Inns,'* 1921 London, Heinemann.
341. Cecil Charles Aldin, p.105, *'Old Inns,'* 1921 London, Heinemann.

of the Inn remains. Treasured pieces of furniture surround you which are never disposed of, even to the ubiquitous American.[342]

In 1922, using the labour of the craftsmen that worked at the Lygon Cottage workshop a high-level timber bridge, was erected, which linked the main building to the west wing; this was a project Sydney had wished to construct ever since he had acquired the property to the West, now the Tavern, during the Great War. He hada feeling now using these crafts men with local builders the next phase of improvements to the Lygon, could move on at pace.

As it grew, Gordon's new venture meant he needed a new employee to run the successful antiques business. Already as soon as pieces were repaired, they were sold. Henry Keil[343], who came to be known

---

342. Cecil Charles Aldin, p.106, *'Old Inns,'* 1921 London, Heinemann.
343. Young Henry Keil was born in 1900 into a family with historic roots in the furniture trade. His father, J W Keil, born in Middlesex, South Hackney, two miles from Shoreditch,

as Bill, had in 1919, like many returning soldiers wanted to build a new future, a new career path. He had taken full advantage of the additional educational opportunities to returning service men offered by the authorities.[344] In his latter days at college, he had won several prizes: first place and a silver medal in his final examination at the London Institute City and Guilds, achieved bronze in the Royal Society of Arts in Design and Craftmanship assessment and taken to opportunity of valuable work experience. In April 1925, the year, after his marriage to Violet Webb, he moved to join Gordon Russell, and to run the antique furniture division from the Russell workshops, at the rear of the Hotel.

In 1926, the organisation of properties on Low Farm and Sands Farm were sufficiently advanced for a small private company to be formed to handle the 'modern furniture' side of the business. The title of Russell Workshops Ltd was altered to Gordon Russell Ltd, from then on Gordon navigated the technically complicated transition from hand made to machine made furniture. He was determined to adhere to his vision of clever design and aesthetics, which was not an easy road. Don concentrated of the hospitality side of the business.

Historically, for several years there had been an unofficial arrangement with the owners of 35 High Street, across the road, to provide dormitory accommodation in its long attic room for the

---

was a carpenter who became a master cabinet maker at forty-four. Henry, one of five children in Camberley, Surrey, had at the outbreak of the Great War volunteered for war work. He was placed as an apprentice in the experimental section of the Royal Aircraft Establishment at Farnborough as a pattern maker.

344. He was awarded a scholarship from 1919 -1923 to study design and technology, linked to woodwork, at Guildford School of Art Training in Design and Technology and later the Victoria and Albert Museum. Guildford was known for its woodwork courses during this period.

chauffeurs who had driven their patrons of the Lygon Arms.[345] Any improvement on this arrangement was to be welcomed.

By 1926 funds had been found for yet another new wing. The whole would provide garages for twenty-four cars, a heated workshop for running repairs, with rooms above for the chauffeurs, and included a clock tower. Petrol pumps were to be installed in the courtyard shortly after the build.

Again management was aware the work was tantamount to breaking eggs, they would be removing the former garage, and absorbing a section of back lane, thus compromising the width of the rear access but they felt the improvement would be spectacular.

1926 Leslie Mansfield's plans for garages and chauffeur's accommodation, west of the Lygon site. The garages were converted to a conference room mid 20th century and in 2018 to guest suites. (quality poor as originals are missing)

---

345. Information from the owner of 35 High Street 2015.

The next obvious candidate to improve the Hotel's offer was the Power House. The Hotel desperately needed an efficient central heating system; coal in the bedrooms had always been perilous, especially when guests left their rooms and the fires necessitated staff constantly running up and down the flights of stairs, with heavy buckets. The pre-war plant was hopelessly overloaded and there was no certainty as to when a proper electric supply would reach Broadway. Following Mansfield's garages, absorbing yet more of back lane, Mansfield designed and had built his curious, contemporary apsidal, semi circular ended Power House, which looked as if it would have been more at home in an Asian landscape than Broadway.

Internally, the generator was hugely impressive, especially for that period.

Inevitably, this was, of course, not the end of it. Even with the Power House, in such an old building adding a central heating system, accessing so many levels, proved to be an onerous task.

On the completion of the garages, chauffeurs' rooms, and Power House, more minor changes became pressing; in the main building more bathrooms, basins, and lavatories were essential. This not only required finance but whilst the work was being done, all the rooms were unusable, therefore, the cost of the work was even greater. There was no alternative, to be successful the Lygon needed to set new superior standards to attract new custom.

Through his experience in man management during the Great War Don had a keen eye for what was important to those who worked at the Hotel, so he turned his attention to both the staff and guests. He instigated a menu of improvements, organising staff training, improving working conditions and importantly for repeat business increased levels of customer service. These innovative programmes resulted in higher levels of service across the board which then made it possible to dispense with outside caterers for the hunt ball and other such functions.

In 1927, brother Dick, returning from architectural studies joined Gordon in the business, together they gained a considerable reputation and were acknowledged as major force at the forefront of European Design.

Gordon (1892-1980) was recognised as one of the first modern designers of the twentieth century. His life, and work is celebrated at the Gordon Russell Design Museum,[346] Russell Square, Broadway.

---

346. In Russell square, on the site of part of the old factory, a short walk down back lane, Gordon Russell Design Museum celebrates Gordon's life and work.

Dick carved out his own career becoming a leading modernist designer, and a Royal designer for Industry (RDI, and Professor of Wood, Metal, and Plastics for the Royal College of Art (RCA). He designed a pavilion for the Festival of Britain and the chairs for the new Coventry Cathedral.

The Iconic Coventry Cathedral Chair by Dick Russell

243

Donald, the down to earth gracious host, who had by 1930 taken full responsibility for the Hotels' running continued the tradition of acquiring and maintaining many of the antiques in the Hotel that gave it its exceptional historic atmosphere.

Sadly, he endured most of the Wall Street crash of 1929, which started in September and continued into late October. Overnight there was a decline in the Hotels' American visitors, both the frequency of their visits and, the spending power of those who did come.

Similarly, the antiques business began to suffer. The success of the antique furniture division, run by Bill Keil, from the Russell workshops, had been in no small part due to his ability to engage with American clients. As sales manager, at just twenty-nine, Keil set sail from Liverpool, 19 October 1929, on the Adriatic, the White Star Line, bound for New York to address the business challenge resulting from the crash. Despite his valiant efforts, he could not avoid the collapse of Russell's international business and the closure of the antique division in 1931.[347]

Despite such monumental challenges, the three boys were well able to steer the ship onwards and upwards when Sydney and Elizabeth retired and became engaged in new ventures.

When Henry Ford, November 1930, purchased the old Cotswold village forge[348] Rose Cottage, in Snowshill, close to Sydney's home,

---

347. Undaunted, in 1932, Bill Keil established his own extremely successful firm, selling English Furniture and Antiques, specialising particularly in oak and walnut furniture of the 16th, 17th and 18th Centuries, which prospered until the early 21st century when it changed direction as the antique market changed.
348. Stanley family, who were the blacksmiths in the Cotswold village of Snowshill from before 1795. The business passed between family members until it ceased operation in 1909 with the death of Charles Stanley.

he was able to find some domestic artefacts from his extended workshop for the three-hundred-year Rose Cottage. When it was completely dismantled, Henry shipped it, complete with bellows, hearth, and quenching troughs, to be re-erected in his Museum Greenfield, Dearborn, Detroit. Sydney and Elizabeth were now free, from the Hotel, and able to take a trip to see the whole in its new home.

By 1933 the old flair and style had returned, still remarkable for its antiquity, architecture, and furniture, at least a dozen of the Lygon's pieces of furniture, were included as the best specimens of their kind in the Dictionary of English Furniture.[349]

The Lygon's offer was enhanced by the outstanding quality of its menus. Sydney had made home grown produce a passion, long before the advertising executives cried 'Buy British.' Seven staff worked tirelessly on the gardens and flowerbeds, producing fine fruit and vegetables. The focus was on homegrown and freshness; the asparagus beds produced 30,000 heads a year, raspberries were grown late into the autumn, there were fresh strawberries, cauliflowers, and a host of other vegetables.[350]

It is worth noting Le Manoir aux Quat'Saisons, Oxfordshire, is famous for its kitchen gardens, but they were not created until nearly half a century after the kitchen gardens at the Lygon Arms.

With its ten boilers, central heating, supplemented by open log fires in every public room, the Lygon exemplified quality, warmth, and comfort.

---

349. Percy Macquoid and Ralph Edwards, 'Dictionary of English Furniture,' London, Country Life, 1954.
350. Noel Carrington, 'Broadway and the Cotswolds,' The Kynoch Press, Witton, Birmingham.

In 1936 Sydney Bolton Russell had two further strokes and on 26 January 1938, Elizabeth's birthday, thirty-five years after he became proprietor of the Lygon Arms, he died, aged seventy-one, and was laid to rest in Campden. A key point made at his funeral was that the business meant for him the welfare of the village, for which he never ceased to care.[351]

The management of the Inn continued under Donald's wing, like his father he too gave back to community having become a County Councillor in 1936, being on Evesham Rural District Council for many years and the Parish Council, and a Trustee of the Lifford Hall, and the Scout Hall.[352]

He remained a keen sportsman and hunted with the North Cotswold Hunt.[353]

It is unsurprising that despite the decline of coaching, even in 1937 horses still had their place in the life of the Lygon. 1 November 1937 the Master, W. W. B Scott opened the Meet of the North Cotswold Hunt at the Lygon.

---

351. *'Evesham Standard & West Midland Observer'* - Saturday 05 February 1938.
352. *'Evesham Standard & West Midland Observer'* - Saturday 04 May 1946.
353. *'Evesham Standard & West Midland Observer,'* Saturday 14 November 1936.

The meet of the Noth Cotswold Hunt outside the Lygon 1 November 1937

Chapter 21

1939 -1945
The Second World War

The year after Sydney died, 1939 brought the challenges of World War II. Immediately, all food came under Government control and in 1940 ration books were introduced. Prices were fixed and the next-door slaughtering of beef and cattle stopped, when slaughtering was centralised; therefore, Evesham's abattoir served the area although the Broadway premises continued to handle pigs, the bacon and pork. Fruit and vegetables were never rationed which was a help given the kitchen gardens at the Lygon, though as in the Great War, the shortage of gardeners became a major issue.

Much of the Sands farmlands, the seventy acres, part of a purchase in 1916, which had kept the Lygon Arms supplied with meat, dairy, fruit, and vegetables then, had been sold on, to enable further expansion of Gordon's design business.

Donald and his staff were spared the Hotel being commandeered as a military establishment, as due to its age and complexity, it turned out to be unsuitable for office accommodation. Restaurants had been immune from rationing in 1940, allowing people to supplement their rations by dining out if they could afford to but like his father and mother before him, Don, supported by his wife Effie, decided to carry on the back breaking work of keeping the Hotel going.

From the onset, Don had a policy, following the example set by his parents, of supporting servicemen, on short term leave from overseas, particularly Anzacs.[354] With the help of the Victorian League, he started off with forty-seven service men of a minimum six ranks, as his guests. Originally the idea was a winner, but eventually most of what Don considered were *'his boys,'* got commissions, so the idea of other ranks was scrapped. In the end he provided a secure haven, free of charge for just over 300 soldiers, sailors, and airman; the stays were sometimes a few days and other times a few weeks.[355] Gratifyingly, by way of thanks, given the Hotel's shortage of staff, many of them took turns to help, carrying out many of the necessary jobs.

Don formed relationships with *'the boys'* and their families. Many an Australian parent would have known of Don who wrote to assure them their sons were safe and had stayed at the Hotel. Effie his wife, helped at the forces canteen and took a great deal of interest in the older people in the village.[356]

Gordon rejoined the Special Police, amazed at the complexity of the tasks and the many jobs the police were expected to manage. When France fell there was a call for Local Defence Volunteers, so he then took a leading role in Broadway's Home Guard.

---

354. Anzacs, a collaboration term for soldiers from Australia and New Zealand.
355. 'Evesham Standard & West Midland Observer' - Saturday 04 May 1946.
356. 'Evesham Standard & West Midland Observer' - Friday 23 December 1960.

Just after Dunkirk hundreds of soldiers billeted in the village enjoyed hot baths at the Lygon and it was at Don's suggestion that his kitchens provided a hot meal daily for many months for evacuee children during the days of the blitz.[357]

The only story of ghosts at the Lygon links to these war years. Peter Smith, a young porter who joined the Lygon in the 1940's, on his second week on nights, was startled at 2.00am in the morning, when the door of one of the rooms accessed from the archway over the yard opened and a woman in white jumped out! He never went passed that door again.

In June 1941, one visiting Australian serviceman from Perth, an able seaman on a naval seaman's course, was young Douglas Barrington. He had graduated with honours in accountancy in 1938, just before the war, and had a lot in common with Donald. A favourite haunt of

357. 'Evesham Standard & West Midland Observer' - Saturday 04 May 1946.

the naval servicemen staying at the Lygon was the buttery bar, the old smoke room, adjacent to the gift shop, which had been renamed Gin corner, as this was the traditional drink of the Navy.

Douglas struck up a particularly strong friendship with Donald, who had no son of his own.

R.A.N. lieutenant Douglas Barrington, was commissioned in 1942 and posted to the destroyer H.M.S Eggesford in the Mediterranean, where it was part of the North African and Sicilian campaigns. Throughout the war he and Don corresponded, and he promised when his leave was over, he would return to the Lygon.

Each time he had leave he immediately returned to England, making straight for the Lygon Arms. Though fascinated with the Cotswolds, Broadway, and the Hotel, at that time he had no idea of settling in England.[358]

In 1944, his leave took him back to Australia to visit his family but, in 1945, just as the war was ending, he was posted back to England to do a gunnery course, and that July took his usual leave at the Lygon Arms. It was on this occasion that Don, discussed his concern over succession planning; at 51 he realised he was getting older, and had decided to find someone else to run the Hotel. The next morning Don asked to see Douglas in his office. At first, Douglas thought one of his naval boys had been up to mischief, so was incredibly surprised to be offered a job as resident manager to be taken up at the end of the War. As a Naval Officer he had never considered a job on land.

358. 'Australian Women's weekly,' 6 January 1951.

Gordon, Don, and his niece had decided to form a private company. With the American's in the war and the H-bomb deployment Japan had surrendered sooner than the Australian navy had anticipated, so six weeks later, discharged from the Navy, still in his demob suit Douglas returned to the Lygon at the age of twenty-four to start at the top, working with Don as its manager; the guest had stayed on to be the host!

Douglas, along with his pet spaniel Jet, would become one of Broadway's most familiar faces walking the High Street early morning. His wartime friend Miss Marien Aitken took on the role of his secretary. When he was appointed to the Board of Directors in 1946, the Hotel had just forty-four rooms.

Chapter 22

1946 to 1985
The Russell Families' Legacy

Over the forty years, 1906-1946, that the Russell family had run the Hotel they had increased to number of useable rooms from very few to forty-six. During Douglas's tenure from 1946-1986 he would do even better, increasing the capacity to one hundred and twenty-five rooms.

Post war the immediate challenge was labour, boys who were partly trained were called up to do National Service and burgeoning industrialisation required large firms to bus workers to their factories or offices.

Offsetting this challenge was the immediate demand for leisure activities such as 'dances.' By introducing regular dances, the Lygon was able to recoup some of the losses incurred during the winter in war years and address occupancy's seasonality, Douglas introduced regular dances, parties, small conferences, cocktail parties, wedding breakfasts, and more. Such events encouraged local people to visit and engage socially.

The fortnightly dances established an air of gaiety, and later helped cover the higher post war costs in the kitchen, this soon led to an outside catering arm, serving local houses, sometimes as far away as thirty miles from the Hotel. In turn this led to the development of residential conferences for up to fifty people, ideal when Broadway was so near the industrial hub that was the Midlands.

On occasion the conferences were international. To serve this demand a temporary canvas supper room that had been used on such occasions, and for weddings was now in situ for around five months, if not more.

Attention to detail drove Douglas: his card index system logged the likes and dislikes of every visitor, including references to their dogs and the table they preferred to be seated at. On arrival guests were greeted by their name, there might be fresh flowers in a room, a pin cushion with pins, a ready threaded needle. There would be note paper and blotting paper, the provision of a forgotten sponge bag, razor strops, big bath sheets, instant hot water, good lighting, and daily shoe polishing.

It was not long into his tenure in 1946 that Douglas was appointed to the Board of Directors. Don, graciously left him to manage, allowing him to learn on the job.

The mid-20th century was a different time; it is perhaps hard to appreciate today the degree to which the Hotel was moving with the times. All rooms had hot and cold running water, which was quite revolutionary for the era, some rooms even benefitted from having 'ensuite' private bathrooms. At a time when few individual citizens had even shared 'party' lines, private phone lines were installed.

Even the menus were strikingly modern with offerings of smoked salmon, shrimp cocktail, steak and kidney puddings, lamb cutlets, coconut pudding, stilton cheese, all washed down with claret at a reasonable cost. The room costs were 27 shillings including meals in winter and 35 shillings during the high season.

In 1948, as his father had done, to give themselves some down time, Donald and Effie moved to Stowick, on the Evesham Road, then began a life of travelling in connection with the promotion of the Hotel and the work of the International Hotel Association. In 1954, to add to his already full life, as he was still a District and County Councillor, Donald became a member of the BBC Midland Regional Advisory Committee.[359]

By 1956 Douglas was appointed Managing Director taking some of the pressure off Donald.

Douglas' next move was to address the need for modern kitchens, and more 'en suite' bathrooms. Another obvious candidate for replacement was the badly ageing canvas supper room, which had become an almost permanent feature in the late forties, and was mid fifties difficult to heat, expensive to repair, and a fire risk to boot.

Dick Russell's architectural practice with support from Hodgson and Leigh was given the job of designing the new kitchens, behind the Great Hall, and the conversion of the old existing east kitchen, that had risen from the converted 19th century stables in 1911, into a permanent supper /dining room which could, if required, host conferences.

The new kitchens were designed to serve both the Great Hall and the new supper/dining room at right angles to the Great Hall.

---

359. *'Evesham Standard & West Midland Observer'* - Friday 08 January 1954.

On completion, in 1957, the converted old kitchens were opened and christened, very appropriately, given the partnership of the three brothers, the Russell Room. The room certainly did meet the exacting standards of a new clientele coming over from America.

Gordon, using newly honed skills, carved the name of the room on a stone plaque that was placed at the entrance 21 June 1957.

Gordon Russell's 1957 carving

Yet more bathrooms were required plus all those fine touches, the finishing and embellishing redecorating, and furnishing, held up by the war years, including the replacement of carpets, and curtains. There is a strong suggestion that the Fleur-de-lys carpet[360] on the Elizabethan stairs and along some of the corridors of the Lygon Arms, came from an auction[361] of the contents of Wood Norton Hall when Henri-Eugène-Philippe-Louis d' Orléans, duke d' Aumale, fourth son of Louis Philippe, (r.1830-1848) returned to the continent.[362]

---

360. *'The dark blue carpet with golden fleurs-de-lis on which kings and queens have walked, covers the halls and stairs of the Lygon Arms'* Also see footnote 358.
361. Mary Anderson, p 91, *'A Few More Memories'* 1936, London, Hutchinson, and Co.
362. Wood Norton Hall, three miles north Evesham, was built by Henri-Eugène-Philippe-Louis d' Orléans, Duke d' Aumale, fourth son of Louis Philippe, (r.1830-1848) who abdicated the French throne and came to England in 1848. Its features wrought iron gates brought from Versailles, carved oak panelling. carved and panelled oak doors. carved oak mantelpieces, two massive oak staircases,

In addition to Douglas running the Inn, Donald was in and out most days, talking to guests, engaged with planning, leading the local British Legion, and taking an interest in the affairs of the Hotel and the ongoing training of the staff. When not concentrating on the Hotel he became president of the Hotel and Catering Institute[363] working with the Ministry of Education and teaching Institutions to initiate training centres which provided national diplomas in hotelkeeping and catering around the Country.

---

and marble bathrooms. Head of the Orleanists he sold Wood Norton and returned to be close to French soil in 1912 in view of renewed energies of the Prince Victor and the Bonapartists.

363. Hotel and Catering Institute was a professional association for the hospitality industry in the United Kingdom launched in 1959, which combined in 1971 with the Institutional Management Association formed in 1938. The HCMIA was renamed the Institute of Hospitality in 2007.

Sadly, mid-December 1960, soon after this triumph, Donald lost Effie, his wife and companion of forty years. The tribute read at her funeral, by her brother-in-law, Sir Gordon Russell, painted a picture of a strong, independent, kind woman. Until 1938, just as Sydney's wife Elizabeth had done, Effie had supported her husband in the management of business, and she had travelled widely on the Continent with him in connection with his work in the International Hotel Association.

Don later moved to the Stone House on the corner of Leamington Road and Colletts Field. He wasn't far from the Lygon and by now the Lygon had started to buy several properties to house their staff, such as the nearby 68 High Street.

In 1960, to the east of the courtyard, replacing the old posting yard stables, behind the Russell Room which had risen out of the rebuilt 1911 kitchen with bedrooms above, a Garden Wing, offering an additional ten bedrooms was added; it reputedly cost of forty thousand pounds.

This extension by Russell, Hodson and Leigh showed the extent to which a modern addition was possible. The stone on the ground floor had two projecting brick storeys with wooden storeys stressing the verticals of the wooden bays. It was not to everyone's taste when it was built. In 2016 during renovations judicious planting and careful painting of the brickwork helpfully further softened the design.

By 1964, the Lygon Arms was considered, by many, to be the best Country Inn in England. This was the year Douglas had the foresight to see that to attract overseas visitors more marketing was required. He would have to go one step further and focus on wooing those in the travel trade. He set about his first gruelling campaign, a marathon American trip covering 13 cities, meeting 126 agents, all in 26 days.

Just as Sydney Russell had wooed the Americans in 1906 so Douglas was succeeding in 1964. His campaign was so successful that even more rooms were needed!

He then went one step further. In 1966 a marketing group of leading privately owned and operated Hotels, known as Prestige Hotels, was formed.[364] This initiative enabled DJB, as he was affectionately called, to work together with others to promote Prestige Hotels worldwide which benefited the Lygon and its other group members.

Meeting of leading hoteliers at the Royal Garden Hotel, London March 1966. The name Prestige was put forward by Michael Chapman – Imperial Hotel Torquay – not in shot. Hotel's first chairman voted in was Michael Blanchard – Whately Hotel – front middle, Douglas Barington is front right.

---

364. Cited: Michael Blanchard who supplied the photograph and the papers.

To meet the need for extra rooms The 1968, Orchard Wing, designed by Russell and Hodgson, built of stone, and rough cast with boxy oriels. was initially described as Arts and Craft brutalist, but over time has mellowed. To the rear of the Garden Room, is a small courtyard.

The Orchard Wing is connected to the main Hotel, the Garden Wing, by a cleverly designed walkway over the courtyard.

Across the walkway, in addition to the bedrooms, a separate conference room was added.

Edinburgh Room – photograph credited to Adam Lynk

It was named the Edinburgh Room, in honour of its first luncheon which hosted Prince Phillip, Duke of Edinburgh, following a tour of the Gordon Russell showrooms, 15 March 1968.

The main kitchen linked seamlessly to the conference room, as it did so cleverly to the Russell Room.

The current store manager Colwyn Thomas who has given fifty-five years of service to the Lygon, joined the Hotel in 1969 at the age of sixteen, when Ron Wagner was head porter. This was a time when the Lygon still had its petrol pumps, as a schoolboy, he had helped on the pumps on a Saturday and Sunday. Anyone who was anyone in the village had an account at the Lygon: those in the Upper High Street including Mme de Navarro and Sir Gerald Nabarro British businessman and Conservative politician an MP from 1950 until his death in 1973 – the names were a little confusing for the staff.

It was good place to work with a hard core of very loyal staff. When Don Russell was the owner, those that had worked at the Hotel for fifteen years became part of exclusive group. It was a tradition continued until the Hotel moved into corporate hands in 1986. Staff even received cufflinks or brooches, to reflect their long service, and every two years were treated to a dinner at the Hotel.[365] There was a staff flat in Majorca and one in London. This level of loyalty, in turn, greatly contributed to its success.

Sadly, in 1970, the quiet man behind the Lygon Arms success, Don Russell, died. By 1970s, 40% of the Lygon's visitors came from overseas. Only Gordon and Dick were able to receive Don's legacy when in 1971 the Lygon Arms became the first Country Hotel outside London to be honoured with the Queen's Award for Export Achievement due to its successful appeal to overseas visitors.

---

365. Interview with Colwyn Thomas.

One third of its visitors were coming from overseas: particularly Americans and recent to the times the Japanese.

Douglas Barrington, the charming lead, Chairman of the International Hotel Association, member of the Board of the British Tourist Authority, took over the reigns fully and received an OBE for his services in 1974.

In 1975 a new Food and Beverage Manager, Kirk Ritchie, a man with the same value and ethics as Barrington, who was sharp, charming, and focussed on quality and hard work, joined the Hotel to support Douglas.

The 1977 Christmas Programme show the extent to which the two of them were working together in a way that impacted the Hotel's offer to its residents.

- the minimum four-day package with private bathroom at £43.00 a night, included early morning tea brought to the room, newspapers, all meals, entertainment – a discotheque, a cartoon film show for the children, lectures on folklore, a Greek bouzouki band, Greek food, and a plate smashing opportunity? The package also included Lord Colwyn's Three B Jazz Band, the service charge and one free limited edition raffle ticket to win a new Ford Fiesta, per each residency. There were 350 tickets implying the Hotel could accommodate up to 350 residents, therefore in the region of 175 rooms.

- There were, if required, packed lunches on departure, cocktail parties to meet fellow guests, and some of the events, typical of the day, were black tie.

- Welcoming sherries were more likely than champagne, and brandy snaps, which are rarely seen these days, featured in the dessert section.

This was a period when the Lygon put on a musical weekend, and enabled residents to have access to H W Keil's private oak and walnut antique furniture collection, housed across the road at Tudor House. As always, the Cheltenham Festival week[366] was highlighted in their programme.

The death of Gordon Russell, in 1980, and Dick in 1981, was a huge upheaval. leaving Douglas Barrington, as owner of the Hotel, to steer the ship just as the White, Sambache, Treavis, and Drury's dynasties had before him. There was no new generation prepared to step up to the plate. The Hotel moved forward with Douglas at the helm supported by the Managing Director, and General Manager, Kirk Ritchie, towards its next phase which would see it move out of private hands into the corporate world.

The Russell family, Sydney and Elizabeth, Gordon and Toni, Don, Effie, and Dick, to a lesser extent as his life was centred around London, had steered the Hotel through good and troubled times for nigh on seventy-eight years. They were almost unique in that they had managed to work harmoniously as a team for most of that time.

---

366. The horse racing-based meeting in the National Hunt racing calendar in the United Kingdom, with race prize money second only to the Grand National. The four-day festival takes place annually in March at Cheltenham Racecourse in Cheltenham, Gloucestershire. It usually coincides with Saint Patrick's Day and is particularly popular with Irish visitor.

The old building had been rescued from being a run-down beer house and awarded pride of place central to the village. The family had worked tirelessly to support and improve Broadway, and offered guests, village visitors and villagers alike a slice of England's history, alongside modern comforts.

It is hard to imagine whether the old building would have even survived, and what it might have become, and how the village might have been impacted if the family had not lent their combined vision and commitment over the years. It was said, without Don, Broadway may never have gained it enviable position.[367]

Douglas Barrington and Kirk Ritchie were a winning formula. In 1985 the Lygon was again honoured with the Queen's Award for Industry and received Four Red stars from the Automobile Association. Its restaurant had three rosettes and the Hotel was nominated as the very first Egon Ronay's 'Hotel of the Year' and was also listed as one of the best 330 Hotels in the World by Harper's and Queen's.

Perhaps inevitably, given it was an ever-rising star hitting the headlines, the Lygon Arms was about to take change direction yet again.

It is rumoured, and these things, are hard to pin down, that Douglas in August visited America to meet up with the agents promoting the Lygon Arms. This is quite likely as the value of the American market

367. 'Evesham Standard & West Midland Observer' - Saturday 04 May 1946.

in the 1980's to the Hotel was considerable. In 1985 on his return, he went on a cruise, and it was on this cruise that an agent contacted him to discuss buying the Hotel.

Chapter 23

1986 – 2016
The Lygon Hotel, out of private ownership, after more than four hundred and fifty-four plus years

In 1986 Douglas Barrington OBE, supported by Kirk Ritchie, negotiated the Savoy Group's ownership for £4.7 million. Douglas became a member of the Savoy Group Board. The Lygon became a member of a prestigious family of Hotels which included the Savoy, Claridge's, the Berkeley, and the Connaught. It was the first time since the building, with the ghosts of its many owners, had been in public ownership since 1532; remarkably it had provided hospitality for nearly 500 years under private ownership, and management – its buildings having evidenced an earlier occupation.

In the hands of MD Kirk Ritchie, within The Savoy Group, supported by their leaders such as Willie Bauer and Ramon Pajares, the Lygon thrived, matching if not rivalling, the treasured memories of Donald Russell and the Hotel's legendry Douglas Barrington OBE.

Kirk's aim was to continue preserving the old Lygon traditions while enhancing them even further by improving its modern comforts.

The Drawing Room

The Charles I Sitting Room

The Inglenook now the receoption

The Cromwell Room

By 1987, there were ten boilers, ten lounges with log fires, sixty-five suites, and double bedrooms for 130 guests, all boasting modern amenities. This was a long cry from the White Hart's original four bedrooms.

These were the days of trouser presses and radios in the bedrooms, early morning tea brought to your room with the newspaper, and garage lock up if required.

The Great Bedchamber

The King Charles I Bedroom

However, the courtyard was a parking area, and even then, a few bedrooms shared a bathroom, which was not ideal but not unheard of at the time!

Characteristically ambitious, the Savoy Group, was also pursuing a long-held desire of Lygon management to offer residents additional leisure facilities. They were fortunate, after years of negotiation, the last remaining member of the Collins family, the neighbouring butchers, had failed to find a successor. In In August 1987, Feller and Son Ltd, of Oxford, purchased their business.[368] Shortly afterwards they sold the Broadway shop with its slaughtering and cutting department,[369] to the Lygon, a transaction marking the end of old tensions between the two businesses, which went back over a century.

The Savoy Group was more than delighted with the purchase which made way for the Lygon Country Club, with its 14-metre swimming pool, hot tub, steam room, spa treatment and changing rooms, a long-awaited offering for its visitors. Rumour has it there is a time capsule in the middle of the swimming pool. It does not seem it will ever be opened!

---

368. Rev R. J. M. Collins, *'Collins in the Cotswolds'* printed by E P Lowe Ltd
369. The business was in the section of the High Street known as North Street at the time.

Whatever arrangements had been made over the years, it had been less than desirable to have a slaughtering and cutting house, lairage, storerooms, garages next door, and Collin's ancillary buildings in North Street running out into 'Back Way,' near the Hotel.

The opening day, in 1990, is said to have been a both a delight and a horror; all the benefit from a delightful relaxing swim and sauna was totally undone, in the 'ladies' changing rooms, by the obnoxious smells coming from the shower drains. Copious amounts of hot water were now for the first time entering the same drains that had been used for the slaughterhouse, the aromas rising made this point very evident that first morning.[370] No harm done, a quick flush by the builders resolved the problem. The testing the day before by some of the staff did not reveal any issues, perhaps the staff at the time were in the male changing room?

---

370. A story from a local Lygon Spa member who was a member at the time of the opening.

Fittingly, after 40 years in the hospitality arena, in 1989, Douglas Barrington OBE, was voted winner of the Lifetime Achievement Catey Award.

Next a Helipad was added in an area beyond the carpark, car parking itself was expanded and the flower garden, with stunning views of the hills, a tennis court, and the croquet lawn were renovated to add to the guest's enjoyment.

The splendidly endowed Great Hall, with its arched ceiling, large ornate windows, open fireplace, heraldic friezes, and 17th century minstrel's gallery set the scene, complimenting the Lygon's reputation for delicious English fare: a choice of Lancashire hotpot, roast Cotswold lamb, jugged steak marinated in Evesham plum wine, for the main course, often preceded by its signature champagne and brandy prawn cocktail.

The Great Hall circa 1990

At weekends, afternoon tea was a splendid 'help yourself' affair, with dainty sandwiches, a range of delicious cakes and fresh baked scones, butter and jam was all laid out on two long tables in the Russell room. The clever ploy was their strategy of permitting guests to eat as much as they wished, appetites were well regulated by the piercing critical eyes of fellow guests, a stern deterrent to the greedy.

The Inn's wine bar, Goblets, though limited in kitchen area provided an informal relaxed dining alternative. In the summer, patio dining was introduced.

Disappointingly, a view particularly felt by local villagers, the successful Lygon /Savoy Group relationship ended in May 1998 when American investors, Blackstone Group and Colony Capital, bought it from the Wontner family who decided to sell after Sir Hugh Wontner (1908-1992) Hotelier and politician, president of the Savory Group died.

On 3 October 2002, Douglas Barrington, OBE, the perfectionist in hospitality, who had managed the Hotel for forty years and done so much for the industry died. A year later in 2003, the American investors decided to sell. The sixty-nine bedroomed Hotel which included Oliver's brasserie, was purchased for around fifteen million[371] by Haydn Fentum, a 33-year-old local man, supported in the venture by his parents and sister Sara Fentum Wicks; The family business, Furlong Hotels, had been built around the buying and selling of Hotels since 1969. They were keen to add the Lygon Arms

---

371. *'The Caterer,'* 01 September 2003, though in such dealings it is hard be sure that was the precise figure.

to their ownership of Billesley Manor, near Stratford-upon-Avon, and Combe Grove Manor, in Bath; previous Hotels had been Homewood Park and Hunstrete House, both near Bath. There were press releases about a further investment of two million, there is always more to do in such a well frequented venue as the Lygon Hotel, especially when it so important to move forward without impacting on its historic integrity. With a two-year contract, in 2004 Martin Blunos took over as head chef of the Lygon, gaining it a Michelin star and two AA Rosettes in 2005 though with other commitments he did not work at the Lygon everyday.

The Fentum's plans included an annual turnover of £6.3m, a profit of £2m improving on the previous £5.4m and £1.4m respectively but sadly this was a short-term venture. By 2005, Furlong Hotels had been acquired by Dawnay Day Hotels, a group who had been set up to acquire the 13 strong Paramount Hotel company chain. With the Lygon and the two other Hotels added to its four and five-star line-up, Paramount's portfolio was boosted to twenty Hotels, an excess of 2,500 bedrooms. Sadly, the Lygon now became one of many.

In September 2007, the privately owned Spanish company Barceló Hotels & Resorts, founded in 1931, operating 130 Hotels in 14 countries, negotiated a 45-year lease to manage the group; this was a delicious variation for local residents with the influx of Spanish personnel and Mediterranean-themed menus. A restoration programme began, headed up by designer Stephan Oberwegner of London-based Max Bentheim Design, to revitalise the bedrooms and public areas. Nothing was overlooked, when local builders, Clarke Cross surveyed the roof, investment was made in roof repairs, and when the same workmen noticed the old Lygon sign was in desperate need of refurbishment a new project commenced.

This was specialist work for those with the knowledge and expertise. The 96 lbs steel sign was painstakingly lowered down by the stores manager Colwyn Thomas, Chef Ian Gill and Dave Canning a local sign writer. Dave then set to work removing layers of old dark gloss paint and using old photographs and an original woodcut found by the Hotel staff, restored the old sign back to its former glory.

The White Hart and Lygon Arms have survived many difficulties: plagues, wars, droughts, the decline of the wool trade, stage then mail coaching, the coming of the railways; the decline of coaching creating a lack of accessibility, followed by two world wars. Its fortunes however were now to impacted even more by the vagaries of this corporate world. After a very short period, in January 2008 to reflect the 45-year agreement, the Lygon and its sister UK Hotels were rebranded as Barceló or Barceló Premium properties. Dawnay Shore Hotels became a Hotel investment company and in July 2008 the Lygon was just one of the Hotels renamed a Puma Hotel. Within four years of rebranding in 2012, the Euro's fortunes and credit issues in the USA impacted upon this arrangement, forcing Barceló Hotels to withdraw from both their lease agreement and the UK market.

The Hotel was back to being managed by freeholder Paramount Hotels and which June 2014, traded as The Hotel Collection.

To an outsider, or a local resident, it seemed managers and staff were moving in and out of the Lygon; it was a revolving door. A chink of light on the horizon came with the rebranding of the Hotel as one of the Hotels that were part of the Hotel Collection; the suggestion was that this reflected the Paramount group's desire to focus on the strengths of each individual unique Hotel. Headed up by Grant Hearn, the new Chairman, supported by General Manager Colin Heaney, and his loyal staff, the four-star Lygon which had grown from 65 to 78 bedrooms, and seven suites, now looked after around 170 guests. The Hotel had six meeting and conference rooms, 190 staff, parking for 120 cars, and full Wi-Fi.

The two AA rosettes restaurant in the Great Hall was complemented by Luke's of Broadway, the smaller 45-seater restaurant to the west of the main building, which had previously been Goblets and before that Barrington's brasserie. Run by rising chef, Luke Thomas, who created a culinary stir locally, with his Mediterranean inspired wine bar serving Italian dishes. However, once again this arrangement, along with the Hotel Collection ownership was not to last.

Chapter 24

2016
London and Regional: The Lygon joins the Iconic Luxury Hotels

In 2016, the Lygon joined forces with the Iconic Luxury Hotels, prestigious owners of the Chewton Glen, Cliveden and 11 Cadogan Gardens in London.

Trading as London and Regional, the owners, brothers, Ian, and Richard, Livingston, announced, at a January weekend event Chewton Glen event, to celebrate the New Forest property's 50th anniversary, that they were close to completing the acquisition of the Lygon Arms in Broadway.

This was a very welcome development, London & Regional, was known to be a global powerhouse, with an impressive, portfolio of private Hotels in Europe.

The brothers had achieved enormous success with Chewton Glen and Cliveden, both grand old heritage ladies, though somewhat younger than their sister, the Lygon Arms.

When the announcement filtered back to Broadway, there was much optimism in the village, as the Inn or Hotel had always been an important focus of village life.

Residents were delighted to learn of Ian Livingstone's comments.

'We are pleased to announce that Chewton Glen and Cliveden House will be joined by the Lygon Arms in Broadway in the near future. It's a long-term project, it hasn't had the love and attention that Chewton

Glen and Cliveden House have had, but we will get there in the end'.[372]

True to their word the Hotel was set for an exciting new chapter. It started with the announcement of a two-year investment, renovation programme to restore the Lygon to its former glory, to become again a must-visit country retreat.

Work commenced in the spring of 2016; over the next 24 months, eighty-six unique guest rooms, and seven suites, were refurbished. Some of the more modern rooms featured décor inspired by Ralph Lauren's private home.

Other were graced by unique period antiques, or the more modern Gordon Russell antiques.

Room 20 The Great Chamber

King Charles I Room

Inspirationally, the Torrington Room, which had in the 20th century been converted from chauffeurs' garages built in 1926, to a conference facility, with rooms above, was in 2018, was itself repurposed to become additional ensuite bedrooms, each with its own private garden.

The Courtyard suites – photograph credited to Adam Lynk

This and the summertime alfresco dining, added a Mediterranean vibe and a completely fresh look to the courtyard, which when it stopped being a posting yard previously served as a parking lot.

Before 2016   *After 2016*

A cocktail bar, a smaller relaxed space, was added.

This doubles as an alternative dining area, in addition to the Russell Room.

The Revitalised Russell Room

Public areas, including the spa, and leisure club were totally transformed.

On a more prosaic level, all the Chimney's were swept, to ensure roaring fires would welcome guests, particularly on chilly winter weekends.

The snug near the entrance

The Tapestry Louge next to the bar area is a wonderful place too meet up with friends.

In the Lobby Louge afternoon tea is an all-year-round affair

It is now served on individual cake stands, the sandwiches are even more dainty, there are small savouries, and sweet cakes complimented by small mousses. The house champagne is often paired to give a total exquisite luxury experience. In house spa facilities are now de rigueur for any luxury Hotel and the Lygon is no exception. All the facilities that guests would expect are in abundance.

In addition, the Hotel guides guests to a wealth of activities such as offsite country pursuits: archery, falconry, clay shooting, and horse riding and places of interest locally, in particular our two Museums.

Across Back Lane the three-acre secret gardens offer fun activities or the opportunity to chill out and just admire the setting, the shrubs, bushes, lawns flowers.

Post acquisition 2016 two new restaurant concepts were launched:

The 75-seat, Lygon Bar and Grill, in the Great Hall, boasts two vast chandeliers made from the antlers of stags, wood-panelled walls, a wooden floor, marble-topped tables, and comfortable upholstered chairs. The historic stone fireplace completes the setting with a roaring fire.

Its laid-back welcoming atmosphere gives a nod to the Hotel's incredible history through the scores of oil paintings, adorning its walls.

The Great Hall – The Lygon Bar and Grill offers menus crafted by James Martin

In early 2023 the catering offer was further enhanced when James Martin, the well-known celebrity chef from Malton in North Yorkshire, who had already partnered with the iconic luxury Hotel Group and opened The Kitchen Cookery School and restaurant at Chewton Glen in 2017, became the executive chef at the Lygon.

James Martin – Photograph credited to Adam Lynk

New flavours, signature dishes, and some of his particular favourites, all inspired by local, artisanal, and seasonal produce are the order of the day.

A small Dining Area before the Lygon Bar and Grill

Next door, the cosy forty-five seat Lygon Wine Bar, The Tavern, with its long history of hospitality, previously Goblets, Olivers, and before that Barrington's Brasserie, previously a lodging house, and before that a beer house called the Baker's Arms, has also been transformed.

The Tavern – Photograph credited to Adam Lynk

Towards the end of 2023, James transformed the 45-seater wine bar into the Tavern by James Martin, becoming Broadway's smallest and cosiest pub, complete with roaring fire in winter.

It now serves traditional pub snacks, scrumptious light bites, the equivalent of English tapas, carefully chosen by James to match the ethos of the Tavern.

From time-to-time he personally produces a tasting menu and uses the Tavern to host an intimate evening with James – amazing recipes with stunning flavours.

TAVERN

JAMES MARTIN
AT LYGON

JAMES MARTIN *Tavern Takeover*

19TH SEPTEMBER 2023

Cotswold Bread
Netherend butter

Sea Bass Ponzu Ceviche
Yuzu mayo, pickled Asian radish, crispy seaweed, chilli fronds

Baba Ghanoush
Aioli, pickles, chilli fronds, crisp breads [v]

James Martin Signature Rosé Wine

Chicken Essence Risotto
Wild mushrooms, Roscoff onion

Wild Mushroom Risotto
Roscoff onion, chive oil, crispy onions [v]

James Martin Signature White Wine

Yorkshire Ox Cheek
Pomme purée, Vichy carrot, jus

Accompanied by a ratatouille gratin

Roasted Cauliflower with a Chickpea Dhal
Golden sultanas, pomegranate, cashews, coriander, minted coconut yoghurt [v]

James Martin Signature Red Wine

The Apple
Apple ice cream and tatin

Marinated Fruits & Sorbet [v]

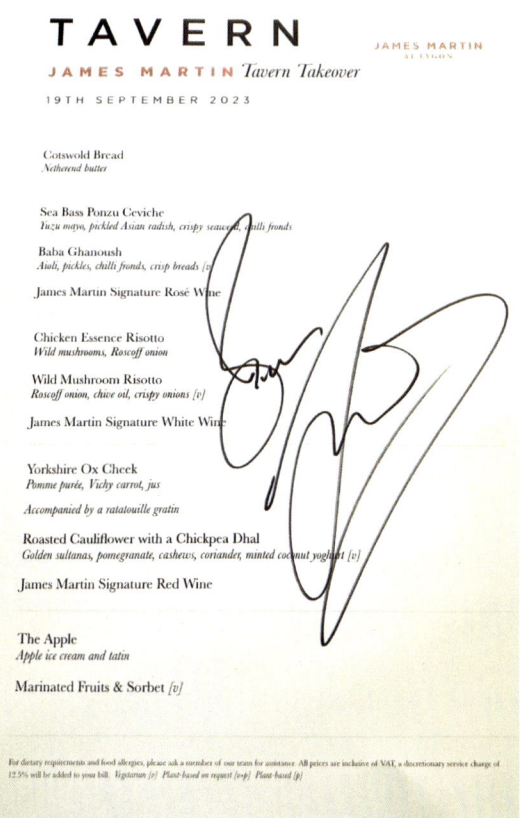

For dietary requirements and food allergies, please ask a member of our team for assistance. All prices are inclusive of VAT, a discretionary service charge of 12.5% will be added to your bill. *Vegetarian [v] Plant-based on request [v+p] Plant-based [p]*

In 2024, on a day-to-day basis, the Lygon is safe in the hands of Graeme Nesbitt, as General Manager, who already had close links with the Lygon for several years, having previously been its manager and its successful Head Chef.

It offers all that could be expected from a Cotswold Inn: stone fireplaces, heavy wooden medieval doors, uneven flagstones, mullioned windows, creaking floorboards – unique history that cannot be easily recreated.

It has come a long way from its late medieval roots, its journey has been a roller coaster, but in the main it is a testament to the constant hard work and passion that overcomes each century's challenges. The 21st century is no different from previous centuries. High finance, the credit crunch, inflation, recessions, and the pandemic have all taken their toll and challenged both management and staff. Nevertheless, its sincere welcome, eclectic quality and accommodation, delicious food, and service have always won the day.

The Lygon has survived the transition from family trusteeship, which brought its own sustainability issues to corporations and PLCs with their changes and challenges.

Leadership and passion have always been the key. Sidney Russell also proved that good management, and community links weave the right results.

The reorganisation has proven to be more than a remodelling exercise. As it has always done the Lygon must keep evolving and reflect the times. The Lygon Arms retains its dual role: offering hospitality while being a guardian of some of Broadway's richest heritage. It is not a museum; that title is reserved for the Angel Inn, which became Tudor House and is now to home of Broadway Museum and Art Gallery, further up the street.

Quite simply The Lygon Arms is unique, with a luxury offering, and a bright future. It has developed and moved forward, certainly over almost 500 years, if not more. I have every confidence it will continue to do so.

Postscript I – A potted history of Broadway before 1532

Archaeological finds such as Mesolithic[373] flints at the top edge of Fish Hill, a Neolithic[374] round barrow, a Bronze age[375] sword, worked, pottery linked to the Beaker or Bell Beaker[376] people, and an Iron Age[377] multi-vallate hillfort with human and animal bones, pottery, and flint flakes confirm Broadway as an ancient settlement. The location of such finds suggests the early settlement was along the southern slopes of Broadway Hill, where there was stone for housing, woods for fuel, streams for water, grazing and arable land, all within easy proximity.

Unsurprisingly, as it lies in the triangle formed by Watling Street,[378] Icknield or Rycknield Street,[379] and the Fosse Way,[380] Broadway was home to a modest Roman settlement. They brought with them small sheep, which survived well on the rich Cotswold Hills despite the cold winters and grew thick fleeces. Recent finds,[381]

---

373. 8000-4000 BC.
374. 4000-2500 BC.
375.3300-1200 BC.
376. 2500–1700 BC originating from scattered prehistoric Western Europe peoples, so called to reflect the shape of their pottery.
377. 800 BC to AD 43.
378. The route, which became one of the major highways of medieval England, linked Dover and London via St Albans to Wroxeter.
379 . Its route ran from the Fosse Way at Bourton on the Water Gloucestershire to Templeborough in South Yorkshire passing through Alcester, Birmingham, Lichfield, and Derby. Buckle Street, to the East of Broadway, on its border is said to be a section of Icknield Street/Ryknild Street.
380. The route from Exeter to Lincoln.
381. Finds during the archaeological investigations before the EA created a £4.1 million Badsey Brook flood risk management scheme 2016-8 to reduce the risk of flooding for 300 properties post the 2007 flood event.

hearth pottery, brooches and the like have confirmed it was a slightly more extensive settlement than had initially been thought.

There is some evidence that one of the salt streets from Droitwich, an important centre for salt in Roman times, followed the line of an ancient Ridgeway, a route used by travellers, herdsmen, and tribal warriors, through Broadway. The original route from Droitwich is thought to have passed down Springfield Road, which became a lane when the railway arrived in 1905, continuing up Broadway Hill.

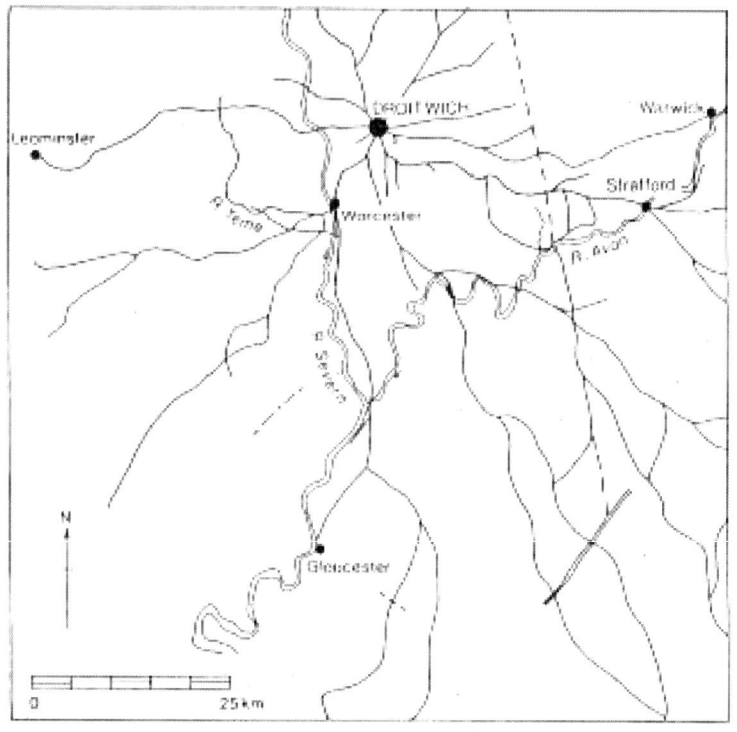

Droitwich saltways

In AD 410, as the Romans pulled out of Britain, leaving a power vacuum, Britain became wide open to continental migrants: Angles, Saxons, and Jutes. However, some may well have originally arrived as mercenaries supporting the Roman Army.[382] Local digs have revealed an Anglo-Saxon cemetery, a Saxon ditch, rich grave goods including brooches, beads, pins and weapons, and several crouched bodies.[383]

AD 577,[384] after the battle of Dyrham (Deorham), Broadway lay within the settled area of the Hwicce tribal kingdom.[385]

382. Seven petty kingdoms of Anglo-Saxon England flourished from this migration in the 5th century eventually the kingdoms were consolidated in the 8th century.
383. A method of burial. A good deal of material was found when 2016 archaeological trenches prior to the construction of a flood alleviation scheme in 2017-8.
384. Della Hooke, 'The Kingdom of the Hwicce' (1985).
385. The Romans called Worcestershire Wiccia.

The footprint of the Hwicce kingdom is similar to that of the Cotswold Natural Landscape (Cotswold AONB) today. Following the Battle of Cirencester, in AD 628, the Hwicce kingdom became one of many of the sub-kingdoms of Mercia, which covered a vast area south of the River Humber. From AD 628 to AD 883, Mercia dominated England, its territory was such that it influenced five of England's six kingdoms: Northumberland, East Anglia, Essex, Kent, Sussex, and Wessex

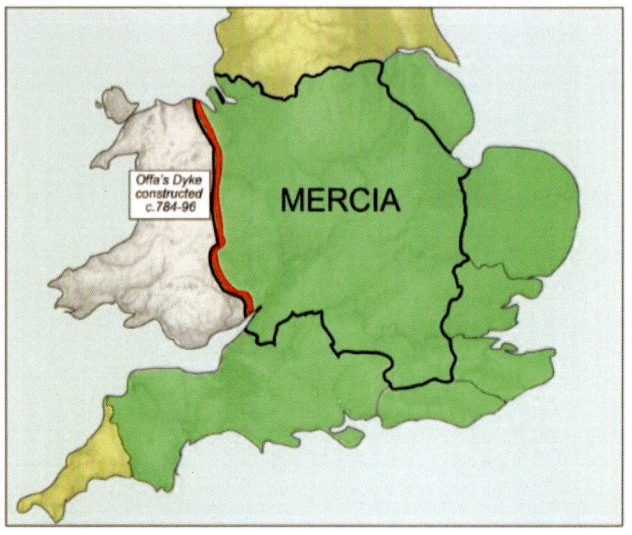

The Kingdom of Mercia and its additional area of influence during the Mercian Supremacy

Around AD 681, Ethelred, King of Mercia, awarded considerable acreage to his nephew, Oswald; part of which, eight years later, supported the establishment of a monastic community at Pershore. Broadway village, a scatter of peasant, single-roomed, houses,[386] settled by those who eked a meagre subsistence life from

---

386. Privacy, bedrooms, and possessions were not part of most lives until Elizabethan times, and even then, only for the rich.

the land, roughly 12 miles from Pershore, does not seem to have been part of this acreage.

At the end of the 8th century, looking for land and riches, northern pagans having found a way to the west, arrived in Northumberland, it was not long before Mercian lands became a target, *'the Mercians stand out as by far the most successful of the various early Anglo-Saxon peoples until the later ninth century when they succumbed to the Viking military threat.'*[387]

The monks of Lindisfarne Priory had a rude awakening in AD 793 when longships appeared on their horizon. Their first encounter was bloody. Vikings were particularly antipathetic to Christian missionaries and the Church. The violence erupted with early hit-and-run raids but led to the arrival of a Great Heathen Army.

They plundered kingdom after kingdom. Worcestershire was frequently the scene of sharp and bloody action. By adopting various strategies including skirmishes, treaties, the swopping of hostages and the payment of geld, only Alfred of Wessex seemed to be able to hold them back. Eventually, in AD 883, Mercia, admiring Wessex's tactics, collaborated thus achieving a degree of stability; in part this was due to Alfred conceding a large swath of Mercia's land,[388] lying to the east of Watling Street, to the Danes.

Such concessions were not atypical. In France, to secure his kingdom, King Charles had approached the problem in much the

---

387. Nicholas Brooks, p 61, *'Anglo-Saxon Myths: State and Church, 400-1066'*, 2000, London, The Hambledon Press.
388. But not always the best land, as translation of old place names, reveal today.

same way as Alfred, brokering a contract with the Viking chief Rollo, ceding Normandy to him.

Broadway, though close to the dividing line, remained within English territory, subject to English Law rather than Danelaw.

Danish Mercia and East Anglia - the areas of England ceded to Danelaw.

Alfred's pragmatic approach brought a degree of peace and united the shires together, under the banner of England. Those under Danelaw settled, farmed, intermarried and many were amongst the first Scandinavians to adopt Christianity.

AD 910 on Alfred's death his older son, King Edward, succeeded. It is his son, Alfred's grandson Athelstan,[389] (r.924-939) who is generally regarded, after conquering Northumbria, as the first effective ruler over the whole of Britain. The period his death AD 939-AD 959 the start of King Edgar's reign was coloured by Viking activity, a series of short-term monarchs, instability, and court manipulations, all at different times. Kingship was peripatetic, there was no fixed capital city and the court moved from one royal estate to another, four or five times a year.[390] According to John of Worcester, each winter and spring Edgar would travel round the kingdom to enquire whether the statutes he had promulgated were being observed and whether the poor were being unjustly treated by the powerful.[391] One feature of Edgar's reign was his monastic reforms, in favour of the Benedictines, particularly in Wessex and Mercia.

In AD 967, that the Manor[392] of Bradanuuege or Bradanwege, (Broadway), was named in documents as a dependency of the monastic Church of St. Mary at Pershore.

---

389. Also spelled Aethelstan or Ethelstan.
390. Frank Stenton, (1971), p10 'Anglo-Saxon England (3rd Edition)' 1971 Oxford, Oxford University Press.
391. Reginald Darlington, p.427, The Chronicle of John of Worcester (in Latin and English). Vol. 2. 1995, Oxford, Clarendon Press.
392. Manor, comes from the old French word manoir, meaning dwelling place. It does not necessarily mean a building, it could be a simple farm, a more prestigious building or just an estate of land. It was the feudal lordship that controlled and had rights to exercise certain privileges, and exact fees.

Pershore Abbey today

The charter outlined the 10th century route to London from Wales, coming from Worcester, via Pershore which entered Broadway from the Hinton/ Childswickham direction, turned to cross Tuck Mill land, went across the land to Pry Lane, down Pry Lane to cross to West End, then turned at Bury End to climb the escarpment via Coneygree[393] Lane.[394] The Charter reconfirmed the settlement was centred around the area of its Roman/Anglo-Saxon origins, near St Eadburgha Church.[395]

---

393. Coney Green – rabbit field.
394. Later in the 15th century, this route was ratified by exemplification of a Decree by Henry IV (1422-1461). Later the core of the settlement around the Church shifted to those areas around the green and old Ridgeway/salt street up the Hill. The old Coneygree lane route slowly became, by both neglect and deliberate act, a much-deteriorated rural byway.
395. St Eadburgha's Church is said to have Saxon foundations.

From the 10th century, until 1539, the dissolution of the monasteries, excluding short periods when Pershore Abbey burnt down around 1002,[396] and for the second time in 1287,[397] or was deprived of their possessions by others, the village of Broadway was part of the lands of the priory of Pershore. The church shaped Broadway's social and economic development, in addition to influencing its built environment, and the surrounding landscape through its land uses. Agricultural land was divided between the fields managed by the Church and cultivated directly, called demesne land, and the rest. Most of the fields in Broadway were cultivated by local peasants who made payment to the Priory through their agricultural labour on church land or through tithes.[398]

However, there appears to have been periods when the relationship fell back to the Diocese of Worcester, it is quite possible that at such times the administration of the lands in Broadway, were influenced by Worcester. After Edward the Confessor, many of the places mentioned in the charter of Edgar passed out of the possession of the Abbey.[399] Some lands which may have included Broadway, were not restored to Pershore until early in the 13th century, in the reign of King John (r 1199 to 1216).

When, in 1002, a nervous and suspicious Æthelred II,[400] who had married a Norman (who were Danes) to protect his throne, ordered of the massacre of Danes, in certain Anglo-Saxon towns,

396. John Leland, p, 242 and 244, *Collectanea, 1 The Itinerary of John Leland the Antiquary, 3rd ed, 9 volumes in 5' 1770, Oxford.*
397. Nash, Treadway, Russell. p.244. *'Collections for the History of Worcestershire, Volume II'*
398. A tenth of the produce or earnings from the produce – a church tax churches providing income, to support the parish priest, or the Convent, and might even contribute to the needs of the poor.
399. Nash, Treadway, Russell. p15. *'Collections for the History of Worcestershire, Volume I'*
400 Frequently named Æthelred the Unready, though he was, in fact, ill prepared.

in the area under Danelaw, it set-in motion a series of reprisals: invasions, counter attacks, his flight to Normandy, and restoration on his return. These 'head-to-head' encounters went on until Æthelred's death April 1016. Edmund Ironside, Æthelred's son, inherited the consequences of his father's acts but lost in battle November 1016, to the Dane's leader's son, Cnut.

Cnut ruled all England from 1016-1033. On his death Æthelred's son, Edward the Confessor (r 1042-1066) was crowned. Unfortunately, though a good ruler he was catastrophically indecisive on the question of a successor.

The battle for the English Crown, the Battle of Hastings, between Harold, brother of Edward's wife and the man who understood Edward had promised him the crown, William Duke of Normandy followed.

The arrival of the Normans had an immediate impact on England and its settlements. The language changed. The Normans used their architectural skills to stamp a physical authority on each local community, determining village layouts; villages with greens suitable for marketplaces and churches would survive, others would not.

The Domesday Book, 1086, outlines the changes in Broadway between the first survey referenced in King Edgar's charter, AD972 and 1086; in the 10th century before the Normans, Broadway was a village of 20 hides, with its streams, ditches, and streets, in the 11th century after the Normans, Broadway[401] was a village of 30 hides, owned by the church, a sizable place of 30 taxable units paying

___

401. p.284, 'Domesday Book a complete translation' 2003, London Penguin.

geld,[402] 51 households (around 220 people), 42 villein class or peasants, with 22 plough teams and in demesne[403] three ploughs, a priest, and eight servi or enslaved people.[404]

By 1130, the Normans had remodelled the old Church in Pershore into an Abbey and Broadway's small church had been rebuilt using some of the original stone for its changes; Norman columns with large diameter bases and simple scalloped capitals now supported the nave arcades.

St. Eadburgha's Church

8 August 1251, Broadway Manor, became one of the last lordships[405] benefiting from Henry III's free warren, over the demesne lands, the sole right previously jealously guarded, to hunt certain beasts and fowl within a given area; pheasant, partridge, hare, and rabbit.

---

402. Tax paid to the Crown. Anglo-Saxon period, taxation were land taxes, custom duties and fees to mint coins. After the Norman Conquest of England in 1066, the geld continued to be collected but was eventually replaced with taxes on personal property and income.

403 A piece of land attached to a manor and retained by the owner for their own use.

404 Slaves had no property rights and could be bought and sold by the Lord.

405. The Lord was the incumbent Abbot.

The Benedictines of Pershore also obtained a grant for a permanent weekly market,[406] a Friday[407] market, (the monk's Wednesday market of 1196 had ceased), and a 3-day annual fair, commencing 24 June on the eve of the Feast of St John the Baptist, to sell wool, wool produce, and other commodities.[408] [409]

The Normans, landowners and clergy understood Broadway's potential; its land was good quality. Broadway's agricultural expansion coincided with the rearing of sheep for commercial rather than domestic reasons. By the end of the 13th century the increasingly, heavily industrialised, areas of Europe, were dependant on the export of English bales. Church administrators, connected to Europe through pilgrims, crusaders, and migrants, moving to and from Rome, even those in Pershore, were very much alive to this new business opportunity, their potential prosperity from wool.

The Cotswolds[410] area was, and still is, ideally suited to sheep; its water quality offered a fair degree of softness, which is essential when dying and finishing cloth. The Romans AD 43–410, had

---

406. Page & Willis-Bund, 1924, 33-43, and Brooks & Pevsner, 2007 *A History of the County of Worcester: Volume 4,'*.
407. Some say Tuesday. The Friday market and the market on the eve of St John the Baptist seem to have lapsed in the time of Edward III due to the plague, as did St Eadburgha's feast day, set as the Wednesday in Whitsun week. A pleasure fair was still held until the 18th century, which today could be said to survive as a 2-3 day 'wake fair', held by a travelling company, on the Wednesday after Whit Sunday. Its length is dependent on the weather.
408. Page & Willis-Bund, 1924, and Brooks & Pevsner, 2007 *'A History of the County of Worcester: Volume 4,'*
409. Habington *'a mercate on every Friday, and lastly a fayre on the eve and feast of St. John Baptist with the next day following.'*
410. The harsher weather, mainly our winters, necessitated sheep be kept in 'cots' or enclosures, sited on the 'wolds' or hills. A literal translation of Cotswolds is 'sheep-hills.

introduced to the area the Cotswold Lion, a breed valuable for both its meat and long, and strong staple.[411]

A Cotswold Lion

Its wool, desirable for heavier broadcloth, was ideal for our English climate, and with the right finishing, the cloth was favoured by the Italians.

Everyone who had access to land: the church, its tenants, and peasants moved more seriously, into the raising of large flocks and began to count their wealth in terms of sheep. The sale of wool, then fleece underpinned Broadway's economy; as its flocks increased in size, so the church's wealth increased.

411. They naturally formed cluster or locks of wool fibres, not a single fibre, a factor which determined the end use of the wool.

The Charter is thought to have instigated the next step enabling Broadway to evolve from a village settlement to a town or Borough.[412] Its main street where the trading was done was called Portstret. Compared with existing towns only 25% of rural settlements became boroughs. By the time of the charter the town had grown to around 400 - 600 people, in line with England's population growth,[413] and a list of Broadway taxpayers, dated 1280, shows the increase in both the number of freemen,[414] and the growth of the borough's economy, and size.

Speed carried the Black Death, which reached England in the middle of the 14th century. In 1348, it reached the Midlands and lasted until 1350 'there was such a shortage of servants, craftsmen, and workmen, and of agricultural workers and labourers ... [*that*] churchmen, knights and other worthies have been forced to thresh their corn, plough the land and perform every other unskilled task if they are to make their own bread.'[415]

---

412. The word borough probably derives from the burghal system of Alfred the Great. Alfred set up a system of defensive strong points (Burhs); to maintain these settlements, he granted them a degree of autonomy.

413. At the time of the Romans the population of England was thought to have been around 4 million, on their departure and due to a European plague, it shrunk dramatically. By the 7th and 8th century England's population had increased enough warrant the Vale of Evesham being cleared and cultivated. By the time of the Domesday survey England's population was back up to 2 million; it then grew rapidly to about 5 or 6 million in the 13th century.

414. Peasants who had purchased or worked out apprenticeships to become free of their obligations to the Lord, save possibly the paying of rent on their properties, and taxes on their market stalls. Charter status for the village, becoming a Borough, in 1251, brought with it further obligations connected to the running of the Borough and to the Church such as an obligation to be involved with the dispensation of local justice.

415 . A chronicle written at the cathedral priory of Rochester between 1314 and 1350, includes a firsthand account of the Black Death, describing the changes in the everyday lives of people across the social scale.

As elsewhere, in Broadway, there were no peasants left to work the ridge and furrow cultivation on the side of Broadway Hill.[416] Much of the higher common lands were abandoned forever. This was the start of a long decline in Broadway's population, reducing the thriving borough back to a village.

In the 15th century, the rearing of sheep and the business of wool continued to bring wealth to the village. A conventual lease,[417] dated 1490, between the Abbot and convent of Pershore and two residents Robert Handy and Robert Faulkes, underlines the importance of wool as an economic driver. The lease was to be renewed for 31 years, at £30 per annum, and covered 'all the site and manor of Bradeway: houses, lands, meadows, leasows,[418] and pastures, as well as demesne lands[419] all manner of pasture for sheep upon the hill, under and about the hill, which used to belong to the Abbot and Convent of Pershore or their tenants, and all the houses of the Inner Court.' The lease mentions a wool house. On ensealing, Robert Handy was to be delivered of four hundred sheep.

In the 15th century after the 14th century challenges: famine, disease, and the Great Plague had impacted all levels of society the decline in population was still an issue, especially in terms of labour. Larger landlords increasingly abandon direct management of their estates in favour of copyhold tenure,[420] a system used by the church. Though not yet evidenced fully, I feel more will reveal itself in my next book, The History of Broadway. Sadly, for now there is little to add to the Inn's story.

---

416. The track off the upper High Street that runs under the A44, signposted to Chipping Campden, curves up the hill, then branches to the right before running straight and uphill, through fields where long ridges and dips, evidence the abandoned medieval acres.
417. Library of Birmingham BLS Barnard Rees Price collection no 28, d/1, Sheldon Micellanea,
418. Rough pasture
419. Land and property attached to a manor and retained by the owner, the Abbot, the Church's use, almost all in Nether End and on the southerly slopes.
420. Tenure by copy of the record of the manorial court.

Postscript II-A snapshot of the Lygon Arms' visitor book, 1909-1912

The Lygon has always attracted amazing visitors. Location, heritage, the imposing 1620 façade, its stories, the visitor ripple effect, and good food all played their part.

In the early years it offered practical accommodation for those travelling to Broadway to do business, mainly connected with the business of wool, then was a significant stage then mail coaching stop.

Ten years before the Great War, 1904 to 1914, it became an even more sought-after venue. With the development of the charabanc, then motor car, a new phenomenon, tourism, took a hold, and Broadway was 'on the map.' The Lygon Arms became a destination, no longer a staging post.

King Edward VII motored to Broadway in 1905 as did his grandson King Edward VIII in 1913. Where they led the English middle classes followed.

A visitors' book was not a new thing then. It added to those, diaries and passages written by distinguished travelers: Byng, Gissing, Hissy, each of whom left their compliments.

Leafing through any one of the Lygon's slightly distressed maroon leather visitor books, the reader is struck by the extent to which the world came together in Broadway, not the Broadway of today but the Broadway of over 100 years ago, at a time when travel was more difficult and communications neither instant nor necessarily far-reaching.

An analysis of the entries from October 1909 to May 1912, as expected, showed indeed there were visitors who had travelled to be at the Lygon from all corners of Britain: Wales, Ireland, Scotland; North-West Cheshire is heavily represented.

Visitors from the major cities Birmingham, Glasgow, Manchester, Leeds abound but London visitors represent a clear 33% of the British entries. Entries highlight London's most fashionable quarters: Park Lane, Hampstead, and Kensington. Unsurprisingly guest's home addresses included references to Castles, Halls, and Manors.

The Empire, Orient, and New and Old World are represented in the book, particularly the American states. The high percentage of Americans reflected both the changing times and increasing references to Broadway and the Lygon Arms in American travelogues and newspaper articles. The American visitors' seasonality was very evident; they increased during the summer month to such an extent that the dining room may well have seemed like an American convention.

Visitors from Brazil, Canada, China, Denmark, France, Germany, Italy, India, Jamaica left their signatures; the changing times were reflected in their references to Persia and Southern Rhodesia.

Peppered amongst the signatures are the military – Captains, Colonels, Majors, Rear Admirals, the ennobled - Baronesses, Lords, each Lady, a Viscount, and his Viscountess and the exotic – the Maharajah and his Maharanee. Sirs and Reverends, academics from Oxford and Cambridge are frequently noted. There are hints of accommodation for the chauffeur or the maid, of course, never named in person; proud references to a third or sixth visit can be seen in the margins.

The whole book reflects the tone of the Lygon during that pre-war period vividly. Not everyone signed the visitor book but over the 32 months covered in the visitor book analysed, around 1167 visitor entries are recorded: 290 - 20% are from addresses London, 254 - 30% are from the USA and some visitors, of course, had addresses in both.

The Hotels' association royalty included: King Edward VII, Princess Marie Louise, HRH Princess Henry of Battenberg, Queen Mary, The Queen Mother, Prince Phillip, the Duke of Edinburgh[421], The Queen of Rumania, HRH The Prince of Wales an impressive list.

---

421. The Edinburgh Room was named in honour of his visit.

Postscript III- Actors, Artists, Writers, Prime Ministers who have stayed …..

Over the years the Hotel has also played host to many celebrities, the visitor books a good number of famous signatures: actor Mary Anderson, Prime Minister A J Balfour, writer J. M. Barrie, essayist and poet A.C. Benson, the legendary actors Richard Burton and Elizabeth Taylor stayed in 1963, before they married, at the height of the scandal surrounding their affair,

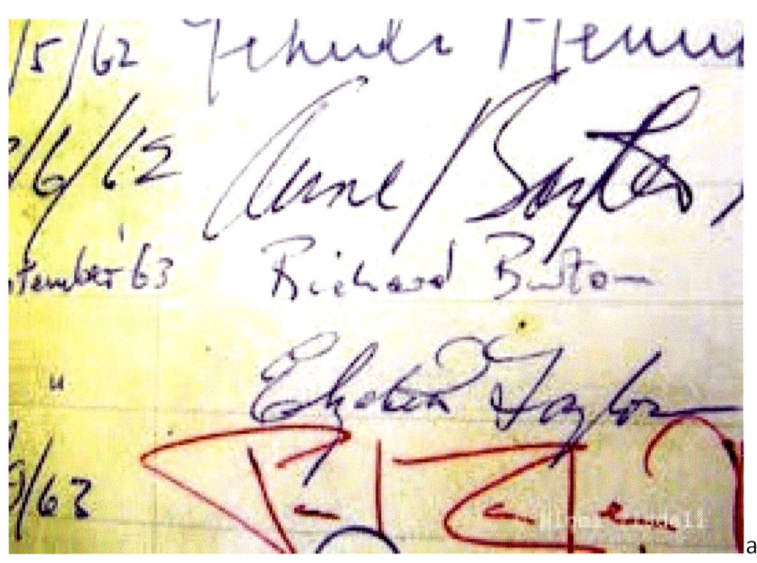

actor Pierce Brosnan – James Bond, actor Claudette Colbert in May 1952, actor comedian, screenwriter John Cleese, industrialist Henry Ford, broadcaster, writer, adventurer Ben Fogle, swimmer Duncan Goodhew, actor Cary Grant in August 1966, Slade guitarist Dave Hill, actor Dustin Hoffman, actor Elsa Lancaster, actor Charles Laughton, actor Vivien Leigh in July 1955, actor Sophia Loren, writer and poet Rudyard Kipling, caricaturist Phil May, Prime Minister Teresa May, singer and actor Kylie Minogue, actor Mary Pickford in June 1955 with her third husband actor and jazz musician Charles Buddy Rodger, actor Michael Redgrave with his wife actor Rachel Kempson in July 1951, who signed herself Rachel Redgrave, singer Paul Robeson November 1959, actor Charles 'Buddy' Rogers, writer George Bernard Shaw, actor Moria Shearer who at the time, April 1953, was much better known than her husband Ludovic Kennedy, actor Rod Steiger November 1959, actor William Shatner – Captain Kirk, singer Barbara Streisand, actor Ann Todd May 1953 and her new husband David Lean, she signed herself Ann Todd Lean but was in fact the third Mrs Lean, the French aviator Aumont Theville, who spoke no English and landed his balloon due to fog in the Thames Valley, on Broadway Hill, and stayed for breakfast, writer and novelist Evelyn Waugh, actor Dennis Weaver – Mc Cloud, actor John Wayne in the early 1970's to name just a few. It seems at times, looking over the visitor books or reading its history, that everyone, who was anyone has stayed at the Lygon Arms.

Postscript IV-The Lygon Arms – a star of the silver screen

Finally, the Hotel itself was at one time a film star, and at another part of a documentary. In 1927, the Lygon became a star in an American silent movie. In the silent version of Warwick Deeping's 1925 novel, *'Sorrell and Son,'* the Lygon Arms masqueraded as the Pelican Hotel, in the film of the same name.

BRITISH and DOMINIONS FILM CORPORATION Ltd. present "SORRELL AND SON" with H. B. WARNER
Released thru United Artists   Made in U. S. A.

United Artists production - outside Treavis's 1620 entrance.
H B Warner as Sorrell, Louis Wolheim Head Porter,

The film crew were in Broadway for ten days to shoot scenes internally and in the High Street. H B Warner, had his British studio debut in the film, having gone to America in 1905, aged thirty, only to return for the movie in 1927.

Alice Joyce who played the sympathetic companion of the sacrificing father in Sorrell and Son (1927).

The film is a faithful transcription of the book which describes the harrowing post-war experiences of Captain Stephen Sorrell, M.C. a decorated ex-British Army officer whose returns from the War to a faithless wife who abandons him and no job, thus leaving him doing what ever he can to educate his son. He goes to work at the Pelican (Lygon Arms) as a hotel porter. After many years he lifts himself out of the ruck and finds happiness with the Inn's housekeeper.

It was released on 2 December 1927, and nominated for the Academy Award for Best Director at the first Academy Awards the following year.

Some of the reviews could have been kinder. *'H.B. Warner is too lachrymose in the role of Sorrell, and entirely too self-sacrificing to be human.'*

'This does not look like box-office material. Disguise the issue as you may, the essentials of motion picture drama are not present. Action, suspense, and sex interest are missing. And only in very few instances has it been possible to successfully dramatize a state of mind, a tortured mentality, for screen purposes. The exceptionally fine array of names may attract patronage, and the many readers of the novel should be interested in seeing the photoplay.

But it is doubtful whether the Deeping enthusiasts will approve the film version. While the shell of the story has been preserved on the screen, it is served up in a pale and emasculated form. Thus, the love affairs of Roland and Kit are entirely eliminated, and the relationship between Sorrell and Fanny merely intimated.

The men who were red-blooded in the book, appear as "virgin men" who are stereotype and uninteresting. And the girl whom Kit finally marries is portrayed by Mary Nolan, the former Imogene Wilson, as a simple English-countryside damsel, rather than the thoroughly sophisticated and modern young writer created by Author Deeping.'

'There is a profusion of sob stuff, some of which gets over fairly well. But there is no denying that "father-love" is licked to a frazzle by "mother-love" as screen materials.'[422]

However, Photoplay Magazine reviews were kinder.

---

422. *'Moving Picture World,'* November 19, 1927

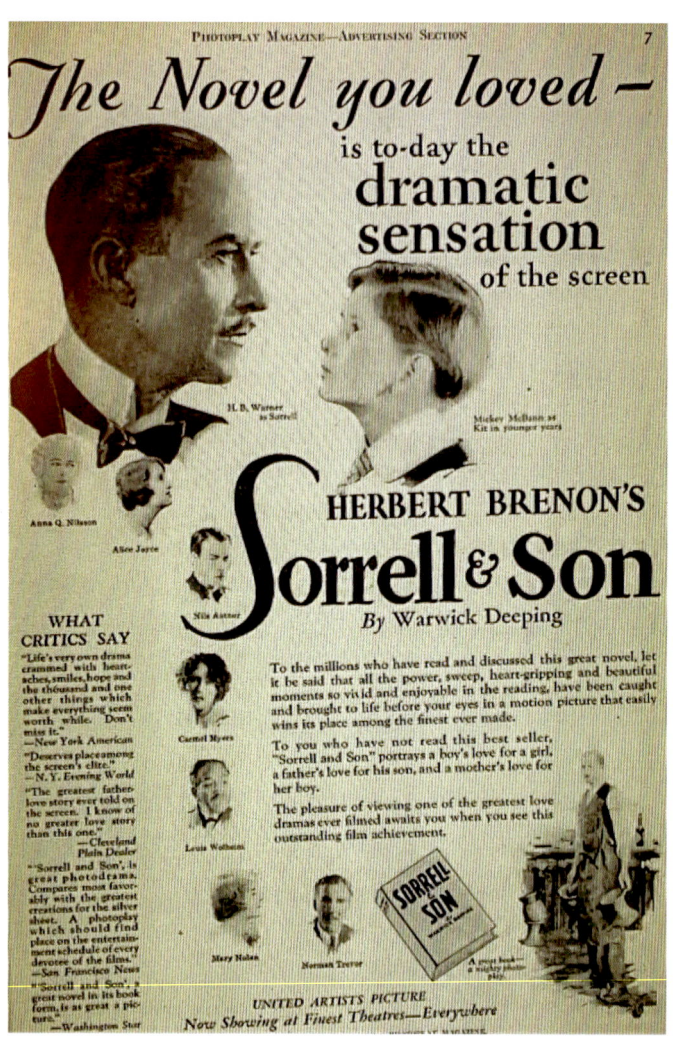

Sadly, and rather touchingly during the 1939-45 war, life to a degree
mimicked art. Major, John William Poston, MC + Bar, 87368, 'A'
Squadron, XIth Hussars (Prince Albert's Own) attached to General Sir
Bernard Montgomery's staff as Liaison Officer, [previously A.D.C and

the 1st Royal Tank Regiment] was killed in action on Saturday 21st April 1945, aged 25.

His obituary reads 'John was a good sportsman and horseman. In 1938 under pressure from his father to gain meaningful employment, John was employed at the Lygon Arms Hotel where he began at the bottom of the ladder as Hall porter and general 'Dog's body'. Later he worked in the bar where he excelled at making cocktails mostly for the American guests; it was also here that John fell in love for the first time with the under-manageress Helen……'[423]

In 1934, a talking picture version was produced and reached Sydney, Australia where it was shown at the Mayfair Theatre.

It also became an ITV mini-series in 1984.

In 1986, in true Domesday tradition, to celebrate the 900th anniversary of the Domesday Survey, the BBC launched a new ambitious Domesday Project, to record a snapshot of everyday life in words, pictures and graphics, across the UK for future generations. There were 250,000 pages, 24,000 maps, 50,000 photos and a vast amount of survey data. A million volunteers took part, in this project, and of course, the Lygon featured in footage.

Finally, today there are new, simple methods, for the Lygon to share its photos and stories; the internet, YouTube, and Instagram provide a wealth of information, allowing the world to engage with its offer and historic past.

---

423. *'Leamington Observer'* Roll of Honour - 1945 - 1947 .

Postscript V - Specific features to look for in the Hotel

The Jacobean Entrance

The Snug

Immediately to the east of the Lygon Arms entrance is a small lounge with a sizable stone fireplace and a fireback dated 1671.

Originally, this area may have been part of the entrance hall. At one time it was described as a pantry. In the early 20th century, a corner cabinet, in this room, held a collection of old English Jugs.

The reception, for many years known as The Inglenook

Along the passageway to the west of the entrance hall is the reception, with an excellent open fireplace spanned by a large wooden lintel at its east end. For many years it was a public sitting room, known as the Inglenook.

A painting of the Inglenook circa 1722

It is lit by two window openings to the south. Given the buildings age these openings may at one time have been closed by wooden sliding shutters, rather than windows with glass.

In the fireplace is a fine 17th century wrought iron 'chimney crane', and old black 'pot hanger sway' which would have held the cooking pot. These imply the room was at one time used as a kitchen.

Several early culinary utensils including steel spits, are displayed above the mantle though some may be displayed in the corner lounge, previously an old buttery.

The cast fireback is dated 1620.

The survey plan dated 1904 shows the inglenook was at that time partitioned into a smoke room and passageway.

Above reception hangs a copy of one version of the famous 'Warts and All' portraits of Cromwell by Peter Lely,[424] the original is in the National Museum of Wales. Cromwell insisted that Lely paint him truthfully, capturing every detail, including his pimples, and warts. The phrase "warts and all" encapsulates this commitment to authenticity and transparency. Although there is no definitive

---

[424]. Peter Lely (1618–1680), a Dutch-born artist was principal painter to the English royals. He became court painter to Charles I in the 1640s, before serving Oliver Cromwell and finally Charles II after the Restoration of the monarchy in 1660.

evidence that Cromwell explicitly used these words, the story has persisted, emphasizing the idea that leaders should be portrayed honestly, even if it reveals their imperfections

The Medieval Door at the end of the passage before the Lobby Lounge

At the far end of the passage is a large medieval strap hinged oak, arch-headed, back doorway, which led to a yard behind the property. The door is now permanently held open.

Halfway along the passageway is another medieval door, again permanently open which led to room which was originally a medieval kitchen. It is now the reception.

The two low doors, in the Lobby Lounge were, until the 18th century, doors from the posting yard to a cellar and a pantry. The one nearest the passageway, the old pantry, became a porter's room, and is now a small office.

In the north-east corner of the Inglenook's panelling is an old wooden staircase, behind a small wooden latched door. This corkscrew or newel staircase led to the first two upper chambers and the eaves. The access to the chambers is closed. It now only leads to the eaves.

The Halberd opposite the door to the reception

A Halberd,[425] is a weapon, approximately six feet in height, attached to a pole on an upright beam at the cross passage near reception. It comprises three parts: the axe head blade for slicing through armour, the pike for thrusting, and the hook that enabled a skilled soldier on the ground to take down an opponent on horseback quickly.

Halberd attached to the wall near the cross passage in the entrance to the Lygon Arms

---

[425]. Possibly the one mentioned in the landlord's will (Thomas White) of 1555.

It may have been a souvenir of the War of the Roses, 1455- 1487. It is mentioned in the will of the first known innkeeper Thomas White, who was born in 1488 just after the end of the war, so teases us to wonder if the White family lived in the building before 1500.

The Saddle Room.

In the southwest corner of the reception is a small 16th century Tudor arched doorway that looks as if it has been reset. The arch leads to a small sitting room, decorated with equestrian artefacts; historically, it had been used as a bar area. Its moulded chimneypiece is said to have come from Merton Abbey or Priory, an early 12th century Augustinian building lost during Henry VIII's dissolution, however, Sydney Russell suggested it came from Merton Place the nearby home of Lady Hamilton.[426] At one period it was a more extensive public 'smoking' room accessed from the Buttery and then a bar area.

---

[426]. S.B. Russell, '*The Story of an Old English Hostelry*,' Letchworth at the Arden Press.

The Old Buttery

Beyond the Saddle Room to the right is a sitting area with a range and cooking implements above the mantel, previously a buttery, then a smoking room, which was primarily accessed from Inn's posting yard.

The old buttery 2015   *Door from the yard to the old buttery*

The kitchen after the first extension

Beyond the Elizabethan staircase on the ground floor is a square south-facing room originally a former kitchen, then a small dining room, now a sitting room adjacent to the Great Hall. Above its curved entrance is carved 'Now good digestion wants on appetite and health on both.'

The original small dining room

The small dining room outside the Great Hall

333

Its simple stone fireplace has a medieval tree of life fire back. The rooms oak panelling was taken from Babington Hall, Derby, the eminent 17th century home of Simon Degge, a notorious sheriff, barrister, and judge whose mansion was demolished in the early 20th century.[427]

Medieval vaulted ceilings

These can only be seen in the individual rooms, or on the landing accessed by the 1665 staircase at the rear of the Great Hall.

Room 20 – The Great Chamber

[427] S. B. Russell, *'The Story of an Old English Hostelry'* Letchworth at the Arden Press.

The Cromwell Room on the first floor

The Oliver Cromwell Room, with all its historical connections, is accessed via a staircase leading from the first landing at the top of the Elizabethan staircase. It is one of Treavis' most ornately decorated rooms.

Mullioned windows have been added, and the room is enriched by an early 17th Century plaster ceiling and decorative frieze running around the walls which bears some similarity to a ceiling at Aston Hall in Warwickshire. Treavis as well as adding the Lygon's (*White Hart*) entrance, added the plasterwork ceiling to the Cromwell Room, making it 400 years old.

This fine private dining or small meeting room boasts a grand carved Jacobean stone fireplace enhanced by a magnificent mantelpiece.

The room reflects that period of the Civil War and links to Cromwell.

To the left of the fireplace is a copy of King Charles II 1660 Proclamation from the first month of the Restoration.

It demands those responsible for the execution of his father King Charles, I turn themselves in for murder & treason.

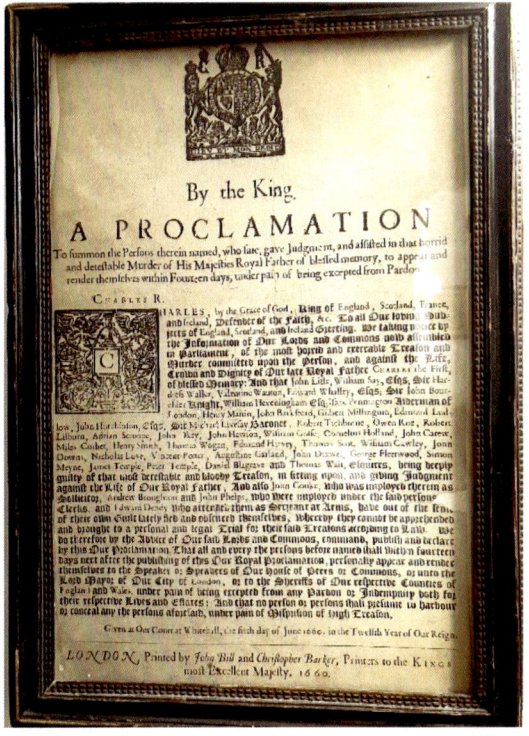

Reproduction of the Proclamation

In the fireplace sit a pair of Elizabethan cast iron fire dogs and a fire back dated 1632

Fireback Cromwell Room

A small mullion window originally an Oriel 'bay' window, which pre the Assembly rooms looked out on to a garden, now looks into the Great Hall.

Oriel 'bay' window

Finally, there are acres of the peaceful gardens to enjoy.

Postscript VI-The Remarkable Story of HMS Broadway, World War II

On the landing near the Drawing Room is a ships bell which used to belong to HMS Broadway.

In 1948, Donald Russell, owner of the Lygon Arms, offered to keep
the bell in safekeeping upon the decommissioning of HMS Broadway.
It is likely he knew of the decommissioning and the possibility of
acquiring the Bell, thanks to his general manager, an ex- Naval
officer, Douglas Barrington, who had convalesced at the Lygon during
the second world war, and later when he was discharged from the
navy stayed on as manager at the Lygon at Don's request, then
became its owner.

The painting on the landing near the bell depicts the moment at
which three British naval ships, on patrol in the North Atlantic, South
of Iceland, located and captured the German U-boat 110, on the
morning of 9 May 1941, despite the efforts of its German captain to
scupper it.

The capture of a U-boat on the high seas was a rare and considerable
achievement.

In the painting, HMS Broadway is on the left, HMS Bulldog is on the right and HMS Aubretia is at the rear of the U-boat.

The engineers on HMS Broadway's motorboat are en route to assist in the removal of items from the submarine – including – unknowingly - a naval enigma machine.

The British, at the time of the capture, had no information about German naval coding and this capture was one of the seminal moments in the history of the War. It is said to have shortened the War by two years.

HMS Broadway[428] (H90), was a converted Clemson Class destroyer, USS Hunt (1920)

HMS Aubretia (K96) was flower-class corvette, built for the Navy

---

428. HMS Broadway, formerly USS Hunt, was one of the 50 World War I American destroyers transferred to the UK, to help our war effort, as part of the USA/UK Lend and Lease agreement in 1940. These ships, known as the 'Gift Horses,' protected our convoys of merchant ships crossing the North Atlantic.

HMS Bulldog (H91), B-Class was built for the royal Navy

It was HMS Aubretia's echo sounder that had picked up on two U-boats and HMS Broadway that dropped the depth charges which damaged U-boat 110, the other got away.

With its rudder and instruments lost, panic had set in. U–boat 110 rose to the surface and its crew abandoned the ship. They were picked up by HMS Aubretia and HMS Broadway. The prisoners were placed in the bowels of the ship so they could not see or hear anything.

The Commander of HMS Bulldog, in charge of all three ships, sent a boarding party, in a 23 ft whaler, to the submarine; the swell took the whaler to the bow.

20-year-old David Balme, in charge of the boarding party, bravely walked along the deck of the submarine to the conning tower and opened its hatch. With the help of his men, all removable items were brought to the deck.

As their boat had been destroyed by the swell, HMS Broadway sent engineers in a motorboat to assist. All items were taken to HMS Bulldog, it was there that a radio operator discovered one item on the U-boat was a coding machine; later it was found to be a naval Enigma machine complete with its code book.[429]

---

429. David Balme, '*Enigma,*' The untold story of the secret capture

Postscript VII - The mystery of the ownership of Back Lane – the story so far...

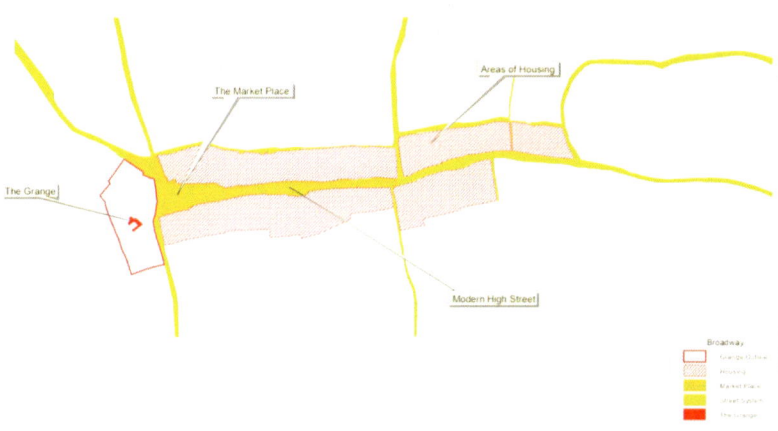

What was it for originally?

The layout of the medieval settlement of the village shows a lane which not only gave access to the rear of each burgage property, on the main street, but gave access to Broadway's common fields, wastes, and the northerly lands extending up Broadway Hill. Now called back lane, at one time called Back Way, ordnance survey maps show that the land north of Back Lane comprised of at least five different parallel parcels of land, which were at that time primarily planted as orchards. In 1900, in a deed, Backway was referred to as a public road.

Who owns the Lane?

Joseph King, of Broadway, according to the census of 1891 and 1901, was a retired fishmonger from Islington. He had purchased a property, two doors down to the east of the Lygon Arms, for £355 in

347

1894, called the Lygon Cottage, previously called the Old House, due to its great age. Mr King's purchase seems to have involved a mortgage, as, 15 November 1901, the property and land owned by Mr King was auctioned by order of the mortgagee. The purchaser at £650, was Mr J Jewsbury. This sale particulars do not mention back lane.

A 1908 Evesham County Court case, between Mr Russell, Lygon Arms and John and Bert Collins, butchers, for damages and an injunction to cease accessing a small area of Mr Russell's land, a small strip adjoining but south of Back Way, behind Mr Collins land. A metal way led from Mr Collins back gate to Back Way. The track and orchard show well on a later plan, but it is copyright. The strip 15 chins in length. When Mr Russell first came to Broadway in 1904 two residents use the land to exercise horses, and someone paid Mr Russell 1s to cross the west end of the enclosure. (? Miss Davies occupier of Mr Foss's cottage)

Witnesses came forward, in the Evesham County Court proceedings, to expand on whether Back Way was Private or Public.

Joseph King said *'he purchased the orchard* (in question*) in 1899.....* *and that he was the owner of the whole of the Back Way and the Orchard, from the small cottage now owned by Mr Foss to the Lygon Cottage on the other side of the Lygon Arms Hotel.* 'He also said '*he sold it to Mr. Russell in 1905 and conveyed it to Mr Russell.'*

Use by the Public

Mr Dudfield, *'had never known any of the public stopped whatever. There was a metal road from China Square to Bell Yard, and at no part of the Back Way was there any considerable width of road except at the rear of the Lygon and Mr Collins.'* (Mr Collins shop, is now Hayman Joyce Estate Agents at the front)

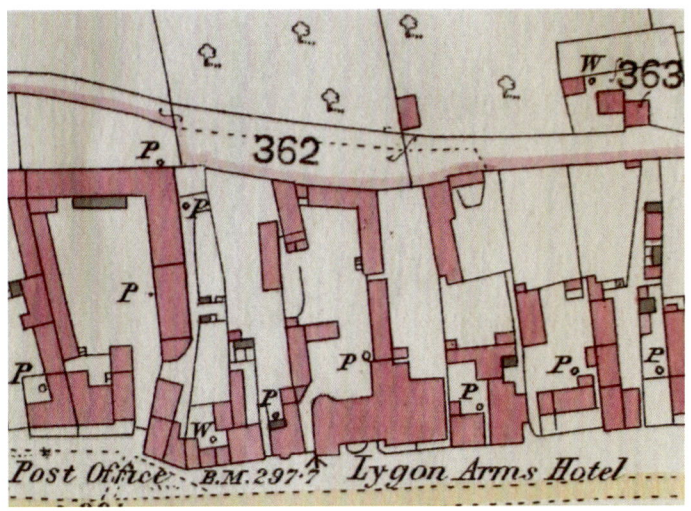

1880 ordinance survey map above shows how narrow Back Way was other then the area behind Mr Collins and the Lygon. A small area of orchard to the southwest of the no. 362 on the map, was the small orchard area under dispute, it shows clearly on a 1904 map.

Mr J. T. Haines (66), veterinary surgeon, said *'he had known Broadway for over 50 years. He had never known any of the public restricted in using the highway, either on metal road or the roadside waste.*

William Kempson (85) mason, born in 1823 lived in Broadway all his life and had worked on every home down the 'Back.' *'He had always known the public to use the Back Way right from Issac Averill's yard. '*(back of OKA).

Chilian Clarke (56) labourer, lived for 50 years in a cottage at the Back Way. In his opinion *'the roadway and the grass at the side were free to the public and he had never known anyone obstructed.'*

Then there was the matter of Gates?

Charles Collins snr (66) a labourer, said *'There were formerly gates across the Back Way.'……'Mr Drury (*Charles Richardson Drury 1874-1894*) put a fence up, but he had to take it down. He was going to enclose it; in the end the hurdles were all taken away.'* He did not know when the gates were taken away.

[More recently, in a letter dated 28 July 1974, a resident mentioned that Gordon Russell had gateposts at the entrance of Back Way, with gates, and that it was understood they were brought out of store and erected once a year to prevent the road becoming a public one, however the writer of the letter had not found anyone who had ever seen this happen. The writer added the present gates were replacements of a very broken down one.

Back Lane, Back Way or The Back remains a complex issue. The width of the lane, on maps – area 362, and as mentioned in the 1908 Court case, was much larger between the Lygon Cottage and Foss's than the rest of the lane from China Square to the Bell Yard, almost three times wider. Overlays show the absorbed lost land is now part of the Lygon Arms. And we must consider what Mr King said when giving evidence.

That there is a public right of way in place confirms the public had free passage.

Postscript VIII- The population of Broadway over the centuries

Year	Population	Families	Houses	Acreage	Comments
1086	200				
1251	600				
1348	250				Black Death
1550	350	240[430]			
1563	400	74[431]			
1620	700				
1776	900	240 [432]			
1801	1117				
1805[433]	1517				
1820[434]	1117		249		
1831[435]	1517		320	4,800	
1840[436]	1517			3,950	
1851[437]	1629				
1861[438]	1568				
1868[439]	1700				
1870[440]	1566		361	4800	
1871[441]	1627				
1891	1536				

---

430 Article Worcester Journal 1871
431. George Griffiths Free Schools of Worcestershire.
432. George Griffiths Free Schools of Worcestershire.
433. Bentley's History of Worcestershire - Broadway
434. Lewis Worcestershire Directory 1820.
435. Parliamentary Gazetteer of England and Wales 1851
436. Bentley's History of Worcestershire - Broadway
437. Census
438. Census
439. Noakes Guide to Worcestershire
440. Imperial Gazetteer of England & Wales 1870
441. Census

351

1894/5[442]	1536	4990
1901[443]	1400-1414	
1911	1793	
1914	1793	
1921	1860	
1931	2138	
1940	1517	3950 men joined Army
2011	2545	
2021[444]	3500	Incl. Leedon's expansion

---

442. The Comprehensive Gazetteer of England & Wales, 1894-5
443. Gissing
444. Broadway's Neighbourhood Plan 2023

Bibliography

PRINT

Aldin, Charles, *Old Inns,* London, Heinemann, 1921.

Anderson, Mary, *A Few More Memories,* London, Hutchinson, and Co, 1936.

Balme, David, Enigma: (Captain Peter Hore editor) *The Untold Story of the Secret Capture, Vol. III of The British Navy at War and Peace,* Whittles Publishing, 2017.

Barnard Rees Price collection no 28, d/1, Sheldon Micellanea, Library of Birmingham BLS

Benson, Athur, *Edwardian Excursions 1898-1904,* London, John Murray,1981,

Broadway's Neighbourhood Plan 2023

Brooks, Nicholas, *Anglo-Saxon Myths: State and Church, 400-1066,* London, The Hambledon Press,2000,

Browne D, *Historical Collections of Private Passages of State: Volume 7, 1647-48,* 1721, London, Proceedings in Parliament February 28, 1647.

Bund, John Willis, *the early history of Evesham Abbey,* read before the Worcester Diocesan Architectural and Archaeological Society, at the Guildhall, on January 25, 1895

Bund John Willis, J *The Civil War in Worcestershire, 1642-1646, and the Scotch invasion of 1651,* London: Simpkin, Marshall, Hamilton, Kent, 1905.

Byng John, *The Torrington Diaries, Volume I,* London, Eyre and Spottiswoode, 1934.

Carrington, Noel, *Broadway and the Cotswolds,* Birmingham, The Kynoch Press, 1933.

Chartris, Hon, K.C Evan *John Sargent*, London, Heinemann, 1927.

Clarendon, Edward Hyde, Earl of, *The history of the rebellion and civil wars in England,* Oxford, University Press, 1839.

Collins, Rev R.J.M. *Collins in the Cotswolds,* E P Lowe Ltd

Cookson, Barbara, *Robert Newton Chadwick*, Campden & District Historical and Archaeological Society, 2012.
Darlington, Reginald, *The Chronicle of John of Worcester, Vol. 2*Oxford, Clarendon Press, 1995.

Eason, Marion, *The Best Little Hunt in England,* Empire, Leeds, 2019.

Eyre, Elizabeth, *History of the Angel Inn,* Willersey, Vale Press, 2022.

Fea, Alan, *Nooks and Corners of Old England,* New York, Charles Scribner's, and Sons, 1908.

Gordon, Dr Catherine, *The Coventry's of Croome,* Phillimore and Co Ltd, 2000.

Harper, Charles G, *The Old Inns of Old England Vol. II a picturesque account of the ancient and storied hostelries of our own County,* Ed. J. Burrow & Co, Limited, London, 1927.

Harper, Charles G, *The Holyhead Road Vol 1, The Mail-Coach Road to Dublin*, Chapman, and Hall, 1902.

Habington Thomas, *A Survey of Worcestershire Part I,* Oxford,1895.

Hissey, JJ, *Across England in a Dog-Cart from London to St David's and Back*, Richard Bentley and Son, 1891.

Hooke, Della, *The Kingdom of the Hwicce,* Manchester University Press, 1985.

Hunt, Margaret, *The Middling Sort Commerce, Gender, and the Family in England 1680-1780,* University of California Press, 1996.

Knight, Sid, *Cotswold Lad,* London, Aldine Press Letchworth, 1960.

Laird, Francis C, *A Topographical and Historical Description of the County of Worcester,* Sherwood, Neely, and Jones, George Cowie & Co, 1815.

Leland, John *Collectanea, 1 The Itinerary of John Leland the Antiquary, 3rd ed, 9 volumes in 5*, Oxford, 1770.

Macquoid, Percy and Ralph Edwards, *Dictionary of English Furniture*, London, Country Life, 1954.

McLean, Elliot, *The Cely Papers*, Ed Henry, London: Longmans Green, 1900

Mundy, Richard, *The Visitation of the county of Worcester made in the year 1569 : with other pedigrees relating to that county* Publication of the Harleian Society, Edited by Phillimore, W. P. W, (1853-1913), 1888.

Murphy, Thomas Dowler, *In Unfamiliar England - A Record of a Seven Thousand Mile Tour by Motor of the Unfrequented Nooks and Corners, and the Shrines of Especial Interest, in England; With Incursions into Scotland and Ireland.* L C Page and Company, Boston 1910.

Noake, John, *Notes and Queries for Worcestershire, 1856,* London, Longman – referring to *Book of Compositions for not taking the Order of Knighthood at the Coronation of King Charles* I. 1630—1632.

O'Connell, Sean, *The Car in British Society: Class, Gender and Motoring 1896-1939,* Manchester University Press, 1998

Parsons, Derek, *Broadway a village history,* 1996, Cornmill Press, 1996.

Paterson, Daniel (1739–1825), *Paterson's Road, being an entirely accurate description of all the direct and principal crossroads in England and Wales, with Parts of the Roads of Scotland published by the British Army Office.* 1829, London, Longman, Orme, Brown, Green, and Longmans

Pevsner, N, *The Buildings of England: Worcestershire*, Harmondsworth: Penguin, 1968.

Pevsner, Nikolaus & Alan Brooks, *The Buildings of England, Worcestershire,* Penguin Books Ltd, 1970.

Price, Richard, *British Society, 1680-1880,* Cambridge University Press, 1999

Ridley, Alison, and Garfield, Curtis, *The Story of the Lygon Arms,* Porcupine Enterprises, 1992.

Rose, Susan *Calais: An English Town in France, 1347-1558,* Boydell & Brewer, Boydell Press, 2008.

Rudder, Samuel, *A New History of Gloucestershire,* printed by Samuel Rudder, *1779.*

Rushworth, John (1612/1690) *Historical collections of private passages of state: weighty matters in law. Remarkable proceedings in five Parliaments. Beginning the sixteenth year of King James, anno 1618. And ending the fifth year of King Charles, anno 1629 Charles I, King of England, 1600-1649. His Majesties declaration to all his loving subjects, of the causes which moved him to dissolve the last parliament, March 10. 1628,* James Astwood, 1682.

Rushworth, John, *Historical Collections of Private Passages of State: Volume 6, 1645-47,* London, 1722.

Rushworth, John, *Perfect Occurrences, January 21 — 2S, 1647,* Henry Walker (cleric)- a weekly newspaper which became the semi-official mouth piece of Parliament in 1647.

Russell, Gordon, Designer's Trade Autobiography of Gordon Russell, George Allen, and Unwin Ltd, London, 1968.

Russell S. B, *The Story of an Old English Hostelry,* Letchworth at the Arden Press, 1914 and 1924,

Scott, Eva, *Rupert, Prince, Count Palatine, (1619-1682), Great Britain -- History Civil War, 1642-1649,* G P Putnam and sons,1899.

Squire, J.C. *The London Mercury, Volume 33*, Rolfe Arnold Scott-James Field Press Ltd, 1936.

Stenton, Frank, *Anglo-Saxon England (3rd Edition'* Oxford University Press, 1971.

Stokes, Peter A, *King Edgar's Charter for Pershore (AD 972)* Cambridge University Press 2008.

Stone DD, Rev. James S, *Over the Hills to Broadway,* Philadelphia, Porter, and Coates, 1893.

The Stonor Letters and Papers Vol. I and 2, ed. E. Charles Lethbridge, for Royal Historical Society (Great Britain); Camden third series, 1919

Stow, William, *Remarks on London being an exact survey of the cities of London and Westminster, borough of Southwark, and the suburbs and liberties contiguous to them.... places to which penny post letters and parcels are carried, with lists of fairs and markets... to what inns flying coaches, waggons and carriers come, and the days they go out.... keys, wharfs, and plying places on the river Thames... description of the great and crossroads from one city and eminent town to another, in England and Wales... the rates of coachmen[sic], chairmen, carmen and watermen...* London, T Norris and H Tracey, 1722.

Stroud, Dorothy, *Capability Brown*, London, Faber,1975.

Symonds, Richard *Diary of the Marches of the Royal Army, April 10, 1644 - February 11, 1645,* the Campden Society, 1838-1901, London Longmans, Green, 1859.

Tarrant, Emily, *Topographical collections, correspondence, and papers of Sir Thomas Phillipps*, Bodleian Library, 2019.

Thorold Peter, *The Motoring Age, 1896-1939,* Thistle Publishing, 2016.

Titow, J Z *Some Evidence of the Thirteenth Century Population Increase.* The Economic History Review, Economic History Society, vol. 14, no. 2, 1961.

The Lygon Arms Visitor Book, 1909 to June 2012.

Williams, Dr Ann and Martin, Professor G.H., Editors, *Domesday Book a complete translation,* London, Penguin, 2002.

Worcestershire Record Office 12th-19th Century - 705:962/8965 leases, deeds, and wills.

On-Line

https://www.badseysociety.uk/village-life/the-way-london-vale-evesham-roads 1350-1880

http://www.british-history.ac.uk/cal-state-papers / domestic /chas 1 Hamilton, William Douglas, ed. 'Calendar of State Papers Domestic: Charles I, 1644, 1888, London.

http://www.british-history.ac.uk/rushworth-papers/vol 6

http://www.british-history.ac.uk/topographical-dict.
https://www.british-history.ac.uk/vch/worcs/vol 4 A History of the County of Worcester: Volume 4, William Page, J.W. Willis-Bund (editors) 1924.

https://www.british-history.ac.uk/vch/worcs/vol 2 Victoria County History, London, *'Houses of Benedictine monks: Abbey of Evesham.'* 1971.

http://earlywelshleigh.blogspot.com/2017/03/ancestry-of-dorothy-oakley

https://eprints.oxfordarchaeology.com/2975 Archaeological investigation report, former Gordon Russell Factory Site, 1996

https://famoushotels.org/news/meeting-cromwell-a-piece-of-english-history
Morby, Adrian

https://historicengland.org.uk/listing/the-list/list-entry/1000896 - Spring Hill House

https://historicengland.org.uk/images-books/publications/historic-farmsteads-preliminary-character-statement-Section 4

Historical Collections of Private Passages of State: Volume 7,' 1647-48. *Originally published by D Browne, London, 1721. Proceedings in Parliament February 28, 1647.*

https://mcnygenealogy.com/book/eastman-theatre-1927-06-26.pdf - Sorrell and Son - Film

www.northcotswoldhunt.co.uk - History North Cotswold Hunt

MAPS

John Ogilby, p.2, *'His Majesty's Cosmographer, and Master of His Majesty's revels in the kingdom of Ireland. BRITANNIA, Volume I or an Illustration of the Kingdom of England and Dominion of Wales thereof.' 1675 LONDON,* Printed by the Author at his House in White-Fryers.